Gorgeous DISASTER

THE TRAGIC STORY OF DEBRA LAFAVE

OWEN LAFAVE
AND BILL SIMON

Books co-authored and by Bill Simon

The G.O.D. Experiments (Simon & Schuster, 2006)

A Cat by the Tail (SelectBooks, 2006, in production)

iCon: Steve Jobs – The Greatest Second Act in the History of Business (Wiley, 2005)

The Truth About Medium (Hampton Roads, 2005)

The Art of Intrusion (Wiley, 2005)

In Search of Business Value (Select Books, 2005)

The Art of Deception (Wiley, 2002)

The Afterlife Experiments (Simon & Schuster, 2002)

Driving Digital (HarperCollins, 2001)

High Velocity Leadership (HarperCollins, 1999)

On the Firing Line (HarperCollins, 1998)

Lasting Change (1997, Van Nostrand Reinhold)

Beyond the Numbers (International Thomson Publishing, 1997)

Profit from Experience (International Thomson Publishing, 1996)

Shortcut Route to Winning Backgammon (Minerva Publishing, 1986)

Beyond information based on my own personal memory, the quotes and incidents presented in this book come from interviews with the people involved, and from official documents in the case.

Quotes throughout the book, including from Larry King, Greta Van Susteren, and other interviewers, have been edited for continuity but without altering the sense or meaning.

Many of the names used in the book are, of course, fictitious. Details about some people have been changed to further protect their identity.

ISBN: 1-59777-534-7
Library of Congress Cataloging-In-Publication Data Available

Book Design by: Sonia Fiore

Printed in the United States of America

Phoenix Books
9465 Wilshire Boulevard, Suite 315
Beverly Hills, CA 90212

10 9 8 7 6 5 4 3 2 1

For Arynne, Victoria, Sheldon, and David;
and for Sallie and Amy

Contents

What is lust made of that it drives one
to risk everything for its consummation?

—Sarah Dunant, *The Birth of Venus*

Beauty is a player, stalking the streets bare-breasted,
stiletto heeled, fly unzipped. Its power is
luminous and monumental.

—Nancy Friday, author, as reported by
Kate Stone Lombardi in the *New York Times*

ARRESTED

WITH POLICE TAPE recorders running, 14-year-old Jack Carpenter says into the phone, "Well, you enjoyed yourself yesterday, right?"

On the other end of the line, unaware she is being set up, gorgeous 23-year-old Debra Beasley LaFave answers, "I did. Did you?" She's speaking in her squeaky, little-girl voice. And giggling, constantly giggling, like a sexy, flirtatious teen playing up to a boy who has lit her fire.

Until just a few days before, Jack was, by his own account, still a virgin. One afternoon with a reading teacher from his school has changed that. As if this rite of passage, this much-sought event in a young boy's life, had matured him overnight, he's the one who sounds like the grown-up of the pair.

He answers the question about whether he enjoyed the sex with an impassive, non-committal "Yeah." But after their third tumble, he had talked about calling it off. The teacher, still with the voice and language of giggly schoolgirl, looks for reassurance that he's willing to continue.

"So it's not *over* over?" she asks.

"Nope," he replies. And then, all unaware, withdraws the small bit of reassurance he's just given. "Not yet."

Perhaps touched by a twinge of remorse, the teacher picks up on his phrase, playfully twisting it to a different meaning. "Why couldn't you have just said 'No, not yet?"

A moment later, she adds, "Oh, Lord—what am I going to do with you?"

The boy replies simply, pathetically: "Sorry."

Finally he says, "All right. Well, I guess I'll talk to you later."

Earlier in the conversation she had addressed him affectionately as "my dear." Now, hanging up, she says, "Okay, honey."

A couple of hours later the same day—Friday, June 18, 2004—the boy places another call to the teacher. The scene is being played out in the living room of the Carpenters' 1,700-square-foot, three-bedroom home on Woodland Ridge Drive in Temple Terrace, Florida, outside Tampa, where Jack lives with his mother, Carla.

Like the first call, this one is being recorded by a police detective, Mike Pridemore. This time Pridemore has coached the boy in saying things designed to draw the teacher into acknowledging more specifically that she has had sex with him. At one point during the call, the boy says, "I'm a little worried...."

"Why?" she asks.

The youngster's response is a set-up, a crucial moment for Pridemore in deciding whether there is a criminal offense here. The boy says, "Like, I don't want you to like get pregnant or anything. I was just thinking about it and I was just thinking if next time, now that we've had sex about three times, if I should use, like, a condom or something."

Pridemore waits for the response. Will she deny it? Will she become incensed and hang up? Will she become suspicious and wary she's being led into a trap?

None of those. Her response is like a confession, an acceptance of the statements the boy has made. "Oh, you're being weird," she says. "Why are you being weird?"

"What do you mean?"

"I don't know," she answers. "Why are you being worried?"

The youngster, inexperienced in romantic conversations with an older woman, has no cogent answer. After some idle chit-chat, he asks, "So do I need to worry about it or no, do you think?"

"I don't know," the teacher replies. "What's the matter?"

"I've been thinking about it because I haven't used...." This time he can't quite manage to get the word "condom" out with his mother listening from the next room. "I'm just scared."

"Oh," she answers. "That should be the least of your worries." The remark is more on target than she realizes.

In the next call, a brief one, she wants to know, "Are you pure?" She means it as a way of asking if he's okay. But in the circumstances, it's an eerie choice of term.

At 8:30 Saturday morning Pridemore is back, picking up with the interview, eventually getting to the crucial information: asking the boy to tell him things about the teacher's body that only someone who had seen her naked would know.

Betraying the woman he has a crush on and been intimate with, Jack stammers a little as he describes Debra's tattoos and the tan lines on her belly. And he gives a detailed description of her pubic hair, which he says is light brown, trimmed in a rectangular shape, with the vagina itself shaved clean.

The boy places another phone call a little after 11. "There's like 20 kids here screaming," she says.

Moments later the conversation enters strange territory. "Pam has a newborn baby," she says. "So I'm kind of holding her right now."

"Oh, really?" he answers. With his every word being recorded, it's not surprising that his answers are unemotional and guarded.

"Yeah. Watching all the.... My ovaries are hurting listening to all these frigging kids screaming."

He responds with a little laugh.

The boy understands the role he has been given. He ignores what must sound to him like girlfriend talk and starts to bait the trap.

"So do you have any plans for Monday?"

"Nope, I don't think so."

He has a connection to this woman. It's a connection no young boy should have to a teacher, but it exists and it carries strong emotions. Despite all that, he tightens the noose. "Do you want to try to do something Monday?"

"Yeah," she agrees. "That's cool."

The whole sorry episode had begun to unravel when the boy's Aunt Marianne saw her son with Jack and a good-looking blonde lady. What was Jack doing in Ocala, an hour-and-a-half away from home? And why were the two boys in the company of that blonde lady? She called her sister, Jack's mother, to share her suspicions, her mother's instinct. That evening, driving Jack home after picking him up at the playground where he spent many of his summer days, Carla insisted he tell her the truth.

The boy broke down in sobs and confessed: the lady was a teacher at his school and he had had sex with her.

Shortly after they reached home, Debra called. She apologized, saying she needed to buy a gift for her husband and had invited the boy to keep her company, but realized she should have checked with his mother first, and she was sorry. Mrs. Carpenter was careful not to say she knew the teacher had had sex with her son. She pretended to accept Debra's explanation.

Mrs. Carpenter hung up and called the police. A few minutes before 10 that night, on-call Detective Pridemore answered the phone at home and was assigned the case of "a possible sexual battery" involving a victim under 16. He drove first to police headquarters, picked up a tape recorder and telephone monitoring device, then drove to the Carpenter home. He parked at the curb and walked up to the house, a trim and handsome structure, the house itself and the attached garage done in white with tasteful black trim, the windows framed by black shutters, and the front door set off by an overhanging balcony. The well-trimmed lawn and groomed front shrubbery add to the sense that the family living here are people of means and good taste.

Police officer David Thornton, already on the scene, filled Pridemore in on what he had learned. He had spoken to the Sex Offender Division in the State Attorney's office; they had recommended recording phone calls between the boy and the suspect. Detective Pridemore was ahead of them. He had Jack sign a consent form, with his mother signing as a witness. Then he set up equipment to record phone conversations on the boy's cell phone.

Following instructions from Pridemore, Jack twice tried to reach Debra's cell phone, without an answer. By then it was quarter past one in the morning. Detective Pridemore drove Jack and his mother to Tampa's Crisis Center. There Jack had to keep his complaints to himself as a pair of nurses combed through his pubic hair; later, a laboratory would analyze all of the loose hairs retrieved by this embarrassing process to determine whether any of Debra's pubic hairs were present.

Even worse was what came next. One of the nurses rubbed a swab on the inside of his mouth, and then another on the other side, to collect samples of his DNA. Then she swabbed on each side of his face. After that, the most humiliating of the entire experience, she used four separate swabs on his penis, rubbing the length and the tip. The crime lab would later analyze the swabs for signs of any DNA other than the boy's. A DNA match would provide conclusive proof of the crime. But Pridemore knew it would be weeks or even months before he would receive the results.

The three arrived back at the Carpenter home at 2 A.M. In a case like this, experienced officers know that the victim might be making up the story—for revenge, out of jealousy, or for some other motive. Detective Pridemore had the boy repeat step by step the details he had already shared with Officer Thornton. Finally, around 3 A.M., the detective said he was through for the night and left, allowing Mrs. Carpenter and Jack to turn in after perhaps the six most humiliating hours of the boy's life.

Monday, June 21—three days since Detective Pridemore first walked into the Carpenter home. It starts as another gorgeous day in the Tampa Bay area. Clear skies but hot, as usual. The temperature had only dropped to the mid-70s overnight. By the time Detective Pridemore's reinforcements—Detectives Steven Sutter and Bernard Seeley—have arrived around 9 A.M., some clouds are visible in the distance. But they just trap the heat; the thermometer has already started its climb toward the 90s.

The wiretap equipment is set up again and, when Detective Pridemore gives him the okay, Jack dials the teacher's cell phone. The youngster asks what she's doing and she replies, "Driving. I had to take Owen to work today."

The boy's mother knows that the terrible scene Jack is now acting out is only happening because she herself called the police. And what lies ahead for the boy? What horrendous ordeal has she called down upon him?

In the next exchange, the teacher who has been having sex with a teen student at her school expresses concern over a far more modest sin. When the boy asks, "So what time are you planning on heading over?" she replies, "Are you sure? Like, I just feel…I mean, I don't want you lying to your mom."

It sounds as if the lady is getting cold feet and might not come. Jack offers reassurance.

"It's all right. She's gone in a sales meeting, like all day."

"You're sure?" the teacher asks.

"Yeah.

The teacher turns apprehensive, which is more justified than she could imagine. "Positive? Because I'm like, scared. I don't want, you know...."

"Yeah, I'm positive."

As if trying to bolster her own confidence, she says, "I mean, I just—I know you wouldn't, you know, do it unless you were sure."

"I am."

"I mean, we were just so close last time, you know?" And then, "Are you *sure*, sure?"

"Yes."

Still in her little-girl voice, she says, "You wouldn't lie to me, would you?"

"No."

"No, what?"

He asks, "Why are you saying that?"

She lets him see a bit of her vulnerability. "I don't know," she says. "I'm just scared." Remembering that three days earlier they had been spotted together, she goes on, "It was a little freaky last time. And you were just like really dead-set on, you know, taking a break."

"Well, I just want to... I just wanted to see you. I thought you wanted to see me, too."

"No, no, no, no, no, no," sounding even more like a schoolgirl. "Don't take it the wrong way. It's just, you know, I'm looking out...."

"Yeah," he says, the actor playing the role he has been assigned, telling lies he's been coached to tell. "But I know we're fine today."

"All right. Well, whenever, I guess."

"All right. In fact, earlier the better, because...because my mom is at a meeting."

"What time is she supposed to be.... Is she already gone?"

"Yeah."

"You're positive?"

"Yes."

Her voice coming down the phone line again sounds teasing and flirtatious. "All right. Promise?"

"Yes," Jack answers.

"Pinky promise?" The adults exchange glances. *Pinky promise?* The *teacher* is talking as if she were the one in middle school.

"Say 'Pinky promise,'" she coaxes.

He complies: "Pinky promise."

"All right," she says. "Well, tell me a time." She wasn't reluctant, after all; she was just toying with the youngster. In this dangerous game the two are playing, she is the one who decides when and where they will have sex, what sex acts they will engage in, and what, exactly, each will do to the other.

A little before 10 A.M., Mrs. Carpenter's phone rings again. By now Detectives Sutter and Seeley are outside, waiting in two separate unmarked cars. Jack picks up his cell phone.

"I'm almost there," the woman says, in that same little girl voice. "Is everything clear?"

Moments later her silver two-door Isuzu Rodeo Sport SUV rolls into sight, cruises up the block, and pulls up at the curb. Detective Seeley pulls his car in front of the SUV while Detective Sutter blocks the car from behind. Detective Pridemore steps up to the car to speak with her. He says, "We need to take you to the police department to talk about the relationship you've been having with Jack Carpenter." Debra looks at him blankly for a moment. Then she nods her head up and down slowly.

He has her step out of the car.

Any mother in Mrs. Carpenter's unhappy situation would be picturing the teacher as a plain, dried-up young woman with pallid skin and stringy hair, the kind men walk past and never notice. This lady is nothing like that. She's blonde, blue-eyed, and very young, simply dressed, with an excellent figure. *She could have any man she wanted. Why would she pick on a 14-year-old?* Yet for a fleeting moment, as the handcuffs are put on, the boy's mother feels a wave of sympathy for the young woman.

Leaving her with the other two detectives, Pridemore returns to where Mrs. Carpenter and Jack have been watching. He asks the boy to confirm that this is the lady he had sex with. Jack acknowledges: this is the lady.

Debra LaFave has had intercourse with a teen student on three occasions. Her fling is over. For whatever pleasure or satisfaction it may have brought, for whatever deep internal need the boy may have briefly satisfied in her, those three brief moments have in many ways destroyed her life.

Chapter 2
DEBBIE GROWING UP

FOR THE CHILD who grows up on the mean streets of the inner city where joining a gang is expected, in a household with a father in prison and a grandfather who served prison time in his day, we can hardly be surprised when he follows in their footsteps. The patterns surround him. No matter how hard his mother may try to implant solid values, for many youngsters in this setting the lessons are too strong to overcome. Those who survive and achieve despite the odds win our awe, admiration, and praise.

For the child who grows up in a home built around devout religious beliefs, with two dedicated parents—a family that sits down to dinner together every night and says grace before eating—we're not surprised by a certain amount of rebellion in the teen years but have the reassurance of knowing that, like a family-values Hollywood movie, most things will turn out fine in the long run. The usual doses of accident, illness, pain, disappointment, and heartbreak will be compensated by the standard measures of laughter, satisfactions, friendships, and loves.

When something goes awry—when the child turns out to be someone far different than we could have expected, far different from the person we thought we knew—we're left to search for answers. How could this have happened?

As the man who would eventually marry Debra, I came to know her mother and father, Larry and Joyce, when I began dating their daughter in my junior year in college. They had both grown up in the Tampa area, as had their own parents. Mostly from British stock, the families had chosen to settle in the small town of Ruskin, Florida, 20 miles south of Tampa, a working-class community nestled among fingers of water from Tampa Bay. Its 8,000 residents live in what are, by today's standards, incredibly inexpensive homes, with a median value of only $80,000, and very few rentals for more than $500 a month. (In 2000, with home prices soaring in many locations, one listing showed not a single home in Ruskin worth as much as $300,000.)

Larry and Joyce became close at East Bay High School, where she was two years behind him. He chose the Army when he graduated and after basic training received orders to Germany. Joyce was desperate for a way out of her home—she came from an abusive household, Debbie later told me—and the two married so that Joyce would be able to accompany her new husband to his overseas post.

If you were to meet the Beasleys now, you'd have a pretty good idea of what they must have looked like at their wedding. Joyce, petite and attractive even if no longer as slender as in her wedding pictures, has blue eyes and naturally blonde hair. Larry is a bit below average height, with light brown hair, a mustache, and glasses. These days he's growing something of a paunch, his hair is thinning, and he's unnecessarily self-conscious about a slight disfiguration on his nose where a skin cancer was removed.

Neither family was in a position to send the newlyweds off on an exotic honeymoon. Instead the couple headed down the coast to the inexpensive beach town of Englewood, Florida. It was obviously a happy time: Englewood Beach was to become the Beasley summer vacation spot, year after year.

After Larry's Army service in Germany, the couple returned to Florida and settled in Ruskin, close to her parents, eventually buying a small house on 12th Street where they still live today. They had two children, a daughter they named Angela and then, in August 1980, another daughter, Debra Jean.

As a young man just out of the Army, Larry worked for a time in his father's house-painting business, then left that for a job with Tampa Electric. He was strong and had no reservations about working with his hands, even though the new job would mean years of wearing out heavy-duty work gloves, slinging an axe to dig ditches for power lines. It was back-breaking work, and some men didn't last long. Larry, with family obligations and a strong sense of responsibility, stuck it out. He would be rewarded through the years with pay raises and increased responsibilities.

Joyce, too, helped support the family, first working in a local bank and then, much later, in a job she found much more satisfying, as a hairdresser.

It might seem surprising for such a small town to have so many churches. Ruskin has one for the Episcopalians, one for Methodists, and one for the Catholics, plus a Church of the Nazarene, with the Lutherans and the Mormons served in nearby Apollo Beach. That's a reflection of the character of the community and of the Beasley home, a character set by the stronger of the two parents, the girls' mother. Joyce, a devout Christian, expected her children to accompany her to regular church services, participate in church socials, picnics and the like, and to live by Christian virtues. Larry attended services with her in the early years but then gave up accompanying his ladies.

Though the family was Baptist, they didn't go to the Baptist Church in their local community because Joyce had decided she didn't care for the style and teachings of the pastor there. She didn't mind driving the extra distance to another Baptist church more to her liking.

Joyce lived what she preached. Neighbors and church friends describe her as sweet, caring, and hardworking. They saw frequent examples of her generosity to people in need, sometimes donating things from her own house, sometimes buying things to make other people's lives easier, like an annual shopping spree for two of her nephews—kids from a part of the family to whom the Beasleys seemed well-to-do.

But there was a dark side to the family dynamics. Just as the father in the LaFave family of my childhood had been remote and difficult to know, so was the father in the Beasley family. Larry had a brother who he was on good terms with, and a couple of close friends. Beyond that, he largely walled himself off, even from those closest to him. Mother Joyce was the order-giver and the rule-maker. Father Larry was willing to abdicate decisions to his wife, in particular decisions about the bringing up of the girls. Debbie resented that her father was so reserved, showing little love and affection to his daughters.

From an early age, Debbie worshiped her older sister. Angela thrived on her kid sister's adulation, yet, as older siblings will, she sometimes heaped complaints and criticism on Debbie. Overall, though, when young they both lived by values that won their mother's approval. They attended church without a fuss, made friends with other kids from the church, and brought home the kind of report cards that make parents proud and offer reassurance about the children's future.

Why wasn't Angela more angelic to her adoring kid sister? It would be hard to have a younger sister like Debbie and not be envious. Even from a very early age, Debbie was gorgeous. Adorable face, shining blue eyes, a mane of golden hair, a radiant smile.

Gorgeous females attract attention, even very young ones. The attention isn't always welcome, and it isn't always healthy. Much later Debbie told me of an incident from her childhood, when she was about five or six. On a sleepover at a friend's house, she woke up in the middle of the night, upset. She got out of bed, went to the phone, called her mother, and asked to be picked up. She was disturbed but couldn't say why. The few sleepovers she went on after that always ended with her calling Joyce in the middle of the night pleading to be picked up, which of course her mother always did. Today Debbie suspects she was molested the night of that first upset, but blocked out the knowledge. Still today she isn't certain what happened. Whatever took place, it was serious enough to leave her unable to enjoy a sleepover ever again.

Attracting unwanted attention, or attention from the wrong people: Call it the curse of the gorgeous. Call it the perverse tornado of beauty.

Debbie loved to sing and was blessed with a voice as gorgeous as her face. This proved to be another passport for her, if only temporarily. Among her friends in Ruskin were the children of the Carter family. Debbie was sometimes hired to babysit the younger brother, Aaron. There was also an older brother, Nick, who was a musician in a fledgling band playing local dates and chasing the ever-elusive recording contract. For readers who don't recognize the name, Nick Carter, with his puppy-dog eyes and cascading blond hair, would become a famous heart-throb ingredient when his striving band became the platinum-selling Backstreet Boys.

Debbie at 13 was already a talented singer. Nick decided to tap what connections he had in the music business to see if he could provide any career help for his kid sister's friend. Nick's group had been put together by promoter Lou Pearlman, who had devised a formula that was to prove golden. The CBS program *60 Minutes 2*, in an episode on Pearlman and the Backstreet Boys, described the formula this way: "A young one, a cute one, a sensitive one, a jokester, a bad boy, and the older hunk—all between the ages of 12 and 20." Pearlman would also later be the wizard behind creating NSYNC.

Nick went to Pearlman and wheedled a professional contract for Debbie. Using the stage name "Alana B," she went on tour, opening for small groups and covering artists like Celine Dion. She didn't make much money at it, and in any case it didn't last long. Still, it was an extraordinary experience for any teen.

Meanwhile Debbie was living a secret life, the first of several risky and potentially dangerous escapades carried on behind her mother's back. Despite the close and loving connection between mother and daughter, Joyce Beasley exercised a high degree of control over her two girls that would eventually explode in her face. She was domineering and controlling, rarely allowing her daughters to make any decisions on their own, instead making all decisions for them.

Angela, by then a teenager, turned rebellious. She began ignoring her schoolwork, slipping out to "have a good time," and butting heads with her mother. Their arguments shook the house.

Debbie, still only 13, was having her own problems, much graver ones that will likely haunt for the rest of her life. At her middle school, Debbie came to have a little crush on one of the boys, and he for her. Pancho was 15 and should have been in high school but had been held back. Joyce disapproved of the boy—an astute judgment, as it turned out. The way Debbie told me the story, one day Pancho cornered her in an empty classroom, lifted her skirt, and forced himself into her.

This was rape. But it was more than that. Debra Beasley had lost her virginity in the cruelest way. Her first introduction to something that should be sweet, fulfilling, and wondrously gratifying was instead a sordid forcible attack.

Worse, Debbie says, after that first time the boy continued to corner her and force himself on her.

Debbie shared all this with me later on, when we were at a difficult point in our relationship. Perhaps she was really testing me: Did I love her enough to stay with her despite the things she had been through?

If it was a test, I passed by her standards. Looking back, I failed by my own.

Victims of childhood abuse respond in many different ways. This experience that Debbie suffered at age 13 might have been the trigger, the root of all the worst troubles in store for her.

Debbie's next relationship proved to be another example of the curse of the gorgeous; if she had been plain or just another pretty girl, this would likely never have happened.

A musician associated with the Backstreet Boys, a guy I'll call Sammy Blye, several years older than Debbie, took a liking to her, and Debbie started seeing him. He was another poor choice for a sensitive young girl from a religious family. Debbie thought it was a serious relationship. For Sammy, it was just another notch on his belt. Worse, he was uncaring and abusive.

On one occasion Debbie told Sammy she couldn't have sex because it was her time of the month. He spread some newspapers on the floor and said, "Lay down and let's go."

It makes me sick to remember her telling me that story. I felt so sorry for her when she shared it with me. Now I'm revolted that she would have allowed herself to be treated like that, revolted that she should have told me the story, and appalled at myself for not hearing it as a warning.

Debbie's life at this time was a tragicomedy of highs and lows. Mistreated by two boys in a row, hiding her secret sex life from the mother she really loved and depended on, while trying to be just another middle school coed. But there were some unexpectedly gratifying times as well. Joyce entered Debbie in a few beauty pageants. Those led to modeling assignments—a mannequin for teenage girls' clothing at department store fashion shows, and posing for catalog fashion shoots. Even though the pay wasn't on the Heidi Klum scale, it was quite a heady thrill for Debbie. And for her doting mother.

The high school for kids from Ruskin is East Bay, a few miles to the north toward Tampa, the same school where Debbie's parents had met. The incoming freshman class in September 1994 included 14-year-old Debra Beasley, who was quickly acknowledged one of the prettiest girls in the school of some 2000 students.

The captain of the football team, an alpha male in any high school, more often than not *the* alpha male, has the pick of any girl he wants. Turning down an invitation for a date with the football captain would be like turning down a dinner invitation from the White House. Debbie was chosen to be on the court of East Bay's Homecoming Queen. The team captain, a senior, didn't ordinarily pay much attention to freshmen, but his eye lit on Debbie, he asked her out, and for time became her guy.

That school year produced two traumas for Debbie, very likely related. The first shook her world. She may have been defying her mother and rebelling against her in serious ways, but Debbie was still very much bonded to Joyce, very caring and concerned, very dependent on her. When the doctor discovered breast lumps in mommy Joyce, the whole family was alarmed. The biopsy showed that she had malignant tumors on both sides, and she immediately began radiation and chemotherapy and underwent surgery.

The idea that she might lose her mother was almost more than Debbie could handle. Shaken by the news, she responded by withdrawing, unable to bear being around her because the fear was so great. Joyce's close friend Cindy scolded Debbie and kept on her case for not showing the love and affection Joyce needed more than ever at that point. But Debbie was deaf to the pleading. Her panic was emotionally crippling.

Cancer kills five hundred thousand Americans every year. Even with improvements in detection and treatment, even with the decline in the number of people smoking, the annual cancer deaths continued increasing each year. (Not until 2006 would the number for the first time show a slight decline.) Joyce, though she lost her hair and gained weight, and though the aftermath of her surgery was as distressing as to any other woman, was soon pronounced by the oncologist to be clean, fit, and healthy. She had defied the statistics, and the good news brought Debbie back to her side.

Joyce's reaction was a sword that cut two ways. She told Debbie, "It's all right. Don't be sorry. There's no need to apologize." That was always Joyce's attitude when one of her children misbehaved or disappointed and then wanted to make things right again. It was always "That's okay." And "There's no need to apologize." It sounds like a wonderful attitude of an understanding and forgiving mother.

Maybe in some families this approach works effectively. It didn't with Debbie. Over the years, it simply taught her that she had no need to take responsibility for her actions. Debbie came to believe that whatever she did could be made okay. This lesson learned from childhood at her mother's knee would have devastating consequences.

The second of Debbie's traumas I'm convinced came about because of her disastrous romantic choices—her selection of guys who for the most part left much to be desired in the gentle-and-caring department. But I could also be equally as persuasive about the notion that it was a way of trying to announce she didn't want to be so under her mother's dominion and control.

Another girl in our school, a classmate of mine, began cozying up to Debbie and befriending her. (I'll refer to her simply as "Maria." Though she came forward and did a television interview after Debbie's arrest, giving her real name, she asked that her real name not be used here, and I'm honoring that.) With Debbie, it wasn't just a friend Maria was looking for. It was a bedroom playmate. I always found a sharp quality to Maria that I was uncomfortable with. I thought she was forceful and controlling, sometimes with an edge of abusiveness. Over a period of weeks, she exercised her full powers of persuasion. Debbie's mother met the girl, took an instant dislike to her, and tried to warn her daughter off. That may have been the deciding factor. Debbie gave in to the girl's pressure.

They met at the house of a classmate, a girl who was, as we say, playing on same team. Apparently Debbie found something pleasing in the sensual experience because she came back for more. Several times. Not that this is so very uncommon; the 1986-87 Minnesota Adolescent Health Survey found that 27 percent of girls 15 and older reported having had sexual contact with another girl. *Twenty-seven percent.*

But in the Florida Bible Belt, girls who played with other girls kept very quiet about it. Debbie might soon enough have satisfied her curiosity and the rebellious instinct that drove her into another girl's arms.

So many people seem to relish seeing the mighty fall. It's part of what keeps the tabloid newspapers in business. Whispers spread around the school like wildfire: Debbie Beasley was making it with Maria. Smart, gorgeous, popular Debbie was a lesbo. Every time she walked down the corridor on the way to her next class, kids would snicker and elbow one another. Cruel, cutting remarks were exchanged just loud enough for her to hear. For Debbie, it was bitter and devastating.

The PA system clicked on over speakers throughout the school. The principal's voice was heard, interrupting classes.

"There will be no kissing in the hallways or anywhere on school property. There have been reports of same-sex kissing. This is never allowed."

Just about every one of the 2000 students knew that the remark about "same-sex kissing" was aimed at Maria and at Debra Beasley.

The relationship led to a steamy scene. As Maria tells it, one day at school she and Debbie went to the Girls' Room together, where Debbie passed out, perhaps from eating so little to stay thin for her singing career. Maria was trying to revive her, she says, when an athletic teacher, one Ms. Stebbins, walked in and found them.

A tornado had hit Debbie's life.

Of course, if what Ms. Stebbins discovered was really one student helping a friend who had passed out, the helper would probably have been showered with praise. In reality the scene was more likely something quite different. Debbie never shared the details with me, but it doesn't take much imagination to figure out what the two girls were most likely up to.

As soon as Joyce heard the story from the school principal, she began making arrangements to pull Debbie out of the East Bay and transfer her to another suburban Tampa high school, Bloomingdale, where Debbie was to spend the rest of her high school years, safely out of reach of her lesbian girlfriend.

Not long after the transfer, Debbie went into the bathroom at home, took a razor blade out of the medicine chest, and cut her wrists. Her father discovered her there a short time later. The wounds weren't deep; she had lost little blood. There was no need for an ambulance. Joyce, strong and calm, in her familiar take-charge mode, got Debbie settled down and comforted.

More a cry for help than a serious attempt to take her life, for Joyce it was an alarm bell.

Chapter 3
YOUNG OWEN

RACINE, WISCONSIN, WHERE I was born in June 1978, served in earlier times as a refuge for runaway slaves. When one slave was captured and jailed by federal marshals, a crowd of 5,000 broke into the jail, freed him, and saw him safely to Canada. That slave's freedom could be a symbol for a freedom choice I would face much later.

The city stands on the bank of Lake Michigan, at the mouth of the Root River, a drive of about an hour and a half north of Chicago. First settled in the 1830s, it became a factory town from its earliest days. Today its boosters brag about its industries and about the local office buildings and homes designed by Frank Lloyd Wright.

My father was a factory worker at In-Sink-Erator, the company founded by the man who invented the garbage disposal. Invited one day to visit the home of a man he worked with, Larry LaFave met the man's sister, Sallie. Larry and Sallie "both acted stupid and star-struck," she remembers. They married when she was 19. When I was born, she chose Kristian as my first name because it was a name she had always loved; my middle name, Owen, was a family name. Their marriage lasted only until I was three.

When I started school, the teacher looked at my name and, misreading it, called for "Kristina." My classmates settled on calling me that for the entire year. I realized my only means of survival would be to go by Owen.

For my mother, the following years were an all-too-familiar story in America—torn between longing for the traditional role of staying home and raising her son, and the need to provide the family income. Her pangs at having to spend her days away from me were all the greater because I was plagued by sinus problems and allergies, requiring frequent trips to the doctor.

We moved in with my grandmother. Her home, a small yellow house on Carter Street, reached up a steep driveway and had tiny rooms. Though the house was probably only 1400 square feet, I had my own bedroom. The rear yard featured stately old trees, a swing set, and in time a sandbox built especially for me.

Mother found work at a local publishing company driving a forklift, working long hours. But she was dedicated to the idea of my being well-educated and forming good values. She took advantage of an employee program that made company products available at a steep discount, which was a blessing because the firm published the wonderful Golden Books series, and she acquired the entire set for me. One of my fondest memories of those years are the times mother would find to sit with me reading from the Golden Books and teaching me to read from them. Though I longed to see more of her, the time we did have together was precious.

My grandfather was a sweet and gentle man, a tire salesman whose father had been the president of Pugh Oil. My grandmother I found to be lovable and kind. I was in my teens before I realized the friction and drama between her and my mother. When I was five, my grandmother divorced my grandfather, sold her home and remarried, following her new husband to Arizona. So we moved, joining a larger family—my mother's sister Libby and her three children. The two boys were several years older so my companion was mostly Lisa, two years younger than me. She wasn't the best of companions.

Whether to manipulate me or to manipulate her mother, Lisa was forever getting me into trouble. We'd be playing and suddenly she would smack me on the back of my head and run away. I'd chase her. She'd run to her mother pretending to cry, and between sobs she'd whimper, "Owen hit me again." That happened often enough to create continual friction in the household about the rotten behavior of bad boy Owen. The final straw came when my mother arrived home one day to discover me locked in a closet as punishment for something I hadn't even done. Though it would be a strain on her budget, she went searching for a place of our own.

She found a small but tidy two-bedroom apartment in a desirable neighborhood. I don't remember much about it except for the green shag carpeting on which I spent so many hours playing by myself.

But it was our own place, and a happy time for me. Though she worked a brutal 12-hour day, she still managed to be a model of a good mom, somehow helping me accept that her long working hours represented an admirable quality. I live by that same ethic today, learned from her in my childhood.

My mother had bigger plans for me than living out my life in the heavily industrial factory town of Racine. Her years at the publishing house had provided plenty of evidence that people with college degrees earned a lot more money than those without. Even after she had changed jobs to work for one of her brothers in a bill-collection business, she remained haunted by those years as a forklift driver and determined that her son would never have to take a job in manual labor. From the time I was three, she had insisted that while she prepared dinner, I sit at the kitchen table and "do homework"—giving me projects like coloring to develop the work ethic. Once I started school, she showed an enthusiasm for my experiences that convinced me learning was not just beneficial but could be fun, as well. At the same time, she also understood a youngster's life shouldn't be all in books. Her office job allowed time for the mommy-chauffeur chores, making it possible for me to take part in sports. Did I ever: football, baseball, and ice hockey.

My relationship with my father wasn't very comfortable. He still lived nearby, kept in touch, and I spent time with him. I guess I always understood that he loved me, but it was an intellectual understanding. He didn't know how to relate to a child. Neither did my grandfather, his dad. I could see that my dad must have grown up with the same feelings of distance from his father that I felt from him, but that didn't make the lack of affection any easier to bear.

For three summers in a row, I spent nearly a month with my mother's mother and her husband Ray in a world strangely different to me in more than one sense: They lived in the desert town of Yuma, Arizona, one of those places set down in the middle of parched, arid land, where you still feel a sense of the Old West. In Racine, the temperature in July rarely climbs above 80, while in Yuma, the July temperature rarely drops below 80. But their house had a swimming pool, which to a nine-year-old of my background meant they must be very wealthy. The luxury of being able to jump into the pool whenever I wanted probably left me with a sense of determination to be enough of a success in life that would day I be able to afford a house like that of my own.

My grandmother and Ray had a friend in Mexico and took me with them on visits to see him. Other than their friend, no one else in the family spoke more than a few words of English. I remember one meal at which I didn't recognize a single dish and didn't like any of the tastes, but could hear my mother's voice in my ear and so ate everything on my plate.

I also remember men casually walking down the street carrying a rifle and with an ammo belt slung over the shoulder, a sight that always made me feel uncomfortable.

Though I had never felt poor, I knew that money was always tight for us. Seeing the little children in the streets of the Mexican town and countryside made me feel fortunate that we lived as well as we did. Another feeling I remember from those trips: the nervousness I always felt at the border, returning to the U.S., when the Border Patrol guard would question us. At that age I was intimidated by any authority figure.

It would be years before those feelings would pass.

I think many parents don't realize how much it can mean to encourage the interests of their children. When I was 11, my mother announced one day that she had saved enough money to sign me up for a week at Space Camp in Florida. At that age I was fascinated by space and had dreams of becoming an astronaut. The idea that she was able to send me came as a complete shock; the thought of going enthralled me. I could hardly wait.

At the airport, she told me there was a purpose in the trip: She was sending me to Space Camp because "You need to know there's more to life than your own back yard." The reality was even better than I could have imagined, with simulations of zero gravity and the chance to watch an actual space shuttle launch. Seeing a launch on film is amazing; seeing it in person, feeling the shock waves rolling past, imagining you can feel the heat from the tongues of flame spewing out of the rocket engine—I can still close my eyes today, fifteen years later, and experience it all over again. With what little extra money she had, my mother was expanding my horizons in many directions.

Age 11 turned out to be a landmark year for me. In addition to another summer in Arizona and Space Camp, I also had my first date. The girl's name was Holly. (Is there anyone who doesn't remember the name of the boy or girl they first went out with?) I smile at writing this—the first of my true confessions in this book: I took Holly to see the movie "Uncle Buck" and we held hands in the darkened theater. When I dropped her off at her front door at the end of the evening, I thought it was too soon for a kiss and didn't try. Later Holly's sister teased me about that. I guess Holly had been ready and willing. It was my first failure with a girl—Holly never accepted another date from me.

The following year my mother remarried and we moved to a totally different part of the country: Vienna, Virginia, a stone's throw across the Potomac River from Washington, DC. My new stepfather, Pete, provided things my real father never had—helping me with my studies, driving me to my games, even going out into the yard to throw a football with me.

My mother had always wanted to paint. She had mostly done portraits in pencil through the years, but the dual challenges of too little time and too little money kept her from pursuing the passion. Now the situation was different. Pete's earnings as a consultant hired by hospitals around the country to solve their collections problems meant that mother didn't have to work and could afford to buy art supplies. She was like a bird freed from the cage, now focusing on landscapes, in oil.

That happy household didn't last very long. The summer before I was to begin high school, we moved to Riverview, Florida, just outside Tampa. My first day there, I walked into a chain store called Winn-Dixie and received a culture shock almost as powerful as the visits to Mexico. There were men out shopping with no shirts on, and barefoot kids with dirty feet. In Racine the rule everywhere was, "No shirt, no shoes, no service." I asked my mother, "Where have we moved to?!"

That fall I started at Riverview's East Bay High School, by then full of notions about laying the groundwork for medical school. I guess that came from the admiration I formed for the doctor who treated me as a sickly little boy, and from a sense that I wanted to help people. My schoolwork was good enough to qualify me for advanced placement in every subject that had an AP track, so medical school looked like it might be within my sights.

Socially, I started off slowly at East Bay. I wasn't very good at making friends in a new situation. But I went out for football and earned a place on the squad. Maybe that helped break the ice. By the middle of the first year I had made a group of friends. And looking back, I realize I was able to cross the dividing lines that usually segregate teenage society. I got along with the jocks, the geeks, and the A-list crowd. The most popular guys in the school were the ones who were smoking, drinking, and doing marijuana. I was friends with them, too, but wouldn't go to their parties. Not that I'm any sort of goody two-shoes, it's just that my mother had drummed into me the messages about making something of myself, starting with doing well enough in school to gain admission to a good college. Alcohol and drugs didn't seem to fit that picture.

By the end of the football season I had to face the fact that I was stuck as a second-squad player and would probably stay there, so I turned to another interest that I thought would serve me better. I quit football for music.

In my elementary school in Wisconsin, band wasn't an option—everybody had to choose an instrument. I began with the viola in fourth grade and switched to the trumpet in fifth, my mother encouraging the effort by paying for additional lessons outside of school. When I transformed myself from a football player to a member of the half-time marching band, it was the saxophone I had my heart set on. But at the time, that was out of the question for me. One day during the summer I had injured a pinky finger playing sandlot football and then that evening, doing kick-boxing, took a blow to the same hand that left the pinky broken and in a cast.

My grandfather had been a trumpet player good enough to have recorded a couple of albums. He restored his own trumpet for me, a fine Bach Stradivarius (though, despite the brand name, with no connection to the famous violin maker). That was enough to push me in the direction of carrying on the family heritage. I took up the trumpet in the concert band and, as well, in the marching band. Ever wonder how the school musicians in those half-time bands master a complicated routine of forming and reforming intricate figures while playing their instruments at the same time? I found it fun, challenging, and intensely annoying, all at the same time. Especially the long hours of practice that involved marching around an asphalt parking lot in the Florida heat.

I guess high school is a time when most kids rebel against their parents. I didn't see any need to rebel against my mom. She was still my most ardent fan and supporter, proud of my excellent grades in even the advanced classes, and I felt happy to have her on my team. Sure, there was a bit of a power struggle, but nothing like what most of my friends at school were going through.

The relationship with my stepfather, though, hadn't worked out as well. He was gone all week on his consulting work. When he arrived at home, he wanted to relax and unwind, barely leaving the house except to rent a video. And I thought he had turned uncivil to my mom. I paid him back by being uncivil to him.

Did you ever notice that kids in America don't make a big deal out of becoming old enough to vote, but turning 16 and getting that driver's license—now that's *really* a big deal. I hadn't been dating much; I guess girls in a big city might not mind going somewhere on a date by bus, but when you live where there aren't many buses, the choices are limited. See if you can find an older kid to double-date with you—good luck. Or ask a parent to drive you—ugh.

I wasn't given a rich-kid's gift of a sexy new car when I turned 16. I was given a car, though, a hand-me-down from my mother of a steel gray Chevy Beretta. I was happy to have it, never mind that it was a beast, and that every time I washed it, paint would come off on the sponge. Regardless, what mattered was that my dating life quickly improved.

The field soon narrowed to a pretty, sweet girl, Danielle, who was also in the band. That meant we were thrown together a lot, at band practice, at performances, on trips to competitions. She was my first serious girlfriend, with everybody in school knowing we were a couple through our junior and senior years. We actually talked about getting married, yet there was an undercurrent of friction between us. We'd have a tumultuous argument over something and break up. And then a couple of weeks later we'd get back together again. Maybe it's that way for a lot of kids in high school, part of the process of learning about relating to another person. Despite the fights, the relationship was a growing-up time for me. With Danielle, I learned a lot about how to work through problems and how to compromise, things I'm still grateful for.

Debra Beasley came into my life during that junior year of high school. Junior year for me, freshman year for her. She was unmissable, with her mass of blond hair, her gorgeous face, and her quick, ready smile. We were both going steady by the time our paths first crossed, and so there wasn't a question of our dating. Still, I felt a strong attraction and it was clear she did too. If there is such a thing as heavy flirting, we were into it.

One day she gave me her phone number, then went to class and asked Danielle if she was still dating me, because, Debbie said, "Owen just asked me for my phone number." When that class period was over, I went to my locker and found Danielle there, waiting for me, in tears. That killed anything there might ever have been between Debbie and me in high school. Perhaps I should have remembered that experience when our paths crossed again. Or maybe I did, and decided it just proved how strongly Debbie had been attracted to me, even back then.

The next school year was when she left East Bay High under circumstances that had the entire school whispering the unexpected word "lesbian." The news surprised the hell out of me, but I didn't think it was anything so horrific. On the other hand, if there were any other girls in the school playing the games that those two were, they were sure keeping quiet about it. From everything the other kids were saying, this was an aberration, unheard of, something to shake your head over or giggle about.

All through high school I knew that I had college in my future. My mother wouldn't have let me *not* go. Princeton was high on my list and eventually became my number one choice, and they wrote inviting me to come for an interview. My mother had sacrificed so much for me, instilling solid values and a powerful work ethic. Still, I was her only child. When I discussed the invitation with her, she said she'd prefer me to remain at home but would support me if I decided to go away to school.

I gave her the gift of my presence. With my nearly-all-A's record, the University of South Florida was glad to accept me. The campus is in Tampa; I would continue to live at home.

In June, I graduated fifth in my class, and in September of 1996 became a college freshman, starting off with courses that included biology—still thinking of medical school. And business calculus—nothing like having a contingency plan.

Even though my tuition was covered by a scholarship, I still had a lot of expenses that my stepfather wasn't going to help me with—gasoline, books, dating, and all the rest. I became one of the legion who soldier their way through college carrying the dual burdens of studies and work. I would put in about 25 hours a week all through my years of college in the corporate offices of the Shriners Hospital for Children, starting in the mail room and eventually climbing my way into hospital administration.

I was dating a girl I had started seeing over my summer between high school and college. She was a stunning girl, half Vietnamese but looking to me more Latin than Asian even with her almond-shaped eyes, which were set off by luxurious black hair and full lips. Light-hearted and playful, fun, with a good sense of humor, she taught me how to be in a real relationship. Her name was Angie; I didn't yet know that Debbie had a sister by the same name.

After my emotionally volatile roller-coaster with Danielle, Angie was a breath of fresh air. This felt like a normal, healthy relationship. And I was crazy about her.

We dated all through my freshman year and were still together when school started again in the fall of 1997. One night she said she was going over to visit a friend for little while. She had done that on other occasions, and been gone for three or four hours. This one night, she gave me the same story. After a while I had no answer from her cell phone, so drove over to her house. Her dad assured me that everything was really okay. I think he knew the truth but wasn't going to tell me. I hung out with her parents for an hour or so and she still hadn't come back, so I left and started driving home.

Angie and I had given each other the passwords to our cell phone voicemail. Okay, maybe it wasn't very smart in retrospect, but it's what the young people we knew were doing with their steadies. I checked in and there was a message from a guy saying, "Hey, I had a great time last night hanging out on the beach with you. I'm looking forward to seeing you again." This was a prelude of things to come that I would remember with enormous pain a few years later.

At that point I turned around and drove back to her parents'. She was home by then. When I confronted her, she admitted she was having a relationship with another guy, sleeping with the two of us at the same time.

This was a girl I felt head over heels about. I was totally crushed by this ultimate betrayal. I told her we were finished, and walked out. A series of tearful phone calls followed. Gullible me, I cared about her so much that I finally agreed...only to find that she was two-timing me the *second* time around. Enough is enough.

Emotionally, that was a hard time for me. But it made me take a look at my life and realize my closest buddies were the same friends I'd had in high school. Most of them seem to care more about partying than about doing anything with their lives. I needed some new friends.

The campus of a university offers an instant solution to this problem. I joined a fraternity, Sigma Alpha Epsilon—SAE. About the same time I also realized that a lot of my friends had been coming to me for advice about their problems. Apparently they looked on me as a pretty good sounding board and source of advice. But this post-Angie period of introspection and navel-gazing made me realize I really, really didn't like trying to solve people's problems.

I gave up thoughts of being a doctor—or a psychologist, which I had also been considering—and changed my major to business.

One day in my sophomore year, my old friend and fraternity brother Richie Maggio and I were sitting outside the Subway sandwich shop on campus when a girl came in and walked past our table. Richie, who had gotten a look at her, leaned over and said in an awed half-whisper, "Wow—that girl is hot." Me being cocky at the time, I said, "I'll go introduce you to her."

I followed the girl into the shop, tapped her on the shoulder, and said, "Excuse me." She turned around and her face broke into a big smile. "Owen!" she said.

My heart skipped a beat.

Debbie LaFave had started that term as a freshman on the same campus. She got her sandwich, came and sat down with us. After Richie left, Debbie and I spent the rest of the afternoon talking in the glorious sunshine of a fine Tampa day. She was clearly as excited to discover me as I was to discover her.

We talked about friends we knew, we talked about campus issues and national issues, we talked about courses we were taking, and about each other. I had dated my share of ditsy sorority girls. Debbie's conversation was light and playful, yet she had something to say for herself.

Along with her stunning looks, that made a killer combination.

Chapter 4
IN LOVE

ON THE ROMANTIC day in February 1999 when Debbie and I first connected in the unromantic setting of that campus sandwich shop, she told me about her current boyfriend, Andrew Beck, who would later move from bit player to major actor in this story. The most romantic day of the year had just passed, and I asked her, "What did the two of you do for Valentine's?"

She answered, "Well, nothing, really. He doesn't make a big deal out of things like that. What did you do with your girlfriend?"

I told her I didn't have one. I was dating, but there wasn't anyone special, no one to buy a Valentine's Day present for.

"He didn't give me a present, either," she said.

I thought she deserved better treatment than that, and said so. She asked for my phone number and pager number, and I asked for hers. The next day she paged me, I called back, and we chatted for a while. Over the next few days I would see her occasionally on campus with this Andrew character. Each time I saw them, the pattern was the same: Andrew striding ahead, Debbie following in his wake, a few steps behind, hurrying to keep up.

We had our first date the next weekend. She sent me a text message a couple of days later to say that she had broken up with Andrew. With similar situations—we both had fathers who were withdrawn and unable to show love, and we were both working to put ourselves through college—I think we felt a pull to each other of something more than just the usual sexual chemistry.

I met her parents quite early on, when I went to her house to pick her up for one of our first dates. Her mother seemed to approve of me, and I found her pleasant, outgoing, and likeable. Her father was much more withdrawn, but in time we would settle into a comfortable relationship that even included going fishing together.

Soon after Debbie and I started dating, she mentioned that "I smoke occasionally." I thought she meant socially. No—"occasionally" just meant she didn't smoke between cigarettes. I told her I couldn't date her if she was a smoker. Apparently even at that early stage, the relationship meant more to her than the cigarettes. She stopped.

We were going steady within a couple of months. The comfortable feelings allowed her to open up to me that she was on medication for depression. After her suicide attempt, her mother had put her into therapy and she had begun taking an antidepressant. Though she had quit the therapy, she was still on the medication. She said that when she was going with Andrew, he used tell her "You're psychotic," as a way of encouraging her to keep taking her pills.

She quit the meds soon after we started going together, saying that she felt as if she were in control of her emotions and wanted to prove it to herself. I thought it was heartwarming that this girl I was coming to have such strong feelings about was gaining confidence from being around me.

Little by little, as we grew comfortable with each other, the stories of her sorry boyfriend history began to come out. The kid who had forced himself on her to take her virginity. And who once stopped her in the corridor at school, she said, pushed her into a corner, and fingered her—in plain sight of anybody who might have walked by just at that moment.

Then the musician, who mistreated her and cheated on her (which, if you believe all the stories you see in the media and on television about music celebrities, is the behavior you would expect from a rock musician, even a very young one).

Next in this saga after the musician was a guy she met through her sister Angie, who sounded as if he should have been Mr. Right. Angie was engaged at the time to a friendly, preppy local guy named Kyle O'Dell. The Beasley and the O'Dell families were spending time together, which was a happy thing in one way because Debbie and Angie had allowed the friction of sibling rivalry to create some distance between them, and the two families coming together eased old tensions between the sisters, drawing them closer.

These shared visits also threw Debbie into the company of one of Kyle's closest friends, Donald, who was an auto mechanic and a bit of a southern country redneck.

Kyle had a protective side to his nature. Distressed for Debbie from the time she had been through with the turmoil over her lesbian affair and her suicide attempt, he was determined to help her find stability. His friend Donald stepped up to the plate, taking on the role of looking after Debbie. Not as a supportive friend, although perhaps that's the way the relationship began, but as a boyfriend. Donald was Debbie's number-one squeeze from about her sophomore year in high school until partway into her senior year.

The motives sound noble enough; the story is more complicated than that. When I was introduced to the family, the Donald I came to know along with the rest of the Beasley and O'Dell clan was verbally abusive and a chronic drinker. As far as I can see, he couldn't have been much of a success in taking care of Debbie because he was not much of a success in taking care of himself. Yet Debbie had been in love with him. There had been other lovers before him, but this was different. Donald had become not just a lover but Debbie's first love.

To his credit, he got along very well with Debbie's parents, in particular her father. Larry was fond of going fishing and so was Donald. With Tampa Bay just down the street, so to speak, setting out for an afternoon of fishing was easy. Maybe Larry didn't see anything out of the ordinary in a boyfriend or husband who with a few beers in him could turn critical or hostile and make life miserable for his woman. He raised no objection Debbie ever knew about to the way she was being treated.

But Debbie did have one champion in the family against Donald. At some point along the line she shared with me stories about a couple of occasions on which her sister confronted Donald about the way he was treating Debbie, and threatened to beat him up. *Beat him up*? Debbie's *sister* was going to beat up Debbie's boyfriend? The Angie I eventually grew to know wasn't intimidated by anybody. She was as aggressive as a bulldog, probably from standing up to the dominating mama Joyce all those years. But for her to threaten Donald that way gives an idea of how badly he must have been treating Debbie.

It was all part of a pattern. According to Debbie, every boyfriend she had had before she started seeing me had abused her in one way or another.

I wonder: if Debbie had ended up married to Donald, would she have had a life anything like her sister's? Angie's existence took some curious and unhappy turns. The man she married was one of those easy-going people who everybody seems to like being around. On the other hand, he wasn't motivated toward any work or career, so he wasn't a very good provider.

One night when Angie and Kyle were visiting at the home of some friends, their host was doing something or other with his shotgun when it accidentally went off. Angie, in the line of fire, was knocked to the floor. She was rushed to the hospital, where the doctors determined that her wounds were not critical. They extracted a load of buckshot pellets from her buttocks and her back. The report that the doctor had for the family, though, was distressing. A lot of the pellets had passed through her skin and launched internally. The doctor warned that with so much lead in her body, she might never be able to bear children. Not long after, Angie became pregnant but as predicted suffered a miscarriage.

In one of those curious quirks that mark so many key events in life, there turned out to be one benefit from the gunshot accident. The insurance company settled with the young O'Dell couple for enough money that they were able to buy a house and newer car, and live a life of comparative ease.

Even the best of good news sometimes has a dark-edged lining. Kyle had never been much of a go-getter to begin with. The insurance settlement made it all the easier for him to drift. He worked for a while in a tire rim shop. He signed up for training to become a computer support technician working with Microsoft Windows, but never finished. Drifting from one job to another, he worked for a while as a waiter at a nearby restaurant in the Chili's chain.

For two years Debbie tried to make a go of her relationship with Donald before finally recognizing the futility of it all. Her next choice was a guy who wasn't a heavy drinker but in other ways wasn't much of an improvement. This was Andrew, the guy she was dating when I met her on campus. As she described it to me later, Andrew was highly controlling and very jealous—in particular jealous of Donald, the previous boyfriend who she had been in love with.

This was an ongoing hot-button issue because Debbie often visited her sister's. Donald, her brother-in-law's close friend, was frequently there at the same time. So in the normal course of affairs, Debbie was still running into her one-time true love. For a jealous guy like Andrew, this was really hard to swallow. Sometimes Debbie would bring Andrew along to Angela's, and the green-eyed monster inside Andrew would stir and rumble.

That monster clawed out of its cage one day. Debbie was at her sister's waiting for Andrew, who was to join her there a little later on. She and Donald decided to go out and have something to drink. When they returned, Andrew was there, seething. He shouted at Debbie, "You're cheating on me." Donald and Andrew started trading blows in a fistfight that was more than just a few angry swings to let off steam. They were really trying to hurt each other. Either because Andrew was a better fighter or because he was the one with the burning rage, he beat Donald savagely. When the two were separated, Angie stepped in and started pounding away on Andrew. By then the police were at the door.

This was the family that I would in a few years be marrying into.

Andrew landed himself into even more trouble with the family later on. He had been a fairly regular visitor to the Beasley home. One day when he knew that the parents and Debbie would all be out, he came over and entered the house, went to Debbie's room and forced the door open. He searched around, found her diary, broke the clasp, and sat down to read. I guess he was simply driven by his jealous nature and couldn't bear not knowing whether Debbie had confided anything in her diary about sleeping with other guys at the same time she was dating him.

When Joyce and Larry found out what had happened, they told Debbie that Andrew would never be allowed in their house again. Debbie abided by that rule. But, incredibly, she kept on dating him.

The Debra Beasley I grew to know once we became a couple I found to be not just gorgeous and intelligent; she seemed grateful to have a guy in her life who wasn't mistreating her in one way or another. And while her dad didn't seem to have many demands for guys she brought into the house beyond their being able to carry on a conversation or, even better, go fishing with him, Joyce was a different story.

On one of our first dates, I found out that Debbie's room, the smallest of the three bedrooms, still had her childhood collection of half a dozen Barbie dolls and maybe twice as many stuffed animals. I know from the apartment my mother and I shared for a few years that it's not easy keeping a collection of child's things tidy, especially in such a small place. Joyce was a thorough, careful housekeeper.

Judging from books I saw around the house, Debbie's leisure reading in those days favored mystery novels, with best-selling author James Patterson apparently a favorite. Joyce's literary taste wasn't hard to figure out: the Woman's Devotional Bible never seemed to be far from her reach.

Though Debbie butted heads with her mother on some levels, on other levels her mother was a crucial emotional crutch. In high school when Debbie had gone on her trips for singing or modeling, her mother always went along. Nothing particularly unusual about that. But now she was a college girl, an age when many young women are out on their own. Yet whom did she call when she needed some emotional comforting? Not me, her boyfriend. No, you guessed it: she called her mother.

Even that part didn't seem really outlandish. I'm sure there are plenty of twenty-something girls who have a similar relationship with their mothers. How many college girls, though, call on their mother every once in a while with the request, "I need you to come to class with me today"? Mrs. Beasley became something of a familiar sight to kids taking courses with Debbie, the lone person of about the same age as some of the professors, sitting there among the students.

Some time around my third visit or so, Mrs. Beasley insisted I start calling her "Joyce." Her husband waited a while longer to see if I was really going to stay in Debbie's life before inviting me to use his first name. I thought I was starting to comprehend the Beasley family M.O., though I would never fully accept the family dynamics—not when we were dating, and especially not after Debbie and I were married.

Larry seemed to take a liking to me; we bonded fairly well and had conversations not just about guy stuff of sports and cars but subjects he took an interest in, especially current events. He respected my passion for history and seemed to enjoy getting me to talk about the subject. For his part, he had an enthusiasm for what he called antiquing, which for him meant going to garage sales. Sometimes I'd go along and he'd tell me all about why he chose the items he was purchasing and why he thought they were worth owning. A small enough attempt at reaching out, but appreciated.

Debbie and I were very soon seeing each other nearly every day on campus, and going out together three or four times a week, sometimes with fraternity brothers and their dates to a local bar, sometimes studying together or renting a video to watch at her home or occasionally at mine.

Being with her was completely different from any of the experiences I can remember with the numerous coeds I had been dating. Initially I had been drawn to Debbie because of her beauty but that had quickly become layered with my appreciation for her brains, starting from that very first long conversation. Though it was easy to tag her for a ditzy blonde, the label didn't fit. And the more time I spent with her, the more I saw signs of her drive, dedication, and intellect.

She had mentioned to me early on that she was going to be flying out to California to spend a little time with a cousin. One day she made a suggestion that surprised and pleased me. Would I like to join her for the trip to California? You bet I would. Just thinking about spending that much time in her company had me in fantasyland.

I was legally an adult at this point, but a child still living at home gives parents a voice they wouldn't otherwise have. When I mentioned the California trip to my mother, she wasn't exactly thrilled by the idea and asked to meet the young lady. And her parents. I set up the powwow. Debbie and I were naturally both a little nervous about how things would go.

We worried needlessly—the adults quickly established a comfort level, my mother approved of Debbie, and we were given a thumbs-up for the trip.

Sometimes even a fraternity guy can be a gentleman. Debbie already had her hotel reservations and knew money was really tight for me, so she suggested we share the room. Her parents didn't even think to ask about the room arrangements, nor did my mother. I'm sure it never even occurred to any of them that we might double up.

Even though Debbie had made it clear that sex wasn't part of the deal, for days just the thought of sharing a hotel room with her stirred my blood, my mind staying on overdrive wondering how the scene would play out.

In bed together for the first time, we kissed and we touched a little. She said, "Owen, let's not, okay?" And explained that she didn't want to start so early in the relationship. Part of me felt the same way. I really wanted to build something solid with Debbie and knew that sex at this stage could be a misstep that might throw things off track and somehow spoil the feelings we both had for each other. Other girls I had slept with on a first or second date without thinking twice about it. This was different.

I had a sense that with a little coaxing, a little urging, a little more touching, she would have changed her mind. It took a truckload of self-restraint but I knew she was right. I hugged her and kissed her and said good night.

Whatever problems she had had in the past and would have in the future with sex, on that trip she was in complete control of herself.

It was only a couple of weeks later when we both let down our guards and shared that most private and most satisfying part of a relationship. We were spending the evening at the home of my mother and stepfather, where I was still living. They went out and wouldn't be home until late. Debbie and I had already come close a couple of times. I suspected that my house might be more congenial for the purpose than her own, which turned out to be right.

She was relaxed, unrestrained, without any reservations or apparent hang-ups. For me, it had been some time since I had been intimate with a girl I had a relationship with and some real feelings for. This was one of those memorable experiences, one of those wonderful shared times that deepens each person's feeling for the other.

In our college years, while I continued to inch my way up in the Shriners Hospital administrative ladder, Debbie worked at a series of part-time jobs, including manicurist, waitress, and bank teller. She wasn't getting singing gigs anymore, but she was still doing a bit of modeling work.

One of those modeling jobs was for a local start-up magazine called *Makes and Models*, a clever play on words. The target audience was guys interested in specialized, exotic cars and motorcycles—so "makes and models," the auto industry shorthand for makes and models of cars. But the publisher's angle was that he would show each vehicle with an attractive, sexily-dressed, or just-barely-dressed girl posed in or alongside it. Debbie was one of the girls hired to do a photo session for the magazine's first issue. She told me about it at the time—this was after we had been dating for about four months—but when the magazine sent her a set of the photos, she refused to let me see them.

The more she stood her ground, the more I imagined the worst. This led to one of our first big fights. When she finally let me see the pictures shortly before our wedding, I felt bad about the fuss I had made. In a photograph labeled "Man's Best Friends," she was posed on a motorcycle wearing a skimpy bathing suit, skimpy enough that she felt cheapened by it—the church-going girl with the devoutly religious mother had done something that seemed to her as bad as having posed for *Playboy*. Okay, the picture was on the sleazy side, but it wasn't any more revealing than any bathing suit she owned. Besides, Joyce had gone with her; even her own mother hadn't objected to the outfit she was being photographed in.

Over time, as Joyce began to recognize that I wasn't just another guy Debbie was dating but was likely to be around for awhile, she started to confide in me some of her concerns about her younger daughter. She explained the suicide attempt by calling Debbie "fragile" and making the obvious remark that "it was a very difficult time for all of us."

I felt warmly toward Joyce and appreciated her concerns for Debbie but by now I had been blinded by my passion. That passion was about to be tested.

After Debbie and I had been dating for about a year, I began to hear a lot of "not tonight" responses when the subject of sex came up. Sure, that happens to couples after the initial flush of newness wears off, but this had to be something else. And when she did say okay, she was very limited in what she was willing to do—like the guy who complained to his friend that his wife only wanted to do it doggie—style: "I sit up and beg, and she rolls over and plays dead."

Something had to be wrong. But what?

Chapter 5
UPS AND DOWNS

WHEN YOU CARE for someone enough, you don't run away at the first sign of trouble. You apply equal doses of determination and patience, and see the problems through. Debbie and I had hit this speed bump about sex something like a year into our relationship. Even if I wasn't ready to speak the three little words that men are told every girl longs to hear, I was deeply committed, with stronger emotions for her than I had ever felt for any other girl. Sex limited to unenthusiastic, only-now-and-then, or even no sex at all, wasn't going to drive me away.

The two of us had enchanting times talking and interacting, connecting on viewpoints, sharing our dreams and goals. We also shared some less desirable qualities. We were both used to getting our own way, both a bit stubborn. Debbie had another flaw, as well: a possessiveness, a jealous streak that would lead to the brink of breaking up.

But the immediate irritation was over her more and more often responding to suggestions about sex with that classic line of so many bad dirty jokes: some variation of "Not tonight, dear, I have a headache." At first she had been so enthusiastic, enjoying each session and in between times looking forward to the next. When she opened up and said, "With you, I don't even need to use lubrication," I took that to mean that our sexual encounters had brought her to new and greater heights of enjoyment.

Whatever the magic was between us that had made K-Y Jelly unnecessary, it seemed to have evaporated. She didn't need lubricant because she wasn't having sex. Or at least, she wasn't with me. After the experience with my earlier two-timing sweetheart, I couldn't help wondering whether there might be someone else. Or was she losing interest in me?

I tried to be sensitive to her needs and desires. I told myself she deserved her space. After a while I started asking myself what could be going on. At that point in my life I had been around girls enough to feel comfortable and confident. Lots of girls seem to find me appealing. But I was growing insecure.

We had spiraled downward from frequent, fun sex to hardly any at all, and something bordering on boring when it did happen. On the surface, about everyday things, we were getting along fine. Yet sex provides an emotional comfort level and a warm sense of security. Without it, I wasn't feeling that close to her emotionally. It seemed more than obvious she wasn't feeling that close to me, either.

Three months went by with sex about once a month. Finally I said, "You know, we rarely have sex these days. And when we do, it's not very exciting. You need to tell me what the hell is going on."

She said, "Owen, I really care for you. I have a very dark past. I have been put through hell. I don't want to take you into that bad space with me. I don't want to bring you into that world."

Then she told me about the rapes when she was 13. I felt heartbroken for her. I felt as if I wanted to wrap a cocoon around us and protect her from all the harms and hurts of the world.

I think she must have felt the protectiveness and support I was offering. Or else she sensed that she was in danger of losing me. Whatever the explanation, the sex frequency started to improve. It had taken about three months to reach the driest stage, and it took about the same length of time till we were fully up to speed again, to the point where Debbie became more active in suggesting sex, taking the initiative to show her interest.

But the physical part of our relationship never did get back to as good as it had been. Some of the spontaneity was gone. There wasn't any more of, "Hey, how about it," and hopping into bed. She began insisting we each had to shower before lovemaking. Okay, I know the old saying about cleanliness being next to godliness. I won't argue there's anything wrong with scrubbing before loving. Still, it felt a lot less like a pair of 20-something young lovers than a pair of 30- or 40-somethings who had lost some of the playfulness.

Looking back, I think maybe that sudden cleanliness business was part of an obsessiveness that I had been noticing in other areas. I had become something of a gym rat, trying to tone up my biceps and abs to give my body a little better definition and a little more size. At first it was a drag but then I started really getting into it. For a while my enthusiasm was a mystery to Debbie. Then she tried it, found she liked it, and started going to the gym regularly. This became one of the first places where I saw early signs of her going overboard. She figured out that this could be a route to improving her shape so she began working out with a passion, taking it to an extreme. From my perspective her shape didn't need improving, but by then she was beyond listening to anybody else's opinion on the subject.

It was only a small step from there to deciding that treadmill and stationary bike were wonderfully satisfying but the results weren't coming fast enough. Some new ingredient had to be added to the fitness formula. As it turned out, the new ingredient wasn't something she added but something she subtracted: food. We'd go out to dinner with friends; Debbie would order along with everybody else. When the food was served, she'd pick at it and move it around her plate, pick something up on her fork as if she was going to eat it, and then put it down again.

Eventually when the busboy would come to clear the plates, hers would have just about as much as when it had been set it in front of her. Then the waiter would come to take the orders for dessert. If there was something on the menu like an apple crisp, or chocolate cake with ice cream, or almost anything with chocolate, she'd order it. And when it came, there wouldn't be any of that pushing it around the plate and not actually eating. In the description of one friend, she'd sometimes order a dessert meant for four people and plunge into the whole thing herself. Apparently in Debbie's version of starving one's self, desserts were allowed.

I shouldn't make a joke of this. Eating that way is a sign of problems. I was a little slow in recognizing that her behavior wasn't just a bit odd, it was dangerous. But then, her parents were slow to recognize it, too.

Sometimes when Debbie and I had a date for dinner, I'd be running late because of schoolwork or held up getting away from my part-time job at the Shriners. I'd always call as soon as I could to say what time I'd be there. It didn't matter. As soon as I walked through the door of her parents' house, she'd start in on me, spitting angry words. It wasn't until months later that I discovered why she would become so furious. She had been starving herself all day; waiting even an extra 20 or 30 minutes before going out to dinner was more than she could endure. Of course, she could have helped herself to a piece of fruit from the Beasley refrigerator to stave off hunger. And once we sat down at the restaurant she wasn't going to eat more than a nibble anyway, until time for dessert. That didn't stop her from throwing what Southern ladies call "a hissy fit."

The eating behavior was bad enough. Another problem was a side effect causing a lot of embarrassment with my friends. She had some bizarre social anxieties that I don't understand to this day. We'd make a date to go out with other couples. When I arrived at her house to pick her up, she'd announce that she wasn't going. This wasn't once or twice when she had a headache or thought she was coming down with a cold. Most of the time she didn't even offer a reason. Just, "I'm not going."

For a social guy like me, evenings at home are fine as long as that's not the only thing on the calendar. I like a lot of friends around me, and all those guys who became instant friends at college when I joined the fraternity still expected me to hang out with them now and then. But it became increasingly difficult because Debbie didn't want to be in that environment. She didn't want to be around those people.

Sure, most of my fraternity brothers were party guys. What's wrong with that? Young, single—what better time of life is there to hang out and party it up? I can understand a girlfriend being suspicious of what we might be getting up to when a bunch of us went out together for a guys' night out. I won't claim we didn't sometimes become a little rowdy, turn a little randy, and grow a little out of control. But never enough to get kicked out of any bar or club.

Sometimes we were like a bunch of *Animal House* characters out carousing—a bunch of guys hanging with a bunch of girls, some of them very attractive, all fixed on having a good time. Did I ever chat up a pretty girl, a sexy girl, a flirty girl? What of it—I didn't take any of them home or spend part of any night in somebody else's arms.

I never gave Debbie any reason to doubt me, but she imagined the worst. Her response when I went out with the guys ranged from annoyed to off-the-wall anger. I put it down to insecurity showing itself as unbridled jealousy. I wasn't used to a jealous, possessive girlfriend. These weren't our finest moments.

I think Debbie herself was insecure in that environment and didn't feel comfortable. She was very self-conscious, insecure even about her beauty. She did not view herself as being attractive. By her own standards she was never pretty enough, never skinny enough, never measuring up in other ways that were still her own secrets.

Debbie's flights of jealousy took a variety of forms. One night the two of us were watching a Britney Spears video. Out of the blue she snapped, "You want Britney Spears more than me!" She wasn't teasing; she was practically in tears.

Another time we were watching *Newlyweds* with Jessica Simpson, who seems to me book-smart but ditsy and naïve, with quirks and behavior like Debbie's. I said, "She's just like you." Debbie answered, "You wish I *was* her, don't you?" After that, she would never watch *Newlyweds* again.

One flare-up was so devastating that it could have ended the relationship. A group of the people I worked with on the Shriners staff would get together now and then for drinks. I would join them when I could, and though Debbie didn't enjoy their company very much, once in awhile she would accompany me, as she did one night when the gang of us were at a bar. Somebody in the group ordered a round for everyone of a drink that was a specialty of this place, a drink with an in-your-face name that offended Debbie: it was called a Blow Job.

It's just a single shot of liquor but served in a wide Bourbon glass. One of the ladies in the group was heavyset, fun-loving, full of laughs. When the drinks were served, this lady picked up hers and managed to open her mouth wide enough to get her lips around the entire rim of the glass. I looked at her and made a crack with an obvious sexual innuendo: "Hey, what are you doing later?" It brought a big laugh all around.

Debbie hauled off and slapped me in the face as hard as she could.

I looked at her and said, "What the hell's the matter with you?"

Red-hot angry, and really embarrassed as well, I walked out. Debbie had driven there in her own car, and I just left her.

When I called later, she cried hysterically but I offered no sympathy. I told her, "That was absolutely ridiculous, entirely uncalled for. You completely over-reacted."

The next day I called her and apologized. It wasn't so much that Debbie was jealous; she was just so insecure that I believe she really thought I was actually coming on to that very nice but quite a bit older and quite, quite heavyset lady.

I can't help but wonder what Debbie would have been like if she hadn't suffered that sexual abuse at age 13. I believe her insecurity, her depression, and a whole range of her uncomfortable behaviors are very likely traced to that gruesome experience.

Somewhere along the line, Joyce must have understood that her daughter was sleeping with me. By then I guess she had come the conclusion that my values, my respect for her daughter, and my determination to succeed in life marked me as the most likely suitor Debbie had ever brought home. So Joyce, despite being so devoutly religious, had apparently overcome whatever traditional values she may have held about sex before marriage.

When Debbie and I were going out together and knew we wouldn't be back until late, sometimes she and her mother would prepare a trundle bed for me in Debbie's bedroom. But in this very small house, her parents' bedroom directly opposite across a narrow corridor made it almost like having a microphone in Debbie's room connected to a speaker across the hall. No way we were going to make out in that setting.

The funny thing is that it was Larry who eventually put his foot down. Even though I had never even sneaked into Debbie's bed on any of those occasions, Larry, the non-churchgoer, was the one who objected to my staying overnight. I wonder if Joyce ever said to him, "They're sleeping together anyway. What difference does it make?" Larry didn't speak very much or make many decisions, but when he did, he was listened to. After that, no matter how late I brought Debbie home, I had to drop her off and drive the 15 minutes to the house of my mother and stepfather.

Every January for the past hundred years, the city of Tampa has held a Mardi Gras-like festivity, the Gasparilla Pirate Festival, which takes its name from a legendary pirate, one José Gaspar, who is supposed to have plied his trade along the west coast of Florida around the beginning of the 19th century. The festival includes two parades—one for children, the other a bit more rowdy. A pirate ship lands near downtown Tampa, crowds of folks parade in colorful costumes, hundreds of thousands of tourists show up, and the streets are lined with booths selling food, drinks, and trinkets.

Naturally the college crowd shows up en masse. At the Gasparilla in my senior year, Debbie and I were there along with half a dozen of my fraternity brothers and their dates. This was a typical Tampa winter day—temperature in the low 70s, but humidity in the high 80s. Debbie and I were dressed pretty much like the rest: me in khaki shorts, tee-shirt, and flip-flops, she looking terrific in tank top, shorts, and sandals.

At one point during the afternoon, while the group was milling around doing nothing in particular, I joined the line at a nearby bank of porta-potties. While waiting my turn, the girl behind me tried to strike up a conversation. I could see Debbie watching me and offered innocent, unenthusiastic replies to my would-be conversational partner, carefully not turning around. Maybe the girl was boyfriend-less and trying to pick me up, maybe she was there with a guy and hoping to make him jealous, or maybe she was the friendly type just trying to pass a few minutes with idle chatter. Whatever, she wasn't catching on to any of my "not interested" cues. She obviously wasn't even bothered by the fact that I never once turned my head to look at her. Given Debbie's history of jealousy, I didn't dare.

Debbie didn't see my obvious lack of response as a sign of reassurance. She looked disgusted, throwing her hands down in anger and annoyance. When I had finished and rejoined the group, Debbie read me the riot act. In front of my friends, she lashed out, shouting, tearing into me.

My surprise gave way to anger and I shouted back at her, "I can't live my life like this. You're being ridiculous."

She looked stunned but I wasn't through. "I'm sick of your jealousy, I'm sick of your anorexia," I shouted. "I'm done. It's over," and I walked away with her hurrying after me.

Though I had calmed down by the time we reached her house, I hadn't changed my mind. With her parents listening to the whole scene, I told Debbie, "I care about you but your anger is tearing us both apart. I'm sorry, but it's over."

What happened then was kind of ridiculous. Joyce started pleading with me, Larry overcame his usual reserve to chime in with reasons why I shouldn't quit the relationship, the two of them talking at the same time with Debbie meanwhile throwing herself to the floor and wrapping her arms around my legs in a desperate attempt to keep me from walking out, pleading and crying. It is a scene that even a daytime soap opera wouldn't risk for fear of their viewers finding it absurdly over the top.

Finally I gave in. I sat down. We all sat down. I said to Debbie, "Look, you used to be on medication for your mood swings and your anxiety. And you used to go to a therapist. You've got the same problems now, and they're making life with you impossible."

I had never talked to her so bluntly about her problems. She was wide-eyed, frowning but quiet. Listening.

I said, "If you tell me you'll go back to your therapist and you'll take whatever medications she prescribes, I'll give this another chance." Debbie's blue eyes filled with tears. She threw her arms around me and hugged me. I didn't need the words: the hug was enough of promise.

It would be a wild exaggeration to claim that our problems were over as soon she was back in therapy and back on medication.

Though the emotional climate between us started getting better, psychological problems never get cleared up that easily, of course. I was deceived into thinking the worst was behind us.

Even though she saw herself as not as good-looking as a lot of my fraternity brothers' dates, and even though she saw herself as plump and round when she was really well-shaped and skinny enough not to even think about taking off weight, to me she was the prize of the campus—great-looking, luscious body, among the brightest of her classmates, and most of the time a pleasure to be with. Despite the occasional stress and turmoil, I felt blessed to have her in my life.

And I felt the envy of other guys. Sometimes you can see that look in a man's eyes, the look that says, "Lucky guy, to have a lady like that for a bed partner."

Larry, Joyce, and Debbie were at home the night of April 18, 2001, when the doorbell unexpectedly rang. Outside were two policemen.

Debbie's sister had been on the brink of seeing a long-held wish come true. By now divorced, she had dated two guys, one a manager at a Burger King, then a man she seemed to have a strong attachment to, a uniform salesman. She became pregnant, this time desperately hoping to prove the doctors wrong and deliver a healthy baby. Five months along, she was doing well and had already chosen a name for her unborn daughter: Madison Jean.

About nine o'clock that April night, she was driving home in her 1998 Nissan Altima after a pizza outing. She stopped at a stop sign, then began to make a left turn, crossing the path of a car approaching the intersection from the opposite direction. That driver also had a stop sign.

The other car, a 1992 Jeep Wrangler, was being driven by Army Captain Joseph Piotrowski, who had spent the day buying a suit and a pair of shoes, and going to a job interview at a dermatologist's office, all in preparation for his return to civilian life. Piotrowski had a dismal driving record. The previous year he had sideswiped another vehicle and driven away from the scene; about an hour later the same night he barely avoided colliding with a police car. He failed a sobriety test and refused a blood-alcohol test, but was not arrested. He was only given a ticket for improper lane change plus leaving the scene of the earlier accident.

Months later, the day before he was due to appear in court on charges from that accident, he was stopped again for drunk driving and once again refused to submit to a blood-alcohol test. That triggered an automatic 18-month suspension of his license.

After his last appointment on the day of Angie's pizza dinner, police reports say that Piotrowski stopped at a liquor store for two half-pint bottles of Jack Daniels, and drank them both in the parking lot.

One of the two policemen standing at the Beasley door, his uniform blood-stained, was holding a bloody woman's handbag. He asked, "Are you the parents of Angela Beasley?"

Captain Piotrowski, drunk again, had slammed into Angie's car.

She was dead by the time the ambulance arrived. Piotrowski's blood alcohol level was about three times the legal limit.

The loss of her sister would draw Debbie and her mother even closer together. Larry, who didn't share much emotionally in the best of times, took it very hard, almost as if he felt he carried part of the blame. He became teary-eyed at times, snapping at the family over small things, even more withdrawn. Worse, he inflicted one of those wounds that can never heal. Debbie had long struggled over the relationship with her dad. In his pain,

Larry said out loud words that Debbie heard as something like "I've lost my only child."

The wound was so deep that she would at least on one occasion blurt out the story to someone who was virtually a stranger. When Debbie began teaching a year later, a teacher she would meet at the school says that "from day one" Debbie told her about that remark of her father's—as if sharing it could ease the pain.

For Larry, though, there was one small benefit out of the tragedy: he went into therapy, something I think the whole family could have benefited from if he had done so much earlier.

Debbie had a satchel full of psychological problems already. Her sister's death would add a heavy weight of ongoing, long-term pain and unhappiness.

In a two-child family, the children face typical younger child/older child issues that either bond siblings to each other against parents as the common foe, or create frictions and bad feelings—mostly, as I understand it, on the part of the younger. Debbie, who had some resentments about the way Angela had treated her, also thought there was some heavy resentment in the other direction—a sharp jealousy over Debbie's short-lived but envy-making career in modeling. Altogether it was enough to keep Debbie from being very close to her sister, even after Angie married and moved out of the family house.

Maybe it wasn't reasonable, but the emotional distance Debbie had maintained from her sister because of resentments still harbored, now made her feel guilty and unhappy with herself, just the way many adults feel guilty at the death of a parent when they have left issues unresolved. She blamed herself for not having been closer. The mantle of sadness that cloaked her family carried for Debbie the added burden of this guilt. I was there with hugs to comfort her, a shoulder for her to cry on, and words of reassurance, yet I knew that feeling of helplessness when nothing you do or say can truly ease the pain.

The funeral was marred by one of those horrific moments like something dreamed up for a penny-novel. After Joyce spoke on behalf of the family, and some of Angela's friends had come to the pulpit to share remembrances, the former boyfriend, the Burger King manager, walked to the pulpit. He spoke briefly, announcing that the baby Angela had been carrying was not from her newest boyfriend, as all the family thought, but was his.

No one could believe what they had just heard. I'm not a fighter but I wanted to punch him out right there in the church. But it was too late for that—the damage had been done.

Debbie came up with the idea of getting tattoos after her sister died, in memory of Angela but also in memory of her grandmother, Joyce's mother, who had been very special in Debbie's life. After her grandmother's death, Debbie had begun to notice lots of butterflies, and it pleased her to think they were a sign that her grandmother was still with her and was saying, "I'm okay." Somehow her sister's death had also become connected in Debbie's heart to the butterfly symbol. She felt the tattoos would be a way of saying about her sister and her grandmother, *They're thinking about me, they're around me.*

When she told me of the tattooing plan, I wasn't enthusiastic. I just don't like tattoos. But it was her body, and she was entitled to make the decision whether it pleased me or not. I voiced my opinion and then stayed out of it. In addition to a pair of butterfly tattoos, she also had her sister's name rendered in Chinese lettering—the symbols for An Ji, which she was told was the closest way of writing the sound of her sister's name, Angie.

In the spring of 2001 I faced one of those life changes that promises to be joyous but brings a full measure of uncertainty and doubt. I would soon be graduating. In addition to evenings spent together, Debbie and I had been seeing each other on campus several times a week, sometimes nearly every day. I wasn't sure how leaving the protected school setting and not seeing her so often would change our feelings for each other.

The job situation faced me with other uncertainties. The people at the Shriners Hospital administrative staff were prepared to offer me a full-time job. From my humble beginnings with them, I had risen to a junior executive position; staying there would be comfortable, yet I couldn't see the opportunity for advancement and success I was hoping for.

Then Morgan Stanley came through with a job offer that sounded like just the sort of thing I had in mind. I never had a chance to find out. Between the time of the offer and graduation, the stock market took its infamous nosedive of 2000, and the job went up in smoke. That left only one good offer on the table: a position in the real-estate credit department of Florida Bank (later to become Mercantile Bank). It seemed to be a place that offered the opportunity to learn about the real estate field and multiple types of businesses, plus stellar possibilities for advancement for a determined young man willing to work hard. And the people I'd be working with seemed bright, friendly, supportive, and enthusiastic to have me on the team. I told them I was happy to accept.

One other piece made me eager for June to arrive. My father said he would fly in to see me graduate. We had never really bridged the gulf between us that had existed since my childhood; I had continued to visit him through the years but had never been able to break through the barrier that seemed to keep him at an emotional distance. His announcement that he was going to come made me think there was hope our relationship might be about to enter a new phase. And I was right.

The festivities took place on a Saturday in June, in the Sundome, the indoor sports stadium of the University of South Florida—a vast arena that must seat 15,000 or 20,000 people. And it was packed. From where they were sitting, I'm not sure my father and the girlfriend he had brought with him, or Debbie and her parents, could spot me among the thousands who were getting degrees that day.

Afterward we all went to dinner together. My father was happily proud of me, the first in our family to get a college degree. He and Debbie's parents gave me gifts of money. Debbie had picked out a gold ring with an emerald and a diamond. Very masculine, very handsome.

Except that I have never worn much jewelry. It's just not me. I made a fuss over the ring when I opened the box, but then virtually never wore it. Debbie was not very happy about that. I felt she had picked a present she thought was right, never mind whether it was something I wanted and would wear.

Another bone of contention between us. Another sign of the differences.

Chapter 6
GORGEOUS BRIDE

"YOU NEED TO get a grip on yourself."

That was one of the things I said to Debbie during the period of her worst anorexia-like eating problems. There was a time when her weight, which at her best was 125 to 130, would drop down to around 107, giving her a thin, gaunt look. For the amount of time she spent working out in the gym, you might have expected her to have a robust, healthy appearance. Apparently no amount of time trotting on the treadmill or pedaling on the stationary bike, plus multiple aerobic classes, can counter-effect the devastated look of the committed non-eater. I still thought she was beautiful; I never stopped thinking that. But I worried about what she was doing to her health.

Caring parents try to give their children support and the best possible nurturing. Joyce was a mother who cared. But her parenting style had made Angie defiant and Debbie blind to the consequences of her actions. Like the classic anorexic, she thought starving herself would make her more beautiful, with little thought for the health consequences.

And then there's the control factor. Starvation and the obsession with being too fat are refuges for girls and young women who feel as if other people or some particular other person has taken away their decision-making power. Short of a feeding tube like the French use on their geese, there isn't much you can do with a girl who refuses to eat. It's one area of life where the powerless can take power. I now understand Debbie was desperate to feel in control of her life. The mother always forgiving her and making all decisions for her had deprived the daughter of any sense of domain over her own life when she was growing up, and Joyce still made decisions for her now that Debbie was my partner.

Once in college I was at the gym with a fraternity brother. We could both see Debbie working up a sweat on a treadmill not far away. He said, "Boy, she's really thin." I answered him, intentionally loud enough for her to hear, "Yeah, she stopped eating. She's got a problem." Later, alone together, she laced into me. "How could you say a thing like that! You should have told him off." I tried to answer, "Other people are concerned about your weight, too. Not just me." Usually when an issue about her weight came up, she would promise to try to be more realistic about her goals and to eat more sensibly. And she really would try, I'll say that for her. It's just that the new good intentions never lasted very long.

I would later wonder whether the thirst for power and control that had been denied Debbie would be a driving force when she found a youngster who was willing to let her be in control.

I began to feel sorry for Debbie. I didn't want to pity her—you can't love someone you pity. I didn't want to nag her. I tried anyway; nagging didn't do the trick. At least it didn't with Debbie. The funny part, if any of this could be called funny, was that she did have big hips and a big butt—two parts of the body that no amount of dieting is going to help. She wasn't going to lose any size in the chest, either. Not that she wanted to. Her boobs were one part of her body that she was content with, probably because she had a voice in their design.

At 18, Debbie had a breast augmentation. I'm not sure why Joyce would have gone along with that. Maybe she thought a more prominent chest would revive her daughter's singing or modeling career, maybe she thought it would raise Debbie's self-esteem, overcoming some of her insecurity. It must have seemed important. Plastic surgery doesn't come cheap. The cost had to be a strain on the finances of a family living on the salaries of a plant worker and a hairdresser. But despite some drawbacks, the result pleased Debbie.

By now my own career was in full swing. I had gone to work at the bank as a Commercial Credit Analyst, which involves analyzing business and commercial loan requests and taking underwriting responsibility. While I felt qualified for the position, they had thrown me into the fray without much training. That just made me learn all the faster. It helped that I found myself working with very intelligent, dedicated people. And some of them, though well established and well-respected in the Tampa community, were quite willing to mentor a newcomer.

My office was in an old building located right on the Hillsborough River. Not that the setting did me much good: I was in a small cubicle with no view. Still I recognized that this was a great opportunity, and I felt pumped about my work. The management of my department apparently admired my work, as well. By the time Debbie graduated, I had already been promoted to Commercial Lending Officer, a position that carried the title of Assistant Vice President.

When I had started dating Debbie, the idea of her becoming a professional singer had pretty much faltered. But she had all along held onto a backup plan. If the singing didn't work out, her second choice was to be a teacher. She had grown quite enthusiastic about dedicating herself to enriching the lives of youngsters. (In hindsight, those words now carry an unhappy, even sinister, meaning.)

After Angie's death, Debbie had thrown herself back into her routine of schoolwork, part-time job, working out, and seeing me. All healthy distractions, but the nightmare of her loss continued to pursue her like a ghostly specter.

In August, the drunk driver went on trial before a military court martial.

Joyce and Debbie both testified. I no longer recall what either of them said so I'm relying here on a newspaper account, which reports that Joyce told the court her daughter sometimes called out to her in the middle of the night because she couldn't stand being alone, and that Debbie was "pretty much of a basket case." (I guess her wording could have been a little more tactful.) Debbie herself, according to the article, told the court, "It's hard to concentrate on anything but that," and complained she'd discover herself angry and "snap at my family for no reason."

"I've been sick," she testified. "I've lost a piece of me."

Piotrowski pleaded guilty, saying he would accept whatever sentence the court saw fit but begging that his pension be left intact for the benefit of his family.

His fellow officers turned a deaf ear to the request.

Piotrowski was sentenced to dismissal from the Army, a fine, plus a sentence of 13 years and six months to be served at the maximum-security military prison known as the U.S. Disciplinary Barracks, at Fort Leavenworth, Kansas. Showing little sympathy for a man who had so disgraced his uniform, they also ordered that he be deprived of his pension, which one newspaper account reported was worth in the vicinity of $600,000.

But that wasn't the end of the matter. A year and a half later, the case would come back to life.

It's standard for an Education student aiming for a teaching job to get experience facing the rigors of a real-life classroom. In the last semester of her senior year, Debbie found herself with an internship at the Weightman Middle School in the nearby town of Wesley Chapel.

She didn't gain as much as she might have from the experience because the teacher she was working under pretty much turned control of the classroom over to Debbie and went off to do other things, which in one way defeated the purpose of doing an internship. In another way, though, the arrangement was a blessing for her. She was thrilled by the teaching; she became passionate about it.

The evaluations she received at the end of the internship period were nothing short of glowing. The school principal, Robert Aguis, wrote in a recommendation letter, "In the classroom, Ms. Beasley maintains a positive, enthusiastic, well-managed learning environment," adding that "she has always displayed confidence and professionalism." Cindy Campbell, the university faculty member who supervised Debbie's internship, wrote that "She was so well-researched and prepared for her lessons," and admired her as "one of those students that stood out." High praise, despite the grammatical error. "She was so professional during her internship," Campbell also wrote, "I still use her as an example in my teachings," and offered the forecast that Debbie "showed promise to be an excellent teacher."

I thought those evaluations were smack on target. Debbie herself probably didn't anticipate how passionate she would be about teaching. As she gained confidence in front of the students, she gained confidence in herself as well. This was a transitional period for her. The butterfly was coming out of its cocoon. I was watching her grow as a person, meanwhile hoping it would mean she could edge out from under her mother's shadow and become a woman of independence—meaning a woman who can make her own decisions, standing tall, proud, and self-confident.

By this time, with graduation approaching, Debbie had some decisions to make about what she wanted. Upscale community, or less affluent? Middle school, or high school? English, or reading?—she was qualified to teach either.

For a while she imagined herself as a high school English teacher. Then she very wisely decided, perhaps because some guidance counselor or professor called her attention to the danger that an attractive girl who looked so young might have a difficult time keeping testosterone-laced high school boys focused on their studies. Since her degree would be in education for grades 6 through 12, she could just as well aim for a job at the middle school level, and that's what she decided to do.

One of the choices on her short list was Greco Middle School in the community of Temple Terrace. The school was not too far from her home, she liked the principal, and it offered a further advantage that she and I rarely shopped in that neighborhood, so she was less likely to run into her students outside of school. The fact that the student body had many students from less advantaged homes was another attraction for her, since it suggested an even greater opportunity to benefit the lives of the kids.

Temple Terrace, situated a few miles northeast of Tampa, is named after the Temple orange and the original terraced landscape of the area. Six square miles in size, the town has a population of 20,000, half of them born out of state, and—as I would unfortunately learn in time—its own police department of 53 sworn officers, headed by Chief Tony Velong, a man who has been in law enforcement for 35 years and is proud of his emphasis on a police force dedicated to community service.

Debbie, guided as usual by her mother, had little problem deciding to accept the offer from Greco, the Temple Terrace school, even though the position available was for teaching remedial reading to middle-schoolers in need of special help, when she had been imagining herself for some time guiding kids to a better appreciation of fine literature.

Her application for a teaching position at the school included a hand-written statement of her principles as a teacher: "I believe that we, as educators, must prepare students to think critically, analyze, and solve problems in order to balance his or her weaknesses. It is my own personal goal to individualize the education of each student.... I hold strongly to the belief that all students can learn. Children's needs must always be first, and I have committed myself to making this happen." This wasn't standard b.s. It was Debbie speaking from the heart.

The references she submitted, from the same three people who evaluated her internship, are in hindsight a little eerie. In answer to the standard question, *Would you employ this person?* one wrote: "Without hesitation. She will be an asset to any school!" (The exclamation point is in the original, not something I added.) Another offered that during her internship, Debbie had "enabled the students to be creative and enthusiastic towards learning.... She is an extraordinary individual, and she would be an asset to any faculty." Knowing what I know now, these words drip with irony.

With references like that, it must have been an easy decision for the principal. Debbie was hired to begin teaching remedial reading at the Greco Middle School following her graduation, at a base salary of $31,112.

Both as a college student and once she became a teacher, Debbie was constantly plagued by the curse of beautiful women. Many people assumed that she got by on her looks and had no need for smarts. Maybe she didn't need 'em, but she had 'em. When Debra Jean Beasley walked in cap and gown with her classmates at graduation, she was one of the very few among the thousands with a grade-point average in her major of 4.0—a perfect grade in every single course she had taken in the Education program.

I'd like to say she looked radiant that day, but of course to me in that time of our lives together, she *always* looked radiant. Larry and Joyce, who had made all this possible, had their pride written all over their faces. No surprise for Joyce, but seeing such pleasure expressed by the taciturn Larry seemed to give Debbie a special thrill.

That her parents couldn't afford to give her a rich-kid's graduation present of a car or a trip to Europe didn't matter. She never thought about buying the kinds of handbags or shoes that came with a fancy Rodeo Drive logo; she didn't harbor any daydreams about living in the best neighborhood in town. We were alike in so many ways, and my heart swelled for her that day.

As soon as Debbie walked into Greco, she almost immediately began meeting people who were to become close friends for both of us. Special among those was Pamela Glas; she and Debbie quickly formed a mutual admiration society. Not everyone welcomed the new teacher, though, and a lady named Aubrette Bobby became a leader of the "Down with Debbie" squad. Perhaps that was inevitable. The school didn't have enough classrooms for all the new teachers; Debbie and Aubrette were two of the three teachers who had to share a single room, a difficult arrangement in the best of circumstances, when all three teachers have the same style and approach of managing a classroom. These three didn't.

Another of the teachers explains, "We had already heard that a beautiful teacher was coming to Greco." (That statement floored me—the other teachers were talking about how good-looking she was even before she arrived ... and not just the men but the women as well!) "Debbie came in excited and very driven. She seemed really nice to me from the first. Aubrette found her bossy and unwilling to share or compromise, but I think it was just that Debbie wanted so much to be a good teacher."

The clashes were so frequent and so unhappy that Aubrette gave up teaching after one year of contending with Debbie.

Despite that area of friction, this was a nearly idyllic time for Debbie and me because from the very beginning things went so smoothly for her with her students. The kids were responding and seemed to be learning; she had the sense that she was getting through to them and making a difference. Her voice would be vibrant with enthusiasm as she told me excited stories each evening about how admirably it was going. The students were giving her very little in the way of problems and, aside from the conflict with her classroom-sharing teachers, she found very little to complain about. She was discovering as she had during the internship that teaching came naturally to her, and she embraced it wholeheartedly.

As you can imagine, her success at work was wonderful for our relationship. The more she gained confidence, the more she became grounded, and the more things became better and better for us.

By that time Debbie and I had been going steady for about four years. We were both ready to take our relationship to the next step. On weekends we began hunting for a place the two of us could move into together, and we soon found one that fit the bill, a townhouse in Osprey Run, a new development in Riverview, then still under construction. The house had a tan stucco exterior, white trim, and a red front door. Inside it was only 1100 square feet but laid out on two floors, with a little pond out back and place for a hammock.

The price was $95,000. I talked to my mother about the idea of Debbie and me moving in together and found her response very reserved. That wasn't a big surprise. My mother had liked Debbie from the start but after awhile began to realize that the warmth she was offering wasn't being returned. Debbie's explanation when I asked about it had caught me off guard, but made sense given what I already knew about her relationship with Joyce. "If I got too close to your mother, my mother would be hurt," she said. Ouch.

So the news that Debbie and I had decided to move in together brought a very measured reaction. "Are you sure you're doing the right thing?" she asked. Much later she told me, "I have no idea how I controlled myself. I thought, *If I flare up and let him know what I'm really thinking, I will lose him.*"

The next step in that conversation offered an example of the kind of extraordinary woman my mother is. I said, "Mom, Debbie and I have found a townhouse we'd like to buy. I don't have enough money for the down payment." She asked without hesitation, "How much do you need?"

Though I didn't know it at that time, my mother then went into counseling and created what she calls "a demilitarized zone" between Debbie and herself.

Even though none of Debbie's money was going toward the purchase, I decided to put the place in both our names. For me, this was just one step in a long-term commitment. But there was a more practical reason, as well. Debbie's mother Joyce, ardent church member, was going to have to give permission for her daughter to move out of the family home and move in with a guy she wasn't married to. I sat down with Joyce and Larry one evening when Debbie was out and shared with them something I wasn't yet ready to share with Debbie: soon, when the time was right, I was going to ask her to marry me.

I think Joyce and Larry both saw me as the only stable, suitable guy Debbie had ever dated. The news that I wanted to marry their daughter was enough to win their approval for our living together.

Debbie and I signed the purchase offer soon after, the bank loan was quickly approved, and the papers signed. Once construction was finished, we began living together.

We settled in like two happy people in a romance novel, delighted to be in each other's company, working out all the details of who does which household chores—bill paying, grocery shopping, cooking, cleaning, and laundry, pleased to spend evenings that ended with both of us going upstairs together instead of Debbie having to drive home. Enjoying sex whenever we felt like it—which usually meant several times a week, with occasional hyper-sex episodes of a couple of times a day, two or three days in a row.

The full-time companionship of somebody you really care about is wonderful but of course comes with a bundle of burdens. There's bound to be a little bit of strain when you put two people together in the same little space. The housecleaning, for example: it went fine, but I gradually began to realize that Debbie had been playing a dutiful-housewife role that didn't entirely fit her.

When Debbie was living at her parents, the house and her room had been neat and orderly. That suited me fine because I'm very orderly myself. But after two or three months, our little place began to look as if it wasn't getting the kind of attention she had given it at first. Not that it was really messy, it just didn't have a well-tended look. And then it dawned on me: Debbie came from a household where her mother had done everything for her.

So it wasn't that she was getting lazy about the housework, rather it was that she was reverting to the real Debbie. She continued to do the deep cleaning, the vacuuming and so forth, while the effort to keep the house picked up and orderly fell by the wayside. But at least she was still cooking—in her plain-and-simple, nothing-fancy style.

The housecleaning issue, though, was a minor blip compared to the larger psychological problems. She continued to struggle with that distorted self-image of the anorexic, staying as slim as she could manage. I much preferred the natural-looking Debbie I had first known.

Even when I was taunting her about her weight, trying to get her to eat sensibly, telling her, "You've got to get a grip," she would still often ask, "Am I fat? Do I look fat to you?"

I was dreaming up something special for the moment when I would propose, yet I was frankly nervous about the idea of hitching myself to a girl who was doing such damage to her body. Sure, I knew it was the anorexia talking. This girl I loved hadn't yet grown out of the feeling that she wasn't in control of any other area of her life—even at a time when she was being much praised at school, much appreciated by her students, and much fussed over and complimented by me. Of course, anyone struggling with an anorexia-like condition doesn't answer to rational explanations or desperate pleadings.

Or anyway, not usually. But in February, she started back into therapy and on medications for the anxiety and depression—Paxil and Wellbutrin.

For me, that was enough to overcome my last uncertainty about moving forward. I kicked my plans for an engagement surprise into high gear. I told Debbie, "There's this real estate deal I've been handling for the bank, and the closing is going to be in New Orleans. I could schedule it so we could go down together. After the closing, we could spend the weekend there."

She glowed, hugging me and kissing me, sending a message, whether she meant to or not, that she had a pretty good idea what I probably had in mind. But I meant it to come as a surprise, so I wasn't going to let her jump to any easy conclusions.

One of the girls at the bank, let in on the secret of what I was planning, was delighted to lend a hand. She drew up a set of phony loan documents, an impressively thick sheaf of papers complete with the address of a commercial property in New Orleans and phony names of the three men who were supposedly buying it.

On the flight, Debbie's excitement about seeing the French Quarter and night-clubbing in some of the hot spots was, I think, only exceeded by her anticipation that she would be flying home engaged, maybe wearing an engagement ring.

After the plane took off and we were comfortably settled in… I opened up my hand-carry bag and took out the sheaf of papers, explaining that I needed one last review to insure that everything was in order. Her face fell. *Oh, it's nothing but a damned business trip after all,* I could practically hear her thinking. Keeping a straight face was almost painful.

We arrived at the hotel about noon and were told check-in time wasn't until three o'clock. There wouldn't be a room available to us before then, but the hotel would be glad to check our bags in the bell captain's storage if we wanted to go out to have lunch or enjoy some sightseeing.

What could I do? I certainly wasn't going to leave a brand new $4,000 engagement ring in the hotel check room.

I told Debbie checking the bags sounded like a great idea and we should do it as soon as I came back from the men's room. I suppose she might have wondered why I needed to take my hand-carry case into the men's room with me; she didn't ask and I didn't offer an explanation. In the privacy of a stall, I fished the ring box out of my case and tucked it into a sock. Though not the most comfortable addition to my wardrobe for a walk around New Orleans, at least it was secure, the bulge hidden by my pant leg.

We spent the next three hours taking in the tourist sights of the French Quarter, with me trying to make sure I wasn't limping from the uncomfortable if reassuring friction of the ring case against my ankle.

Late in the afternoon I guided Debbie to Jackson Square where I knew I could rent a horse-drawn carriage, which would provide the most romantic setting I could think of for a proposal of marriage.

Debbie saw the sign at the carriage stand: $40 for a half-hour ride. She said, "Owen, that's way too expensive. It's a waste of money."

Uh-oh.

I said, "It's expensive, but it's once-in-a-lifetime. Let's do it."

"No," she said. "It's not worth it."

I had it in my mind that proposing on a horse-drawn carriage would create a memory we would cherish forever. A pathetic notion, as things turned out, but I was determined. I pleaded as gently as I could: "It's romantic, I love you, I want to share this with you."

She melted and agreed.

Slipping the coachman an extra $20 bill and whispering in his ear, I got a small nod of agreement that he would take us someplace romantic. Debbie smiled at me as I climbed into the carriage and put an arm around her. The clip-clopping of the horse's hooves on the pavement had a hypnotic effect. In a few minutes we reached the courtyard of a French Quarter hotel with big iron gates opening to a garden rainbow of flowers. Determined to play this with all the drama of a scene in a 1940s romance movie, I surreptitiously fished the ring out of my sock, got down on one knee and said all in one breath, "Debbie, I love you very much, you make me extremely happy, I don't want to go on living without you, will you marry me?"

She sat there, silent as if she couldn't find the words, huge tears welling up in her eyes. I slipped the ring onto her finger. She still hadn't spoken and finally I said, "Well?"

"Yes," she said. "Of course."

On the way back to Jackson Square I had the coachman stop long enough for me to step into a bar and have the bartender shake up two Hurricanes, that knock-you-off-your-ass drink concocted from dark and light rum, lime juice, and passion fruit syrup. The "passion" part made this particular drink seem especially appropriate. We toasted each other to celebrate our new status in life and our new commitment to one another.

When we returned from New Orleans and spread the word that we were engaged, Debbie's mother was overjoyed, mine was accepting, and a lifelong friend of Debbie's family, taking on the role of substitute big sister, insisted on throwing us an engagement party. She meant well, God bless her, and her heart was set on making it an unforgettable event. Only the very best would suffice.

She did a classy job, with an elegant evening function in Debbie's home town of Ruskin at the Bahia Beach Resort, a hotel and marina with a view out to the ocean past private boat docks often crowded with expensive yachts, with the Tampa and St. Petersburg skylines rising in the distance beyond. (We're very big on water scenery here; in Florida, you're never far from a bay, an ocean, the Gulf of Mexico, or some inlet from one of these. The water isn't just the tourist attraction. It holds a big draw for most of us.)

All of our closest friends were invited—Pam and Jeff Glas, Jeremy and Mary Jackson, Bobby and Lacey Cobb, Jeff Hoffman and his fiancé Stacy, Jeremy Butts and his fiancé Zoë, along with friends from my work, Debbie's parents, and my mother and stepfather. And about 70 other people. *Seventy.* Not just for cocktails—this was a fancy buffet dinner, with assigned seating and waiters pouring wine throughout the meal.

That's not all. There was a DJ for dance music and a cake from which the bride and groom—I mean, the engaged couple—cut off pieces and fed them to each other. The truth is, this was essentially a wedding reception without the church ceremony.

Some things you just have to have a sense of humor about; I had no voice in the arrangements. We were registered like a bridal couple and received a typical assortment of dishes, glassware, and kitchen appliances. I couldn't help thinking, *If all our friends are giving us these presents now, what are they going to do when we actually get married—give us another whole round of gifts?*

I would have been just as pleased to have a bunch of our closest friends over to the house with some food, some wine, and a keg of beer. Our hostess had gone to such trouble and such expense over an affair that just made me uncomfortable. And I thought a gift registry for an engagement was embarrassing, though we heard no grumbles from our friends.

It was a lovely function that must have cost quite a bundle. I'm still grateful for the generosity of it all but frankly still a little embarrassed by it. I smiled my way through the evening and hope I never gave a clue about what I was really thinking.

In a supermarket romance novel, I guess the engagement of a girl with a troubled past would mark a new page in the book of her life on which her troubles would begin to disappear. Real life isn't that simple.

Victims of rape, especially victims of childhood rape, can suffer devastating issues of low self-esteem and diminished self-respect. I don't know if all of Debbie's problems arise from those unhappy childhood experiences. I doubt if she knows herself. Whatever the source, I sympathize with the problems. I truly do. Deep-rooted malfunctions of the psyche don't go away just from wishing they would. In many cases, perhaps in most cases, they don't go away at all.

Debbie was making an effort and the medication for anxiety and depression was helping her live a calmer, more stable life. (One drug she was on, Paxil, has since triggered thousands of lawsuits and the manufacturer has paid out millions of dollars in the face of claims that they misrepresented safety data and withheld negative information about the drug. Fortunately, Debbie didn't seem to have any negative side effects that could be attributed to the drug.)

While the anxiety and depression were a little more under control, she continued to be an absolute nut about eating. Checking the nutrition facts on every food package in the supermarket, counting calories as if her whole future depended on it, keeping a detailed log of everything she ate, Debbie was an obsessive battlefield commander trying to marshal the facts on every aspect of the campaign she was waging. Her mother worried terribly over Debbie's compulsive eating behavior, at the same time troubled that her own habit of taking detailed notes on her food intake when Debbie was a child might have led to the current worrisome patterns.

From the turmoil of anxiety and depression to an obsession over foods. Not much improvement to cheer about.

In May 2003, Capt. Piotrowski, the drunk driver responsible for the death of Debbie's sister Angela, came up for a second trial, this time in a Florida criminal court on charges brought by the State Attorney's Office in Tampa. Each of these trials was like reopening an old, painful wound for Debbie, fresh reminders of the guilt she felt and would never be able to escape.

Piotrowski's lawyer had filed several motions to have the case dismissed, arguing that it was double jeopardy and a violation of his client's constitutional rights to a speedy trial—a year and a half had passed since the court martial—but the judge was unmoved. While being tried in a state court after already having been convicted in a court martial is not a routine situation, it's not entirely uncommon. And the reason he was being retried in Tampa isn't difficult to figure out. Military prisoners are eligible for parole after serving only one-third of their sentence, which meant that Piotrowski could be released in just another three years. That possibility was revolting, especially to Debbie and her mother. Apparently the State Attorney's Office saw it the saw way.

In the face of charges not only for the death of Angela but also the death of her unborn child, the defense attorney desperately tried to argue that five months into a pregnancy, the unborn child was not "viable" and therefore that his client should not be held responsible for that death. He also presented evidence about the lead gunshot pellets still in Angie's body, hoping to convince the jury that the fetus had been exposed to dangerous levels of lead that could also have contributed to the death.

These were claims of desperation that sounded like feeble attempts of an attorney to do something, *anything*, for his client.

The two men and four women on the jury weren't taken in by these arguments, spending less than 15 minutes before coming back with a guilty verdict. Piotrowski received a sentence of 15 years, the maximum allowed under the law. As I write, the Army is looking at 2009 as his earliest release date. And even then, that's not a date he would walk free. The Army has a "detainer" from Florida, so when Piotrowski leaves the Disciplinary Barracks in Fort Leavenworth, it will be in the custody of officers from Florida who will escort him out of an Army prison and right into a Florida prison.

Debbie's psychological condition improved after the second, local trial, as if this in some way put a small part of the pain to rest. For a time she was able to function more normally, more like the Debbie I had grown to love.

Before Debbie and I had even started thinking about what we wanted to do for our wedding, two of the couples in our little social circle were married in quick succession. My longtime friend, buddy, and college fraternity brother Jeff Hoffman had become engaged to his girlfriend Stacy about the same time that I proposed to Debbie. Moving faster than us, their wedding arrived before we had even started thinking about a date. The Hoffmans' marriage took place in a Methodist Church right on the beach, followed by a large reception with dancing to hip-hop and disco music. The whole thing was done to perfection. There was magic in the air. It was enough to make us both start thinking.

Then one of the teachers from Debbie's school, Jeremy Butts, stood at another altar beaming while his bride Zoë walked down the aisle. This ceremony was also held at water's edge, this time not on the bay but at a lake. Again it was an inspiration for a couple starting to think about their own arrangements. Zoë introduced us to their wedding planner. By the time the evening was over, we were sold on the idea of working with her.

Does anybody actually make it through arranging a wedding without conflicts, fights, and badly mangled feelings? The wedding planner was receiving her marching orders from Joyce and Debbie, a typical arrangement, except that my mother, faced with losing her only son, was anxious to be consulted and allowed to offer her opinions on the plans. But it wasn't to be. This was to be a Beasley-run function, LaFave input most definitely not welcome. My mother was hurt. Unfortunately for her, the worst was yet to come, and it would be at my own hand.

With plans progressing smoothly for the wedding, the wedding planner hard at work, Joyce busy giving instructions, Debbie decided it was time to go shopping for a wedding dress. At the time, Debbie was filled out to a natural shape and looking healthy. She was, Pam says, "probably a size 6 or maybe a size 4," but was still struggling with that unrealistic "ideal" image of herself as skinnier than a supermodel.

And so she picked what Pam describes as "a wedding dress that was like a size 2." Pam was present when Debbie tried the dress on at her mother's and couldn't get into it.

Debbie still had a few weeks left, and a ton of stubborn determination. Pam Glas remembers that Debbie at this period would starve herself, and worse. "She used laxatives and all kinds of crazy things—crazy diets where she would just eat an apple a day for long periods of time, or just having popcorn and water for lunch, until she didn't look healthy." Plus, she was exercising all the time, and also squeezing in regular visits to a tanning parlor, I guess thinking that the artificial tan would keep her healthy-looking while the numbers on her scale slowly dropped and she gradually morphed to that thin and gaunt look I had always disliked. And that she disliked, too, for a different reason—still thinking she looked too fat.

But it worked. She made it into that size 2 dress in time for the wedding. "I don't know how she did it," Beth says. "She probably lost ten pounds. And she was already really thin. She looked good in the dress."

While Debbie was struggling with her weight, I had my own hassle to deal with: selecting my best man. The guy I really wanted standing alongside me was Richie Maggio, neighborhood friend from when my family had first moved to Florida, college fraternity brother, and closest buddy. But I knew that wouldn't fly. Richie and I had been drinking buddies and carousing pals. Once Debbie and I started going steady, the Richie part of my life became an issue. He still wanted me to go barhopping with him and our other guy friends, and she didn't want me to—which maybe was natural lady-logic and justified, or maybe was her overactive jealousy and suspicious streak in play.

Richie remembers it this way: "She didn't want me in your life. I thought she was going to ruin you. At your graduation, she pulled me aside and said, 'Owen's mine. I've got him now.'" When she and I started living together, as far as Richie was concerned, "It was the nail in the coffin. You were tied to her and you weren't going to get away. There was no going back. You were headed for one big explosion. She didn't want you to have fun." He had all but lost me as a close friend, and he was hurting.

For what it's worth, Richie had his own explanation for Debbie's behavior: "A lot of girls are jealous. Sometimes the prettier they are, the harder it is. People treat them differently. You think you can get what you want because you're pretty."

I really didn't want to give up occasional nights out with Richie and the gang, but faced with the choice between the guys and Debbie, you can guess which decision I made. So Richie was pissed at losing one of his drinking partners, and Debbie was unhappy that I would have even thought about going out on the town with Richie and the guys, no girls invited. She saw him as a black-hat character trying to lead me astray, down a path toward being unfaithful. The bottom line was that she didn't like Richie and didn't want him around, so he became mostly a telephone buddy. And while he would certainly be a guest at our wedding, there was no way I could ask him to be my best man.

The two other guys I felt closest to who I thought would pass the Debbie-test were Amin Molavi, another longtime friend from the same neighborhood of my childhood, or Bobby Cobb, part of our current social circle and somebody Debbie was more comfortable with.

Then my dad said he would fly out from Wisconsin for the wedding, which pleased me. Our relationship had continued to strengthen ever since my graduation. I suppose that was partly because he was proud of me and partly because, out in the working world and out of my mother's house, he was finally beginning to see me no longer as a child but as an adult he could relate to. It meant a lot to me that he and I were becoming closer. So the decision was easy. I asked my dad to be my best man, and he was happy to accept.

On top of that, I then had my mom's injured feelings to contend with. Debbie and her mother had decided on one of those of-the-moment contemporary weddings where the dominant color for the girls of the bridal party, other than the bride herself, is black. My mother found this out after she had already gone dress shopping and picked a becoming number—in black.

When Debbie heard, she said it simply wouldn't do. With the bridesmaids wearing black, my mother couldn't wear black too. She would have to find a different dress. My mother, who already had strong reservations about Debbie, and who so recently had been closed out of taking any part in the wedding plans, was now having more salt rubbed into the wounds. I remembered how she had once told me that Debbie has "an endearing side, but never lets me in."

Another friend of Debbie's, Sandra Hart, had her own explanation of the distance Debbie kept from my mom, deciding it was because of Joyce. But Debbie's relationship with her mother, Sandy thought, "was a lot less mother/daughter—Debbie was Joyce's only close friend, a very large controlling factor in Debbie's life. Joyce had lost one daughter, and was holding on to Debbie as tight as she could." Sometimes Debbie would call Joyce and ask her to come to keep her company—on a school day. "Maybe a couple of times a month Joyce would come and sit in the classroom all day with her," Sandy says, "which I always thought was weird."

Most of the guys who had been my fraternity brothers in college liked Debbie when we were all in school, and liked her still after we graduated, with Richie as an outstanding exception. Richie had been sharing his concerns with Ricky, another close friend who had also been a neighborhood buddy in my first Florida days. The two of them concocted a plan that still leaves me a little bewildered and annoyed, even though I know they had my best interests at heart.

Without saying anything to me, Richie and Ricky went over to my mom's house a couple of days before the wedding (nothing like waiting to the last minute), knocked on the door, and said they needed to talk to her.

I suppose you can guess what's coming. Richie now says, "I knew Debbie would ruin his life. It could only get worse. Ricky and I had to say our piece." He says he knew that talking to me wouldn't do any good. "I think Owen saw the problems but was content with it, especially after they moved in together. He knew how I felt. He's stubborn. He knows what's right for him at all times. I call him 'the boss.'"

So the two of them sat down with my mom and each said what they felt they had to say. Richie remembers telling her, "We could be wrong, but we've known him from age 13. She's not the right person for Owen." Ricky chimed in with more of the same.

"We just knew how wrong it was," Richie remembers saying. "Owen shouldn't be marrying this girl." She was going to ruin my life, he told my mother.

After my mother's initial attempts to strike up a relationship with Debbie, she came to feel, she told me later, that "she could hurt you because she was so self-contained and self-serving."

Richie says about his visit, "We just had to do it; we had to say our piece. We wouldn't be good friends if we didn't."

But "We didn't say, 'You have to do this.' Ricky and I aren't like that. We didn't talk to her like that." My mother was listening to all this and thinking, "Owen is very analytical but he's so infatuated with her that his thinking is clouded." She now says, "I was fearful because of her relationship with her mother, which has left Debbie incredibly insecure. So she uses her beauty to control." My mother had decided that the problem was Joyce: "a nice lady who loved her children but was over-controlling because she so badly wanted them to be perfect."

My mom didn't make the guys any promises, Richie says; he and Ricky both understood there was nothing she could do. "She just wanted us to support Owen, as well. She understood how we felt. I think she thought the same way as we, possibly." But she told them she wouldn't interfere. "I always told Owen he had to make his own decisions, that I would support him but that he would have to make his own way." She told Richie and Ricky, "We have to make our own decisions. If you're a true friend, you'll be there to support him, and you'll be there to help him pick up the pieces." And she said, "If I can show up and smile, so can you."

In the end, Richie says, "We were just comforting each other. All three of us knew we were going to let the timetable unfold however it would unfold."

I never knew about that visit until my mom told me after Debbie's arrest. It wouldn't have made any difference, of course. I knew Debbie came with a truckload of problems but I was crazy about the girl and I truly wanted to be married to her. At that point it would've taken a great deal more than the efforts of my mother, Richie, and Ricky combined to stop me.

Another issue was less of a hassle. Since all our friends had given us wedding-type presents at the engagement party, we had to think up something else they could do for us at the time of the wedding. Instead of registering at a store, we found out we could register at the resort where we were going for our honeymoon, and we passed the word around: anybody who wants to do something for the bridal couple can give us a gift of whatever they feel like toward the cost of the honeymoon.

Debbie and I were married on July 19, 2003, in front of about a hundred people at the Palma Ceia United Methodist Church on "Bay to Bay Boulevard" in Tampa. (This one is not actually on the water, but close enough: it's on a peninsula with Tampa Bay a mile to the west and Hillsborough Bay a mile to the east.) The bride looked glorious in her white cap-sleeve gown, size two—with nobody but family and close friends having any reason to suspect what she had gone through to fit into it. I wore the traditional black tuxedo with white tie and vest. Our wedding photographer was so happy with the way the photos came out that he put pictures of the occasion up on his web site. (After Debbie's arrest, he would make a bundle selling rights to our pictures to various Web sites and TV news/interview shows.)

Richie and Ricky went through their duties as two of my groomsmen to perfection, giving no clue that they had major reservations...or at least, none that I was aware of.

One memorable and very unusual part of the ceremony involved butterflies, that symbol so important to Debbie in memory of her grandmother and her sister. The subject of butterflies had come up in a conversation with the wedding planner, who somehow actually found a butterfly distributor—something I didn't even know existed.

After the wedding ceremony, Debbie and I and all our guests moved into the church courtyard, where one of Debbie's cousins read a poem and then the members of Debbie's family released the butterflies. It was a tender and beautiful moment, unusual and moving. One butterfly landed on my face and Debbie took it as a sign of approval from her sister.

The reception, at the Riverwalk Hotel (yes, on the water), was the traditional sit-down dinner. Debbie read some beautiful and touching remarks to me that she had written, and I read my remarks to her that she seemed to be moved by. I'm not going to try to recollect and record here any of her words or mine, because they would be too painful to recall.

Richie, blessed with a knack for being class clown, had everybody laughing. My dad gave a great speech. Amin and Ricky each stood up with a toast and a few warm words.

There was one other glitch at the reception, a slip of my own that still gnaws at me. In my remarks, praising my new wife as the love of my life and thanking the people closest to me, I somehow neglected to mention the one person to whom I owe the values I live by, the beliefs I hold dear, the things I most treasure.

I had forgotten to mention my mother. When I was through speaking, my mother rushed to the ladies room where she sobbed and sobbed.

I didn't even know it. All through her out-of-sight tears, I was laughing and applauding the remarks of my father and friends. As the old song says, sometimes we hurt the ones we love.

Eleven months later, that's what Debbie would do to me.

Chapter 7
SUNNY DAYS, CLOUDY DAYS

DEBBIE AND I AGREE that we wanted to honeymoon in a tropical setting, some place lovely and relaxing but with a foreign flavor, and not too expensive. The wedding planner came up with an answer that fit our requirements: a resort of the Sandals chain, on the island of St. Lucia, where they offered an all-inclusive package that meant we would never have to think about the cost of anything for the entire week.

St. Lucia is a dot of an island in the Eastern Caribbean, fought over in the colonial era by the French and the British in 14 separate battles, with the British the final victors. Today it's an independent island state but rendering allegiance to Queen Elizabeth as part of the British Commonwealth. For a honeymoon, it's breathtaking, offering warm temperatures, gorgeous stretches of sandy beach, gin-clear water, friendly natives, and one-of-a-kind attractions like the one they refer to as the "world's only drive-in volcano."

We toured the island, visited the local market where they sell trinkets to tourists and just-caught fish to the housewives, and went snorkeling for the first time in tropical waters. At one point in our wandering, two little native boys stopped us and said to Debbie, "Could we have a picture with you?" They were so polite and well-mannered that we didn't hesitate to say yes, and I snapped the photo of the two of them posed one on each side of her. Of course, it was with our camera, so they never saw the picture. But they got to stand alongside the beautiful blonde lady, and maybe that was all they wanted.

Waiting in line for dinner at the hotel one night, we chatted with another couple who mentioned they heard that one of the guests had been stung by a jellyfish during the day. Yes, we knew all about it: the victim was Debbie. Like the little boys, the jellyfish seem to have been drawn to her. Fortunately her wounds were minor and the pain soon gone. It was the only cloud on an otherwise perfect trip.

We spent an idyllic week there, a wonderful beginning to married life.

No marriage is without its problems. We began well but would be running into storms very soon—with the devastating, home-wrecker problems less than a year away.

Two months after our July marriage, Debbie began to wonder if her birth-control medication could be causing a weight gain, and decided she wanted to try a different pill. Her doctor gave her a prescription for Yasmin. Birth-control pills of course work by bringing about changes in a woman's hormones. For many, it's no big deal, while for others, I now know, the experience can be terrible, a situation complicated by the fact that it's easy to overlook the hormone connection to behavior patterns or health problems. When mood changes begin or the body starts functioning differently, you don't necessarily immediately think that the new medication might be causing it. We still tend to think of our doctors as all-knowing, and the idea that your doctor might have put you on a medication that brings severe problems with it isn't the first thing that pops into the mind.

The list of major side effects that can be caused by taking Yasmin is scary. Some of the items are headache, migraine, nausea and vomiting, changes in blood pressure, and weight changes. Also breast pain, vaginal thrush, disorders of the menstrual cycle, and bleeding between menstrual periods.

And as if those aren't bad enough, the list also includes the possibility of depressed mood and changes in sex drive.

None of this means the drug should be pulled off the market. All birth-control pills have a similar list of side effects.

I don't know if Debbie's doctor mentioned any of this to her when he gave her the prescription. Neither of us ever thought that her birth-control pills might have had any role in the behavior changes that started soon after.

Debbie had already begun putting weight back on after the shrinkage she forced on herself before the wedding to fit into that too-small wedding dress. Now her housewifely behavior started going seriously downhill. She essentially stopped cleaning the house, stopped doing the grocery shopping, and stopped cooking meals.

That's not very welcome behavior in any wife. She was suddenly turning her back on cleaning and other chores she had agreed would be hers when we divided up responsibilities five months earlier on moving in together. I was mystified, annoyed, and not a little bit alarmed.

What you do when the person you love and live with suddenly stops taking part in household duties? I tried to talk to Debbie about it, I tried to pressure her. She had no answers, no explanation. While I didn't suspect the birth-control medication, I did wonder if her medication for depression wasn't working any longer. I also wondered again, as I had earlier, whether growing up in a household where her mother handled the housekeeping chores had left Debbie feeling as if cleaning and doing laundry shouldn't be expected of her. Maybe, I thought, Debbie was reverting to her childhood role, expecting that whatever she didn't bother to do would—presto!—be taken care of. And in a way, she was right. I'm a neat person by nature—Debbie knew I would clean up if she didn't.

I felt I was being taken advantage of.

When I'd bitch loudly enough, she'd make an effort. I'd

come home and she would greet me with a smile. "Look—I cleaned up." But she couldn't stick to it. After a few days, she'd be back to the uncaring, anything-goes routine.

One of the other changes wasn't a biggie but was important to me.

All through college at the University of South Florida, I had been a season ticket holder to the USF games, and I kept up my subscription after I graduated. Debbie had always gone to all the games with me. Now she announced that she wasn't going. "That was before we got married," she said. "I wanted to spend time with you. Now that we're married, I don't want to go any more."

There may be a word for that, but I'm not sure what it is. Deceitfulness? Lying—with actions instead of with words? Is it a matrimonial form of bait and switch? I was really upset. But she did, at least, say, "Go and have a good time."

I started calling up one or another of my old fraternity buddies to take along to the games with me.

For the most part, our sex life in our first months of marriage left me with few complaints. We were still getting it on typically once or twice a week—not really ideal for a newlywed husband, but enough that I didn't feel the need to make a big issue over it. Every once in a while we still had one of those flings of twice-a-day hyper-sex. But then there began to be times when she would again say yes only once or twice a month—definitely not a design to keep a newlywed husband feeling satisfied.

Now when I look back at the list of side effects for her birth control medication and see that item about "changes in sex drive," I think maybe it wasn't just Debbie becoming difficult about sex.

I thought the situation was dark but then it became even darker. By late fall or early winter, Debbie would sometimes come home, walk in, close the door, step out of all her clothes, microwave a bag of popcorn, take it to the couch in the living room, turn on the television, eat the popcorn, and fall asleep stretched out on the couch.

I'd come home late from work and find the appealing, tempting sight of a gorgeous, totally naked wife, the picture sadly marred by a tornado of clutter and debris, a trail marking wherever she had been in the house.

What if we have children? I wondered. *Will I be left to do everything?*

But that wasn't an immediate concern. We had agreed to spend a while enjoying life, hopefully managing to see some of the U.S. and maybe even Europe, and building a financial nest-egg, before starting a family.

In various ways most of us live what has been called an unexamined life. Even many of the small things we take for granted or don't bother to think about can blow up in our faces. I was glad that Debbie was continuing to take her anxiety and depression medication. I never inquired about the doctor who was prescribing for her, and who had become my doctor as well.

Therapists don't have the training or the license to write prescriptions, so she was getting the prescriptions for her anxiety and depression meds from our M.D., a man who was board-certified in Internal Medicine but who received his medical education at a school in Bogotá, Columbia, and who was running large ads promoting his services for laser hair removal and varicose-vein "therapy." Maybe those are not the best qualifications for monitoring a patient's emotional and physical reactions to powerful anxiety and depression drugs.

Could one or another of the drugs she was taking cause more than a loss of sexual desire? Could the side effects of one of those drugs be responsible for her changes in behavior that put such a strain on our marriage? Is it possible that a switch to a different medication might have saved her from all that was to follow?

How much of a show of affection in public is suitable? Where does being loving in public cross the line so that other people feel like shouting, "Get a room!" Debbie's fellow schoolteacher Jeremy Jackson remembers being with us at restaurants and dinner parties where Debbie "would talk...childlike...and get lovey-dovey" with me. He says we were "like a young couple in love," Debbie sitting in my lap and talking about "Owen this and Owen that" as if I were her favorite topic of conversation.

Pam Glas's husband Jeff remembers us "openly loving, holding hands, kissing, hugging"—although, to be honest, he thought we went beyond what was appropriate in public. My point is that our friends could see the depth of our love. And to be honest, despite what Jeff thinks, I didn't see any reason to hide it.

I realize now, though, that I was catering to Debbie's style in this. What seemed okay when I was with Debbie no longer seems okay in my post-Debbie life.

At Greco, the reactions to Debbie so varied that it was almost laughable. Pam Glas, who would become Debbie's closest friend and only true confidant, says, "Debbie was a really committed teacher, excited to be teaching."

But in some ways Pam didn't see Debbie as the heroine of her own story when she first arrived at the school, because she wasn't then on antidepressants or in therapy and so was "unbearable to be around." She could be "very nasty and mean and high strung," Pam would later tell Debbie's prosecutor. After a few months, "She got [back] on medication and she was a different person, much more in control of herself." Even so, Pam says, "I never considered her to be stable, even on medication."

Another of Debbie's closest friends at Greco, Avery Hampton, was married to a high school teacher, Beth. When the two first met, Beth found Debbie "down-to-earth, really fun, a sweet person." That came as a surprise because Beth had expected Debbie to be "uptight or snotty or something" but instead found her lovable. As she came to know her better, though, Beth began to see Debbie as someone who couldn't take care of herself and always seemed to be turning to me for my opinion. "It just seemed she always made herself [appear] more weak than she actually was."

Zoë, the wife of Greco teacher Jeremy Butts, found my wife open, chatty, and friendly, as well as "very sexual" to the point of being flirtatious, yet in a way that never suggested she was trying to interest any of the other guys in her. She also found Debbie immature, which I think was fair and on target.

You might expect that a gorgeous woman would walk through the world brimming with confidence, filled with the sense that she could enter any room of strangers almost anywhere and people would seek her out, want to be in her company, want to bask in the glow of the aura that a beautiful woman seems to cast.

Maybe a lot of beautiful women are like that. Debbie is not one of them. Her level of insecurity often translated into preferring to stay at home with me than to go out and face the world—even when that world just meant dinner with our closest friends. Sometimes it was as if she had a social anxiety disorder: she would withdraw and simply not want to communicate. Beth Hampton says, "We'd be planning a get-together and somebody would say, 'Let's invite Debbie and Owen—but they probably won't come.'" The first few times this happened, Beth didn't recognize it as a problem. "I thought this was just something they did. Some people are just that way. Until one day Pam said, 'Oh, it's just Debbie.'"

"She hated leaving her house," Pam says. "She didn't like being at other people's houses all that much. She didn't do well in large group settings. Jeff and I would take our girls and go have dinner at their house a lot."

One friend describes Debbie as "all of a sudden becoming very closed off." She says, "When you would invite Debbie and Owen, it would be hit or miss whether they would come. They would invite us places and that would be great, she would be a good mood. But if we would invite them, a lot of times it would be, 'Oh, yeah, they're not gonna come.'" Something like half the time, in this friend's calculation, we wouldn't show up.

After a while, everyone came to understand. "She won't leave the house again," Pam would say. She and Beth would look at each other and roll their eyes. Finally Pam hung a label on it: "We started to call her agoraphobic."

For me, it was doubly frustrating. First because I didn't want to sit home on a weekend evening when we could have been with our closest friends. And secondly because I found it really embarrassing; I didn't want to call up whoever at the last minute and tell them, "Sorry, we're not going to be with you after all." And I didn't think I should have to. Time after time I would try to insist to Debbie that if she was canceling at the last minute, at least she should be the one to call.

The strategy rarely worked.

And when we did show up for an evening with our friends, they never knew quite what to expect. Just as they differed in their opinions of Debbie's personality, they also differed in their attitudes toward another inescapable aspect of being in Debbie's company: the business about her sexuality.

The thing was that Debbie looked so lusciously sexy to begin with that she could have just sat there not moving and still had everyone else at the table or in the room thinking inappropriate thoughts. At school, Pam, Debbie, and Jeremy Jackson had become a private club, three musketeers eating lunch together every day. Teacher Avery Hampton says that the three "enjoyed each other's company and found things to laugh about together." Avery's first impression of Debbie had been of a "pretty blonde girl, a sweet, nice person," who he soon recognized to be "devoted to teaching."

Avery was one of the people assigned to assess Debbie's teaching ability, standard practice with beginning teachers, and he was impressed. "She had good classroom management and the students seemed responsive. She always had really good lesson plans, and she cared a lot about her kids. In her classroom the kids would be working and intense listening to her. And those were with students who had lower reading scores," which made her success in holding their attention all the more impressive. He concluded she was "an excellent teacher."

She looked so sexy that she didn't need to do anything to heighten people's response. But she did anyway. Her friend Jeremy Jackson says, "She definitely wore things where you'd take notice of her. But, you know, if one woman wears a small T-shirt and another woman does, it can be an entirely different effect."

Any man with a sexy wife is proud of the way she looks, but I did often have reservations about the clothes Debbie selected. We had a lot of conversations on the subject, all a waste of my breath. I'd never know what she might put on for an evening out. Sometimes she'd select things as modest as any other wife in the group, other times she'd select some skimpy, too-tight blouse, or a low-cut top showing off an eyeful of cleavage.

And she talked very openly about private sex things that would have been far too personal for anybody else in the group ever to bring up.

Once when Debbie and I were out shopping we wandered into a novelty store where they had a display of sex toys. The little old lady who worked there started taking each one out and showing it to us, explaining its features. We ended up buying one of the items, a vibrating ring designed for the man to wear, claimed to enhance the pleasure of both partners. We tried it that same night. Though it didn't do anything for me, Debbie enjoyed it so I continued using it to please her.

At a dinner party at our house not long after that, Debbie went upstairs, came down with the ring, and showed it to everybody. She told them all, "You should buy one of these. It's so much fun. It's really great."

Debbie liked attention, and this was just one of the ways she captured it. Maybe it's a sign of insecurity—I'm not sure. But I found the conversation kind of funny. I suppose another blonde pulling something like that would have made everyone think "dumb blonde who doesn't have anything better to talk about." Everybody in our group knew Debbie was smart, and a reader of books, and up on current affairs, always eager to take part in a conversation about events of the day. This wasn't some dumb blonde desperate to get people to listen to her. It was just Debbie being Debbie.

Beth Hampton says about these conversations that for Debbie, it was "always a good time to talk about anything. Nothing was inappropriate." Pam Glas adds, "She talked like that all the time. It was a joke with us. Jeff [Pam's husband] liked how Owen would handle it—he would just shake his head and smile."

The Hamptons, on the other hand, both misread my reaction, thinking that conversations like this embarrassed me. Beth says, "She would do it in a good-natured way, but it would end up embarrassing him. He was just sort of rolling his eyes. But it was all fun. We were all laughing about it, so it wasn't anything I would be ashamed of." Beth thinks she remembers Debbie saying that sex had grown boring after a while and this was a way to enhance her sexuality and bring her back to being excited about sex again. "I wouldn't tell anybody something like that," Beth says, "[but] she was just sort of the fun, carefree one."

Sandy Hart thought Debbie was "inappropriate in her open discussions about sex," especially about showing off that sex toy.

She had heard Debbie talking about sex often enough but thought this was going too far. She was embarrassed and "my husband was embarrassed. It would be one thing for her to show it to me, it's another to bring it down in front of an entire group of people. I don't think she even thought of it as embarrassing to Owen. He just passed it off with a 'That's Debbie.'"

One member of the group especially remembers an evening when, as he recalls it, Debbie announced that "Owen tried to put it in my butt and it hurt." He thought that saying something like this—"as dinner table conversation!"—was completely inappropriate but "just sort of expected out of Debbie...sort of aligned with the whole Debbie thing, her childlike openness."

The other Jeremy—Jeremy Butts, who also taught at Greco—had his own favorite: a time when Debbie told him that she had shaved the hair on her privates into patterns and that I had trimmed mine. Jeremy should do the same, she suggested. The conversation "made me very uncomfortable," Jeremy says.

Another time, at a party at our house, Debbie was lying on the hammock in back chatting with Jeremy Jackson and Jeff Glas about the politics and social impacts of gay marriage when Debbie said something about "back when I was a lesbian..." and when she saw the surprised looks on their faces said, "Oh, did I never tell you about that?" Jeremy told her, "Okay, Debbie, that's more than I need to know already. Let's move on to something else."

Mostly it was just talk. On a couple of occasions, alone with her girlfriends, it turned into something more, with Debbie explaining about her factory-made breasts. "She was quite proud of them," Sandy says. "She normally went without a bra." Sometimes she would let another woman touch them to see what they felt like. But there had been a price: when Debbie and I had first become intimate, her breasts were sensitive; she had the enhancement done in a special way to make certain she wouldn't lose the ability to breast-feed, but the procedure had left her without feeling in them. What she had gained in appearance, she had lost as a part of lovemaking.

At least she had the good judgment not to offer the opportunity to any of the men. Or maybe I should say, not as far as I know.

Sandy was tremendously fond of Debbie, yet almost brutally candid in her observations. "I always thought of her as being like my little sister in a lot of ways," she says. "She's just so young in the way she talks and the way she acts. I loved her because of that. She's brutally honest and she's very open...but very, very immature."

Debbie's sexuality and behavior weren't a mystery to Sandy, after a conversation the two once had. They were talking about the impact on a girl of childhood rape, and Debbie opened up about the experience of her own repeated rapes at age 13. "There's a misconception," Sandy says, "that young girls who are victims of rape may have struggles with not wanting to get involved in relationships with men." Actually, she believes, the opposite often happens. "Young girls tend to become very promiscuous after having been a rape victim.

"So that's sort of how our conversation was," Sandy says, "Talking about what had happened to her, and as a result of that she had become more promiscuous. Your self-worth is lowered and soon you think of sex and love as the same thing."

Yet despite Debbie's sometimes-rash behavior and her difficult background, her friends were able to see the simple girl beneath the surface. Debbie, in Sandy's view, was "very comfortable in her life, she loved the townhouse" and rather than shopping at upscale stores, she "was just as happy at a dollar store or a garage sale."

Sometimes people with keen insight can match the wisdom of a person trained and experienced in a particular field. Sandy's shooting-from-the-hip, parlor-psychology analysis of Debbie was surprisingly on target. Los Angeles psychiatrist Mark Goulston says that a girl who is a victim of childhood rape frequently chooses inappropriate partners. "Many grow up feeling they can't trust anyone. They can't trust authority figures, who should have prevented the attack from happening. They can't trust God, for the same reason. So they may choose a series of inappropriate partners, people who treat them as badly as the rapist, while the girls each time think, *But I'll get him to love me, and it will turn out all right.*"

Dr. Goulston also says these women often suffer from what he refers to as the "Out, out, damned spot" syndrome. "They feel unsavory, and they compensate by pursuing promiscuity with a vengeance, telling themselves, 'I'm no longer a victim, I'm proving it didn't screw me up.'"

But it is, he says, a case of "the lady doth protest too much."

I guess Debbie, and probably her mother as well, looked on my mother as if she was in competition with Debbie for my affections. I squirmed one night when we were all having dinner together at our townhome. My mother remembers that at one point, "Debbie got this look in her eye and said to me, 'You know, you're *not* a loving mother. With my mother, we watch movies together, we hug, and cuddle, we're like buddies to each other.'"

My mother was visibly hurt. I said to Debbie, "I don't think I would want my mother to be like that." About that incident and others like it, my mother now says, "I knew I couldn't say anything. When the walls came tumbling down, I knew you were going to need me."

While Debbie thrived in her routine as a reading teacher, my own career was cooking on high burner. The image was never far from my mind of my mother who had worked so hard and sacrificed so much when I was little. I wanted to do better. So far I had been promoted quickly at the bank and was making good money, meanwhile harboring secret aspirations of doing something beyond banking. I wanted to be a developer, and I was sure I could find outside projects that the bank would permit me to do and that would give me a chance to start learning that business. But at the time, Debbie held me back by her fear of taking financial risks. Coming from a lower-middle-class family, she couldn't think beyond holding a steady job and waiting for the regular paycheck to arrive.

But to give her credit, Debbie wasn't sitting still, either. She and Pam both had aspirations of preparing themselves for promotion within the educational system, and set their sights on master's degrees. They had begun by signing up together for two prerequisite courses, one in K-12 reading education, the other in assessment. The pair of gals would meet after school and drive together to their classes at the University of South Florida. Though it meant less time that Debbie and I had together, we'd make up for it a little by chatting on our cell phones while the two of them wound their way through traffic to the campus.

The "agreement" Debbie and I had reached about putting off starting a family until we had stashed some money in the bank and enjoyed some traveling turned out to be a one-sided deal. Joyce wanted grandchildren and began badgering Debbie. Ever the dutiful daughter, Debbie began badgering me, leading to numerous fights. She always bolstered her case by using the example of Pam and Jeff Glas, able to afford children though each of them was earning a schoolteacher's salary.

This became a leading subject of arguments. Debbie had created a timeline where she would stop taking her depression and anxiety drugs and get pregnant, timed so that she would have the baby over her summer school break. She kept after me and I'd say "Yeah, whatever." We had another of these set-to's shortly before Thanksgiving. Finally, to quiet her down and give me a little peace, I said, "Let me think about it."

Thanksgiving for us meant two meals—with my family in the evening, preceded by a complete dinner with the Beasleys earlier in the day, the little Beasley house always crowded with 20 or 25 members of the clan.

Debbie waited for a dramatic moment when her mother was at the table and every Beasley was digging in, and then said, "Hey, everyone, I've got an announcement to make. Owen and I are having a baby." Everyone lit up with excitement, her mother most of all—"Oh, you're pregnant!"

"No, no, no," she said, beaming. "But we've got a plan." Everybody was befuddled, including me. I said, "Hold on. Baby, what are you talking about?!"

I could see that Debbie was embarrassed and hurt by my reaction. She got up and ran into the other room, fished through her purse, and came back bringing this piece of paper with a timeline written on it, which she shared with the entire family. She said, "I figured it all out." I'm thinking, *Oh, Jesus.* This timeline of hers showed her stopping the behavioral drugs to rid her system of them, then three or four months later stopping her birth control pills, and then the baby would be delivered the coming summer, during the school vacation, so she wouldn't have to take any time away from work.

Out loud in front of everybody—probably not the most tactful thing to do, but I was really upset and feeling on the spot—I announced, "We never agreed to that!"

Everybody looked kind of embarrassed.

Of course, for her to have a baby the following summer, she would just about have to be counting on going to bed that very night and getting pregnant. So much for a timetable with three or four months to rid her system of the behavioral drugs.

When we returned home that evening, we had a very heated argument, another one all over again covering the same ground, this time with the added fuel of my having embarrassed her in front of her entire family.

I finally agreed to discuss the subject periodically, each sharing our views, letting her know how close I thought we were coming to a timetable that would work for me.

Over the next months she told me multiple times how devastated she was by the embarrassment I caused her in front of the family. She brought up the topic of having a child every couple of weeks.

I've since learned from Pam that Debbie was complaining about how down she was that I didn't want to have children as quickly as she did. Pam says, "She went through a period of time where she just had to have a baby, had to have a baby, had to have a baby. She was like, 'If I just go off the pill...'" Pam would tell her, "Don't do that. Just wait—you guys are still newlyweds."

At the time I thought the conflict Debbie and I had over this subject was just one of those disagreements that every married couple has. Now I think these arguments put a real strain on our marriage.

I wish I could say that Debbie's sexy talk and sexy clothing were reserved for private times with me and social occasions with our friends, but that wasn't the case. I have since found out from the other Greco teachers in our group that it was happening at school, as well. Looking back, I can't help but wonder whether Debbie had missed out on her own childhood as a result of the early rape, and was now trying to recover that childhood by becoming like her own students.

Middle school at its best is a difficult society to navigate, the hallways and classrooms filled with young people whose hormones are raging and who are trying to figure out how to cope with their changing bodies, unfamiliar feelings, and rampant sexual desires. I would think the last thing they need is to have a teacher who models inappropriate behavior. But with Debbie,

I'm sorry to say, that is, I now know, exactly what they had.

Even Sandra, who taught at the same school with her, could say, "I definitely thought she had severe emotional problems. She wasn't rational, she wasn't stable by any means—always on the brink of sanity. It was always 'Is she having a good week?' never 'Is she having a bad week?'"

Fellow teacher Avery Hampton, who was a close companion during Debbie's first year at Greco, thought Debbie's inappropriate behavior at school was a result of her medications, even though the pills were supposed to be smoothing off her problems, not causing them. But Avery says, "She was medicated out the wazoo. She would talk about the different pills—'I'm taking this and this together' or 'My doctor just prescribed this for me.' And I just remember thinking, *Wow—that's an awful lot of medication.*

"And when we talked about her sister and what had happened, she'd say she had been having a lot of trouble sleeping."

Pam adds, "When she was on the medication, she could focus better. She could sit down and have a conversation and not be an all over the place as far as moving from one subject to another, or even like sitting down with us and spending the entire lunch period, instead of getting up and leaving."

Defending Debbie, Pam says there was "all kinds of buzz about her" among the lady teachers of the school who were forever scrutinizing the way she dressed and the way she acted. I'm grateful to Pam for having been such a good friend to Debbie during those years. Strangely, as much as people were drawn to her by her beauty, Debbie wasn't very good about making friends. Through my entire time with her, Pam was the only girlfriend Debbie ever had.

So Pam can be forgiven for not liking the way Debbie was criticized by some people who didn't know her well, yet a lot of the criticism was justified—as Pam certainly knows, because she has done her share of it.

Pam and Avery, while admiring her as a teacher, both had reservations about her way of relating to the students, spotting early on the very thing that would lead to her troubles. "Debbie was so close to her students," Pam says. "She was a buddy to her students, where I'm like a parent. She found out a lot about their lives and was very close to them."

To Avery, "It was almost like she would've been a better kindergarten teacher because she was sort of childlike with them," highlighting the childishness that, again, may be a result of her childhood abuse. "The kids would always come to her about problems at home and so on." A lot of teaching, he points out, is classroom management, and she managed the classroom by bonding with the students. "She found that to be effective as far as getting them to do what she wanted. Her attitude was more of, 'Get the kids to love me and then they'll do what I ask them to do.'"

The method worked. "She would often have a group of kids in her room who would just come by there to hang out and talk to her, or they'd be sitting there listening to music with her," Avery says. Debbie was so committed to seeing her students improve their reading skills that she often bought additional books and teaching supplies at her own expense, on one occasion when she had only been at the school for a couple of months shelling out $60 of her (make that *our*) own money. I know—I was the one who paid all the credit card bills for both of us.

One teacher—somebody who was not one of Debbie's fans, so perhaps this should be treated with some skepticism—said that Debbie once went to the principal with a note she had intercepted in class that contained something vulgar about her, saying she wanted the student suspended for ten days. According to this teacher, the principal refused and told Debbie that she "might try dressing more appropriately in front of the students."

Sandy remembers Debbie dressing conservatively in her first year of teaching but becoming erratic in the second year. "She'd come to school some days dressed really to the max. And then some days she come in sweatpants and a T-shirt, with her hair in a ponytail or in a bun—too sloppy for school. She'd pop in a movie and show her kids a movie for the whole day. And that might be several times a month."

But it wasn't just a matter of dressing as if she were going out for a run; on occasion her choice of clothing was much worse. Her friend Pam was a good deal more accepting about this than I was. Pam says, "Debbie sometimes wore really short skirts and showed a lot of cleavage at school, but that was Debbie. She's gorgeous so she can get away with wearing stuff that the rest of us would never wear." The principal, Janet Spence, had spoken to Debbie about watching the length of her skirts. Pam says in her friend's defense, "It was only on occasion that Debbie would dress provocatively."

The principal was with Debbie once when, bending over to pick something up, Debbie's short skirt rode up enough to reveal her butt and her thong underwear. That was too much even for a liberal principal. Mrs. Spence sent Debbie to change into something else.

Because Debbie was highly respected as a teacher by the students, the administration, and many of the other teachers, perhaps it's understandable that the principal didn't want to lay down the law with too heavy a hand to a member of her staff who was doing such a good job.

But this raises a point not to be overlooked: in a middle school or high school, any teacher who dresses in ways that might make kids focus even more on their inevitable sexual thoughts is crossing the line. That should be obvious. I won't argue that Debbie's problem might never have happened if she had dressed conservatively every day. Still, who can say for certain?

These days dress codes are common enough for the students; they should be strictly enforced for the teachers as well. No matter how good an educator the teacher is, school administrators should have a zero-tolerance policy for inappropriate teacher clothing.

In Debbie's case, though, it wasn't just a question of clothing. She was doing things that could arouse the youngsters in her classes well beyond the issue of cleavage and short skirts. She shared with students personal things in her private life, like taking medication for depression because of her sister's death. And about her tattoos, most of them hidden under her clothing so that even talking about them had to conjure up images of her bare flesh.

Sometimes she didn't leave it to the imagination. In her classroom one day, she told teacher Jeremy Butts about her new belly-button ring and then raised her shirt to show him—with students present.

Eventually, Pam says, "Every student in school had seen her tattoos at one point or another. If I were a betting woman, I'd tell you that it's because that's all she's ever known—that's how she's gotten positive attention all her life: using her looks and her ability to flirt."

At times, especially during an energy spurt, Debbie would shift into her high-pitched voice and become what Pam calls "a fast talker and a kid-like talker."

Debbie and Pam were in class one night at USF, presenting together in front of their classmates. Debbie was talking really fast and going on and on and on about their report, as if unaware she was talking way too fast and way too long. Pam wanted to interrupt but didn't want to embarrass her friend.

When Debbie was into something, Pam says, "She'd be really, really manic." Jeremy Jackson saw another aspect of the same quirk. "Sometimes in our conversation she would just jump from one topic to another. You could tell her mind was skipping from one thing to another." Avery Hampton says it happened in the classroom, as well: "I've seen her being so overly excited about a lesson plan that she would just be so involved and really excited, bouncing around the room and helping every kid."

To Pam, Debbie's occasional hyper-energy and unchecked desire to see the kids succeed would sometimes produce odd results. "During her energetic spurts, she'd be happy, obsessed with the projects, working overtime. Where I would take a kid's story and have them do all the work, she would take a kid's story and she'd be anxious to type it up herself. She would sit all night and work on it."

Pam remembers a time when Mothers Against Drunk Driving had organized a candlelight vigil. Because of Angie's death, the work of MADD was of course close to Debbie's heart. She mentioned to Pam that two of the students who were going to the event with her would be coming back to the house to spend the night. Pam remembers replying, "You're out of your mind. Absolutely not, you cannot do that. It's against school policy. And besides, there's the liability. You cannot do that." She must have made a good case; no students ever stayed with us.

A lot of the Greco students, Beth Hampton says, were "kids who were needy, kids with poor home lives." Debbie drew huge satisfaction from helping them, and the kids appreciated her for it. "They looked up to her," Beth says. "And she fed off that." But sometimes it led her into being too close. She would have what Beth calls "buddy conversations" with her students, becoming too involved in their personal lives.

A youngster in one of her classes was a girl I'll call Norma; Debbie apparently befriended the girl and had in-depth conversations with her about the issues in her life. When Norma ran away, it didn't take long to figure out that Debbie should be asked if she knew anything. Beth says, "Bizarrely, Debbie did know where she was." Apparently that didn't surprise Beth very much: "It's a mistake young teachers make sometimes—the difference between being an influence and getting too close."

Confronted by her friend Pam over an issue like this, Debbie would say something like, "I don't understand. Why is that so bad?" Pam's reaction: it was "like she just didn't have clear boundaries."

What would happen when Debbie encountered a young male student who also had a problem with boundaries was something that the entire school and much of the world would find out only a few months later.

Chapter 8
CONTACT

NOBODY WANTS TO come home and find his or her spouse fast asleep, day after day, while the sun is a long way above the horizon. By the beginning of 2004, Debbie was arriving home from school around three or four o'clock, heading for the bedroom, and sleeping for hours—often not waking up until I walked in. That's not unusual for people whose time clocks run on a different schedule from the rest of us—night-shift workers, computer hackers, and at least one Hollywood screenwriter I know about, who work while the rest of us are sleeping and sleep while we're working.

That wasn't the story with Debbie. She would typically sleep all afternoon, wake up for dinner when I came in, then spend the evening preparing for her classes, reading, or watching a pay-per-view movie with me. At bedtime, she'd go upstairs with me and go to bed. She was sleeping eleven or twelve hours a day.

About food matters, she wasn't as obsessed as she had been in the past, though she was following the Weight Watchers program and consistently monitoring her intake, still making a record of everything she ate. There didn't seem to be any reason why a woman in the shape she was in, and working out a couple of times a week, should need to be following Weight Watchers and keeping a detailed log of her eating.

Socializing continued to be a problem, too. By now all our friends knew that when we invited them over to our place for dinner, it was a definite appointment, but if the plans called for dinner at someone else's house or at a restaurant, they didn't have any great expectations of our showing up. Debbie's social anxiety was liable to kick in, triggering a phone call from one of us saying that we wouldn't be coming. The last-minute cancellations were something our friends by then took for granted. They understood that she often couldn't face socializing with a bunch of people and preferred sitting home with me, just the two of us. I suppose in one way you could look at it as a compliment: this gorgeous lady with the great figure was choosing the security and warmth she found in my company over the company of others, even when those others were our six closest friends. She would spend the evening watching television, then go to bed.

But at least she didn't seem to be depressed, which made me thankful for her anxiety and depression medications.

It seems strange, looking back, that I could have been worried about Debbie descending into one of her dark places when she was such a big hit in other parts of her life. She was a hero at school, where she continued to have remarkable success with many of her remedial reading students and was probably the most popular teacher there. And she was considered fun and funny in our social crowd, in part because of, not in spite of, her frequent wickedly inappropriate conversations about sex.

I took it as a very good sign when she continued to bring up a subject she had begun talking about halfway through the school year: looking for a high school teaching job. She had come to a sense of confidence about her ability to maintain control of classes of students much closer to her own age, no longer feeling threatened by the effects of her beauty on 16- to 18-year-old boys. Though she so far hadn't actually filled out an application for a high school job, just talking about it was a healthy sign.

Some things hadn't changed. Around this time, in early 2004, Debbie still wanted children as desperately as when she first brought the subject up shortly after our marriage. There was something magic in the air when Debbie was with the small children of our friends. Even the shy ones were drawn to her as if she had child-magnets running in her bloodstream. Whenever Debbie was around them, she blossomed. Pam Glas's four-year-old, Maddie, formed a special bond with Debbie, a bond felt even more strongly in the other direction. Debbie had a special affection for her because she had such a strong connection with the name: her sister had selected "Madison" for the unborn child who died with her in the drunk-driving accident.

Pam asked Debbie to babysit now and then, something she was always delighted to do, and their kids became very attached to her. Watching Debbie with the children, I could see what a fantastic mother she would make. I understood her eagerness to start a family of our own. But it still didn't make sense to me so early in our married life—though I've since changed my view.

Sometimes I'd try to lighten the air about this subject of friction between us by making jokes about it. Once when the Glases were at our house with Maddie and their newborn, Ellie, I told Pam, "Don't bring your kids around here—it just makes Debbie want some of her own." Debbie was too busy holding Ellie and cooing over her to pay any attention.

Months later, Debbie's conversation with Pam about going off the pill would hit me hard, when I saw a list of Debbie's prescriptions from the pharmacy we had been using. One item came as a real shock. For months, she had been on Yasmin for birth control.

She picked up a refill on January 16. Assuming she bought a new supply early to make sure she didn't run out, the January supply would have lasted her at most until late February or the beginning of March.

The record shows that she had never ordered another refill from that pharmacy. She continued having her anxiety and depression medications filled by them. Did she suddenly decide to use two different pharmacies, going somewhere else for her birth control pills?

That's a possibility. Debbie and I had grown a little uncomfortable with that pharmacist. We joked that he reminded us of the character played by Robin Williams in the movie *One Hour Photo*—a guy who inserted himself a little bit too much into the lives of his customers. Yet this pharmacist already knew from Debbie's prescriptions that she had issues with depression and anxiety, and that she was on the pill. What sense would it make to let him continue filling the prescriptions for psychological problems but try to hide the fact that she was still on birth control?

This only leaves one other explanation I can think of: that Debbie had done exactly what she had talked to Pam about. Not that this is so rare. I'm sure there are thousands of women, maybe tens of thousands, in this country at any one time who have stopped using birth control while conveniently forgetting to mention the fact to their husbands or boyfriends.

The foundation of any relationship is trust. Taking a step like that is a violation of trust. Maybe not as great a violation as a husband who has an affair, certainly not as great as a wife who cheats with a teenager. But between husband and wife, I don't believe there are gradations of trust. This isn't in the same category as telling a lie, where there's a huge difference between a white lie and a whopper. If you break trust with your partner, you break trust. Period!

Perhaps I'm making too much of this. Debbie broke trust with me in so profound a way only a few months later that this first dishonest step, if that's what it was, has lost its significance. Or maybe it was the initial crossing of a line that made the crossing of that much more dangerous line all the easier.

On Debbie's good days, people would see us as a bright, happy pair of newlyweds, Debbie sticking close to me, often sitting on my lap when we were visiting with friends, making me feel loved and in love. Yet I couldn't afford to feel encouraged by her moods. As soon as I'd start to think that maybe the clouds were clearing, the skies would darken again. Not long after New Year's 2004, she went into another slump. Some days I would come home from work and find the old familiar pile of her clothes just inside the front door. She would come in, close the front door, step out of all of her clothes, and I would know that I'd find her sound asleep on the couch, completely naked, with the empty popcorn container alongside her.

From the time we moved in together, her effort with household chores had gone in cycles, Debbie sometimes doing the chores she had agreed would be hers, sometimes doing nothing at all. This time was worse. By February, she had just shut down completely. I could trace her steps from when she walked through the front door by the debris of clothing, books, and popcorn bags. Finding her would have been easy even if we had been living in a much larger house—there was literally a path from the front door to where she had settled. The house wasn't being cleaned, the kitchen was usually a mess. And she was back in that mode of sleeping for half the day.

We talked about it multiple times. To her credit, she never threw at me as a defense any labels that past therapists might have hung on her. But maybe it would have been better if she had offered me an explanation of "depression" or "anxiety" or something even more specific from the list that psychologists use. Instead whenever I'd say something like, "This place is a shambles. I don't want to live like this," she'd say, "I'll try to improve. I'll try to be better."

Though Debbie had given up caring about maintaining the household, she certainly had not given up caring about maintaining her body. On top of going to the gym regularly—at the time it was Gold's Gym—she had lately added regular yoga classes. And she was keeping a jet-setter skin glow with trips to the tanning parlor.

In Debbie's second year at Greco, the school was undergoing renovations and the county had set up a number of small stand-alone trailers, or "portables," each the size of a standard school classroom and equipped with its own tiny bathroom. Debbie had been assigned "portable 44" as her classroom, and became friendly with a teacher named Belicia Guerra, who had the portable directly opposite.

By early spring, Debbie was complaining to Belicia about "headaches that won't go away," and about having "a terrible time" with the anniversary of her sister's death. Then, Belicia says, she began to see changes in Debbie's behavior. Her one-time friend became distant and wouldn't talk to her anymore. And she was growing less professional in her work. "She had been very strict with her students and now became casual with them," Belicia remembered, "often letting them just hang out and watch television." She overheard Debbie telling some students about her intention of adding more tattoos, which Belicia considered entirely inappropriate.

In early May, Debbie suddenly morphed into a different person, someone I didn't know. If this was a movie I was watching instead of my real life, I would've said it was stupid and unbelievable that someone could change so dramatically almost overnight.

She started coming home with CDs of rap music. I enjoy listening to some top 40 rap music, but when Debbie started listening to rap, that's all she wanted to hear. She had become obsessed. When I asked her about it, she shrugged and said, "It's what the kids at school listen to. They listen to it all day and it just grew on me. It's what I like now and it's all I want to listen to." I'd tell her, "I don't want to listen to that garbage—put something else on."

Whenever we were going out to a restaurant with friends and she dressed in one of her tight, low-cut blouses that advertised her cleavage, I always put it down to her social insecurity. Even the dazzling combination of beauty and brains wasn't enough to give her confidence around other people, so she'd bolster herself with the display of her prominent figure, and the sex talk; sometimes launching into a subject with a rapid, unbroken stream of thoughts that didn't give anyone else a chance to speak for minutes on end.

So I was used to Debbie dolling herself up in sexy clothing. But when she started occasionally going to school in skimpy clothing, I'd tell her, "Debbie, that's no way to be dressing for school. Those boys you're teaching have their hormones pumping already. One look at you like that and they won't be able to listen to a thing you're saying."

She'd answer, "They're little boys. They don't care about the way I look."

Was that naïve? Or calculated?

If I thought the way she had been dressing was inappropriate, I hadn't seen anything yet. With the change in personality around May came even more extreme clothing. She started wearing very short shorts, and tight little halter tops. Sure, she looked luscious. But I couldn't imagine any man catching one glimpse of that scene and not mentally undressing her. It was like she was announcing to every guy, "Let me see the bulge in your pants."

At least she wasn't dressing that way for school. Yet.

Also about the same time she began smoking again. Not in the house, but in her car and, I later learned, during breaks at school. I could smell it on her and on her clothes, and it was another problem between us. I told her I couldn't handle the smoking. She said, "That's what I want to do," and went right on doing it.

From Tampa, it takes only about an hour and a half to drive to Orlando, a world tourist destination because of its high density of fun in the form of theme parks. Many of the local schools take advantage of this convenience by offering students the "educational" benefit of going on field trips as a kind of celebration when the end of the school year nears. Sometimes a reward, sometimes in the nature of a graduation present, sometimes just an excuse to break the routine when the class work is finished, exams are over, boredom threatens, but everybody still has to hang together until the official end of school. That year, Debbie took part in no less than four school field trips.

In early May, a crowd of eager students hustled onto a couple of buses for the ride to Orlando and a day at the Universal Studios theme park. Part carnival, part thrill rides, part pure entertainment, a visit to the Universal Park offers two experiences of value to every youngster, and many adults as well: a look behind the scenes at moviemaking that carry valuable lessons. One is a demonstration of movie makeup, themed around applying prosthetics and makeup for actors in a horror movie. The other is a ride based on the 1974 film *Earthquake;* as your car thunders along the tracks, you pass noisy, awesome scenes of the kinds of things that can happen in real earthquakes—ceilings collapse, subway cars collide, gasoline trucks crash and explode. Sure, it's designed to scare and thrill, but in the process you come to understand the sort of movie magic Hollywood uses. I like to think it's a lesson in fantasy and reality that helps kids understand the things they see in the movies and on television aren't real. Of course, if you told the kids there was a lesson to be learned here, it would spoil their fun.

When Debbie was asked to be one of the teacher-chaperones for her school's Universal trip, she readily agreed, especially since Sandy was also going along. Recalling that day, what Sandy remembers most vividly is how Debbie was dressed. "She changed into something totally inappropriate, little tiny shorts hanging below her belly button, which was pierced. One of the other teachers said to her, 'Girl, you need to cover yourself up, because even when we're on field trips, we still have to follow the dress code.'"

So I wasn't the only one unhappy with the way Debbie was sometimes dressing for school and school events.

The following week, the buses loaded up again for another field trip, this time to a different part of the Universal Studios theme park complex, Islands of Adventure. This trip was for students who helped out at school in one way or another—members of the Peer Empowerment Teams, who work with the at-risk students; the Crime Watch, kids who patrol the hallways checking for passes; and the Student Assistants, who are teachers' helpers. Debbie, planning to chaperone again, asked me if I wanted to go along. The idea of escaping the bank for the day, out in the sun, sharing the rides and the junk food with my beautiful wife, sounded way too good to pass up. This time the crowd of students included school athlete Bobby Woodhouse and a good buddy of his, another athlete, Jack Carpenter.

These outings are always an easy day for the teachers. It's not like herding a group of elementary school kids who have to be kept together and watched every minute. The ground rules for the middle-schoolers call for them to check in with a chaperone by cell phone periodically, and to show up at a prearranged point a couple of times during the day. Otherwise they're on their own.

The visit to Islands of Adventure was enjoyable and uneventful, but with an aftermath. The next day, Bobby and Jack, on their way to a class, encountered Debbie. She called them over and gave them some candy, saying she had bought it at Islands for them. The boys didn't know what to make of that. Bobby said later, "Why would a teacher buy something and give it to us? And after that, that's when we first started going to her (classroom). That's how it started. That's the reason we started going to her room."

Debbie had taken the first step of her dark and dangerous dance.

Had she chosen her dancing partner, or had he chosen her?

I would subsequently learn that Jack first met my wife earlier, in April, at a tag football game of a school team that several of Debbie's students played on. She and some of the other Greco teachers went to a number of the games. Jack and Bobby, both on the team, had been noticing the gorgeous teacher who had started showing up. They knew who she was; probably there wasn't a single boy in the school, and probably not a single girl, either, who didn't know Mrs. LaFave by sight.

One day the pair of them walked over to her and introduced themselves.

It was the simple act of a forward, cocky student and his pal.

Much later, another Greco teacher who had Jack as a student, Bernadita Natal, summed up that moment: "I think Jack came on to Debbie," she said. "That's his character."

I do not mean to shift blame here.

I do not mean to shift blame.

This event does not stand in any way as relieving Debra Jean Beasley LaFave of the guilt for what she was soon to do.

I am merely, to the best of my ability, recording the events as they happened.

Chapter 9

HEATING UP

DEBBIE WAS A POPULAR chaperone that year, I think because she was so admired by most of the kids and many of the teachers, and because people seem to gravitate to any gorgeous woman. Or at least those people who don't assume that a beauty will be cold and haughty and likely to snub them. Teachers like that at the school avoided Debbie, which was fine on both sides.

Of the four Greco field trips in the last month of school, Debbie was invited to chaperone every one. Next on the list was another trip to Orlando, this time to visit Sea World, and I gladly joined her on that one as well. Once again Jack was along. This time he wasn't just a face in the crowd. Debbie introduced him to me, along with his friend Bobby.

I still remember the pair from that day, unmissable from the way they were dressed—like a pair of ghetto kids, Jack wearing an oversized UPS jersey and a UPS hat tilted sideways, Bobby wearing an orange Buccaneers jersey, his hat also tilted sideways. Jack, with short brown hair, an athletic build, and an all-American look, struck me as bright, but for some reason he sprinkled his talk with street slang.

Avery Hampton paints a vivid picture of 14-year-old Jack Carpenter, who had been in one of Avery's seventh-grade gifted classes: "He had a mischievous side to him. He could be troublesome. He's also really funny, but he would do it at the expense of another kid, and I'd have to pull him aside and tell him not to."

At the start of the school year the previous September, Jack had come to him and said, "Mr. Hampton, can I be a student assistant for you?" Avery knew he was going to have his hands full that school year. He figured he could use the extra help even though he had some reservations about the boy. So Jack became one of Avery's teaching assistants, helping with miscellaneous chores and even grading some papers. But halfway through the year, Avery, as he tactfully puts it, "allowed Jack to become student assistant for another teacher," and took on a different student in his place.

Calling him "one of those kids who didn't exactly break the rules, but bent them," Avery says, "He would push it to where you're about to give him a referral [a written reprimand], and then back off. He would stir up things. He would say 'Daniel said this about you,' when Daniel hadn't said anything of the kind. He would stir the pot with [other] kids."

Jack was also "cocky" in Avery's view. "He didn't draw lines very well." On another occasion, Avery gave an example to illustrate the point: "He made comments like, 'Ms. Beasley, she's really hot.'"

"I didn't ever hear him talk about any other teacher in the sexual connotation," Avery says. "Other students commented on her looks but not to the extent that he did. At times I would say to him, 'Jack, that's inappropriate. You really can't talk about a teacher like that.'"

He was the type of kid who "didn't really know boundaries all that well. Like he would push the envelope." Jack teased Avery one day in front of a full class of students, referring to Debbie as "your girlfriend." Another day, when Debbie came in to cover for Avery, Jack asked her, "Ms. Beasley, would you date Mr. Hampton?" It's what Avery meant about not drawing the lines very well. "He would tease adults like that," Avery says.

Teacher Bernadita Natal saw Jack as "a manipulator, too big for his britches. Sweet at times, but cocky and wanted to run class his way."

And then there was the issue of boundaries. Not that it would make any difference on the nature and degree of Debbie's crime, but Jack once crossed the line in conversation with Bernadita in a remark that, if true, puts the boy's history in a slightly different light. He said to Berna, "I had sex with somebody you know." She shut him up in a hurry.

But whatever points he was trying to score, his cousin Cliff, who was in a position to know better than anyone else about Jack's experience with girls, believes Jack had at that point never gone any further than kissing. No intercourse, no oral sex, not even much of any touching. Virtually everything about sex with girls still lay ahead.

Berna Natal's problems with Jack, though, went beyond the issue of his talk. "I didn't trust him," she says. On one occasion, Berna arranged a student field trip to Costa Rica. Then Jack signed up to go. She faced being responsible for him on a journey to a foreign country. "I didn't want him on the trip," she says. Yet she knew that saying no to just one student would run the risk of a parental complaint to the principal. Rather than take Jack along, she cancelled the entire trip.

There was one more item on the list of sudden changes in my wife's behavior, a biggie.

Debbie announced that she didn't want children. Essentially she woke up one morning and told me, "I don't want to have children for a long time. Like, ten years."

I was taken aback. This was coming from the lady who had had all those fights with me over her wanting children, with me wanting to wait.

I said, "What's that about? How come you suddenly don't want kids?"

"I just want to wait," she said. "I just kind of realized I'm not ready."

Occasionally after that, she'd say out of nowhere, "I don't want to have kids." Or "I can't imagine having kids right now." Just out of the blue.

Debbie gave out her cell phone number to the parents of her students, and to the students themselves. She explained by saying that she felt sympathy for the kids and "I want to be there for them" in case they had questions about their schoolwork. That's probably inappropriate, perhaps something only a new teacher would do. But I took it as a sign of her very real dedication, an earnest concern for her students.

I think when she shared personal things about herself with the kids, about things like her problems over the death of her sister, her medications, and her tattoos, she sent a message that shifted the social barrier. Kids had begun calling her about personal things like their girlfriend/boyfriend problems. Sometimes these calls would interrupt the conversation between us or our watching a television show together. She'd stop whatever we were in the middle of to chat with the kid, sometimes accepting an invitation to watch one of the after-school sports games, sometimes listening to stories about whatever was on the caller's mind, or sometimes just letting them gossip. Though it didn't happen all that often, I still found it inappropriate and annoying.

Among the callers was Jack, who wasn't even a student of Debbie's.

One thing, at least, was on an even keel. We were having regular sex. No objections from me in that department, other than that she was still so obsessive about cleanliness. It was, "Hold on. If we're going to do anything, we need to go take showers first." She had been like that occasionally in the past but now it became part of the every-time routine. It robs the moment of spontaneity.

Still, it takes two to tango and maybe I was dancing all alone and didn't even realize it. I thought our sex life was fine in those early months of 2004 and Debbie offered me no complaints.

But she was complaining—to other people. Bernadita Natal heard from a fellow Greco teacher Debbie had been griping to that her sex life wasn't pleasing her anymore. To Pam, Debbie shared the news that she "wasn't connecting well sexually with Owen." Debbie told her, "I'm dissatisfied sexually." She complained of the same thing to the other Jeremy, her fellow teacher Jeremy Butts, who was a friend to both of us, grousing that her sex life wasn't up to her expectations.

But in a conversation with Sandy Hart, Debbie told her that the lack of a pleasing sex life "doesn't matter to me." And, Sandy says, "She would always tell me her connection with Owen was about more than sex—she had a deeper connection than that."

I don't have any idea what to make of all this. If she was really unhappy about her sex life, why not bring it up with me, the guy who could do something about it, instead of griping to friends, who weren't going to do anything more than listen and offer empty phrases of understanding?

Or was she perhaps laying groundwork, providing excuses to herself that would justify what she was already beginning to contemplate?

Debbie and I were having a night on the town with dinner at a little Mexican cantina and bar near the university. We had finished eating and were sitting around drinking—Debbie with her standard Mich Ultra, the Michelob ultra-light, low-carb beer, me with a Corona and lime, appropriate to the setting. About 10 o'clock, Debbie's cell phone rang. In her sprightly little-girl voice, she started joking and clowning. In response to a quizzical look from me, she covered the cell phone and mouthed "Jack."

I waited patiently while the chitchat about nothing went on, expecting her to hang up any minute. This was the same kid I had met on the Sea World trip, who I remembered wasn't even one of her students. She kept on chattering, cutting up and cracking jokes, while I sat there stewing. Then the phone on the other end was apparently handed off to some boy named Cliff. I would later learn he was Jack's cousin, a boy who would figure absurdly, painfully into the story that was about to unfold.

I was thinking, *Hey, that's inappropriate. A teacher shouldn't be talking to students like that, joking around, laughing, swapping stories. That's over the line.* But then, that was Debbie. Okay, so it was annoying; I saw it as part of who she was.

But finally, losing patience, I took the phone out of her hand. By this time it was Jack again on the other end of the line. Forcing myself to be tactful because I didn't want to spoil the rest of our evening at the cantina and possibly a romantic interlude later, I said as if I was joking, "Isn't it past your curfew? Isn't it past your bedtime? Don't you need to go to bed?" I was being a smartass and needling the boy. Debbie started saying, "Oh, no, no, no—he looks up to you. Don't be mean to him." I handed the phone back to her. Instead of ending the call, she talked to him for what seemed like another 10 minutes, just talking nonsense. I was steamed.

Should I have spotted something seriously amiss here? I don't blame myself. These were children. I was blind to the truth because it was so incomprehensible. Who could have imagined that one of these two giggling boys would soon be a player in throwing my entire life off track?

There would be other calls like that with Jack over the next three weeks. I confronted Debbie about it more than once, trying to make her see how inappropriate it was, telling her, "You're the teacher, you're not their friend." She tried to pass off Jack's calls as no different than calls from any of her other students. My complaints annoyed and upset her. "If they need me for whatever reason, I want to be there," she'd say, calling her students "my babies."

Except that Jack wasn't one of her students. She taught remedial reading. Jack, besides being an athlete and one of the popular kids of the school, was also bright and capable, not in need of help with reading. And he certainly wasn't a "baby."

Jack's teachers recognized that the youngster was infatuated with Debbie, but they didn't think anything of it—what healthy male wouldn't be? To teacher Berna Natal, it sometimes seemed Jack was playing a game of pushing the boundaries to test the limits of how much he could get away with. "Jack made several comments about what Mrs. LaFave was wearing and how hot she was. On one occasion he said, 'That Mrs. LaFave, she's got some boobs on her.'" But I stopped him with a threat to write a referral for talking disrespectfully about another teacher. Jack could be arrogant and rude to me and to other students. He is very intelligent but can be annoying."

With Avery Hampton he went even further. One day in late May, Jack overstepped even the extra latitude allowed the school athletes. The boy announced, "I'm going to sleep with Mrs. LaFave." There probably wasn't another boy in the school who would have made a remark like that out loud to a teacher. Avery figured it was just one more inappropriate remark from a youngster who was always overstepping the boundaries.

One day near the end of school, Jack showed up for his Spanish class and said to Ms. Natal, "I know this stuff already. Let me go over to Mrs. LaFave's." She said he couldn't go unless Mrs. LaFave gave him the note requesting permission. She thought that would be the last she heard of it but Jack showed up with a note from Debbie asking that for the remaining days of the school year, the boy be allowed to spend that class session in her classroom.

Bernadita figured this meant that Jack would be sitting in on Debbie's reading class. In fact, Debbie didn't have a class that hour; it was a dead period in her schedule, time provided for teachers to grade papers or prepare for upcoming classes. Looking back, Berna now says, "If I had known it was her planning period, that [Jack] wasn't going to attend a class, I wouldn't have let him go." But she didn't know that at the time. She signed off on the permission form, allowing Jack to spend Spanish class for the remaining days of the school year hanging around in Debbie's portable.

That wasn't the only class Jack was able to finagle his way into escaping. In the last couple of weeks of school, he was able to spend part of each day at Debbie's portable. Most of the time his friend Bobby Woodhouse would be there, and sometimes another buddy of Jack's, Walt Grimes. If Debbie had a class, they would sit on one of the sofas and talk while she worked with her reading students.

When there wasn't a class in session, Debbie and the boys, sometimes joined by a couple of girl students, shifted into party mode, even ordering pizzas sent in to the classroom. Bobby later described the scene: "Ms. Beasley was just very friendly, but she just seemed like one of our 15-year-olds, you know, our friends. She didn't act like a teacher.... She'd come over and sit down with us." Walt's description is more specific and blood-chilling: "[Jack and Mrs. LaFave] began flirting and became more friendly."

Walt remembered that "there were a couple of times we'd be sitting on the couch when there wasn't a class going on. She would come sit next to Jack and like he would lean on her or something. Maybe their arms would touch." It seemed innocent enough that Walt didn't think of it as flirting.

Jack was obviously confused about what was going on. Alone with Bobby, sharing his confidence and confusion, Jack would say that it seemed Mrs. LaFave liked him. "But for both of us," Bobby said, "it seemed like that wouldn't be possible. But we would talk about it and he would say like, you know, she gives him clues...(It) kind of seemed like the way she would talk...that that might be possible."

It wasn't just in her conversation that Debbie was growing more forward. In her classroom, she was allowing Jack a degree of physical contact, and brazenly doing it in front of the other youngsters. Bobby remembered, "One time he laid his head on her lap for maybe twenty minutes. He was just laying there. He just kind of laid there and she just sat there."

At the same time that she was tempting the boy physically, she was dangling the bait with words as well. Bobby, again: "Sometimes she would get mad talking about her boyfriend." (These students had known Debbie from the time she first started teaching at Greco, when she was still "Ms. Beasley"; a lot of the students, not just these boys, had never accepted the idea that the lovely, sexy teacher had married and was now Mrs. LaFave. To them she was still Ms. Beasley and the man in her life was still her boyfriend.)

The conversations with Debbie also came to the subject of Jack's dating and what girls he liked. "At the time he didn't have a girlfriend," Bobby relates. "He would bring up girls he might like at school or girls he might try to get with. He would say girls he thought was pretty or whatever, and that he might want to talk to, and she would say her opinion about it if she knew the girl." Bobby says there were "a lot of black girls that, you know, thought we were cute and liked us" and that brought a reaction. "I think Mrs. LaFave just thought it was kind of funny that, you know, so many black girls liked us that year." She got a smile, or pretended to, from the two of them being targeted. Bobby didn't find anything racial about her reaction. "Nothing against them or anything like that."

As an athlete, Jack ranked as one of the top kids in the school. And he was multi-talented: while playing on the Greco flag football team and serving as its captain, he was also a more than adequate basketball player. On Tuesday of the final week of school, Jack and Bobby gathered up their gear at the end of the day and headed over to the gym on 22nd Street for the first basketball game of the summer league. Innocent enough, the games would figure prominently in this sad story.

Greco math teacher Steve Torkelson, the coach of the team that Jack was on, remembers Debbie asking him for a copy of the schedule, and after he gave her one, he saw her starting to show up at the games. She would have been hard to miss. Torkelson remembers her sitting in the stands wearing high heels, miniskirts, and tight shirts.

One day after the boys had been hanging around in Debbie's classroom, Jack says, she invited him to stay after school. He was supposed to go for a haircut. She offered to drive him to the barbershop, waited there with him, and then drove him to his basketball game.

Soon, I now know, Debbie took a step that carried her from hungry observer fantasizing at a distance about the forbidden, to an actor, a player, a woman who had given herself permission to be tempted. She developed a regular routine of driving Jack to his basketball games, sitting there watching the game, and then driving him home. She mentioned none of this to me, and since it all took place while I was busy earning a living as a banker, I was totally unaware. She'd come home late and tell me she had been watching some of her kids in a basketball league. I told her once, "You need a hobby."

Debbie answered, "No, this is what I want to do." Though I didn't much like it, at least it seemed an improvement over her coming home, stripping naked, and going to sleep.

One week she was at the basketball games three nights in a row. I thought it was becoming ridiculous, and I guess I was beginning to grow suspicious. But I'd call her cell phone and always be reassured by the sounds of the game in the background.

The last field trip of the year took a crowd of students and chaperones to Busch Gardens. The name may bring to mind images of horticultural exhibits, but in case you're not familiar with the place, it's another amusement park, with roller coasters and hair-raising rides that are definitely not for the faint of heart. Debbie wanted to try them all.

Three of the young teachers hung out together for the day at the park—Jeremy, Debbie, and Channel Cox, a science teacher. During the afternoon, Debbie steered the conversation to the subject of Jack and his sidekick Bobby. She talked about how they were both really smart and both good athletes.

Jeremy says, "I'd had this same conversation with her once before. One day she and I were walking together past the new gymnasium, and she asked me about the two boys, who were both on the football team." As Jeremy recalled the conversation, Debbie said, "They're really good kids. Do you know them? I hear one of them is really smart. I hear Jack is really smart."

At Busch Gardens, Jeremy replied as he had on the previous occasion. "No, it's his buddy. It's actually Bobby who is like the genius of the two," he told her. "Jack is a really bright kid but Bobby's scores are off the charts."

She went on talking about who Bobby was dating, but that was just the lead-in to talking about Jack and the girls who were after him, whom she described as 'hoochie mamas,' using the language of the teenagers. And she said, "That Jack, he's such a cutie, and he's got all these hoochie mommas all over him. He needs to get a good girlfriend." Again she was speaking the way the kids would say it: "a good girlfriend."

Channel and Jeremy gave each other a look and shook their heads.

"I don't care who he dates," Jeremy told Debbie. "He's a good football player. And if he wants to date a hoochie mama—he's 14, he can date a hoochie mama."

The whole conversation was just like Debbie, Jeremy figured, always saying things a little bit out of left field. "It struck me as a little weird," he says. "But it didn't send up any flags."

Debbie asked Jack if he would be willing to help her clean up her classroom, in preparation for moving her things out at end of the school year. If she was looking for chance to be alone with the youngster, Jack wasn't yet in tune with her intentions. He was picking up signals but not believing them. In any case, he said he'd be glad to help.

The portable assigned to Debbie as a classroom was done up suitably for unobserved misbehavior: the windows were blacked out. "But that wasn't uncommon," Jeremy Jackson says. His windows were blacked out, as well. "Otherwise," he noted, "kids sometimes went by and made faces at the students in the class." Those in the classroom who saw the display would start giggling, and the whole class would be disrupted.

Walt, Bobby, and Jack were spending a good part of the day hanging out in Debbie's classroom. After school, Debbie continued to play chauffeur for the boy, taking him to basketball watching the game, and then driving him home—carefully letting him off far enough away that no one who knew him would notice and drop a comment to his mother.

Jack was obviously in heat; he had reached the point where he could barely wait to be in Debbie's company. From her classroom in the portable directly opposite Debbie's, Belicia Guerra couldn't help noticing the comings and goings, especially when there was something looking not right. Students aren't allowed in that area of the school complex until nine in the morning, and she noticed Jack showing up and hanging around outside the door to Debbie's room as early as eight, always with his cell phone in his hand. She questioned him about it a couple of mornings. The first time he said he was there because Mrs. LaFave had asked for his help.

The second time was on the last day of school. Jack said he was there because he was on detention.

That part was true, sort of. Debbie had asked Jack if it was okay to put him on detention, so he could spend the day in her classroom. He didn't know quite what she had in mind, but it must have sounded like the next step in wherever she meant to take their connection, and he agreed. The next morning, he was so eager to begin his "punishment" that he had showed up an hour early.

By nine o'clock, the whole troop had assembled. Debbie had arrived, and had provided passes so Walt and Bobby could be excused from other classes so they could be there as well. Under her supervision, the boys began packing up her things. I suppose there must have been a festive air, with three months ahead for the boys of no books and no classrooms. Debbie's thoughts, on the other hand, I'm afraid were not on what she would do to enjoy the summer with her husband.

The group took a break, with Debbie joining Jack on one of the two couches in her classroom. Bobby says, "They were both sitting on the couch, his back turned toward her, and she massaged his shoulders." (He actually said, "I think" that's what happened, though how he could be uncertain about whether a sexy blonde teacher gave his friend a massage is beyond me.)

By this time Jack had told his friends that he thought he was going to have sex with Debbie. But at this point, on the last day of school, nothing was certain. It didn't seem to any of them as if such a thing was really possible. Bobby says, "They still weren't yet actually doing things so he wasn't really sure if she was actually going to." Yet with the massage, and the clowning around and childish giggles from Debbie, there was an atmosphere of sexual deviltry in the air.

Walt came up with the bright idea that Jack should ask Debbie to flash the boys—show them her breasts. Bobby described his own reaction: "It was one of those things where he said it and, you know, he would've been happy if she would have, but he wasn't, you know, real serious thinking she would do it."

Jack, always cheeky, took it as a dare and made the brazen request. He said to Debbie something like "Show us your boobs—as a graduation present," since they were all finishing middle school and would be in high school next year. Walt says Debbie laughed and took it as a joke. "She was like, 'Stop it.' She was, like, kidding around. She was like, 'Shut up,' and was laughing." It seemed to him as if Jack and Debbie were "kind of flirting" about it.

Walt and Bobby must have been dazzled by this risky exchange with a teacher because they're vague on what happened next. Walt says, "I think he went and, like, gave her a hug or something. He walked over and wrapped his arms around her. I think she hugged him back. I think they were still laughing."

The other two boys left around midday. Jack stayed behind in the classroom. After his friends were gone, he says, Debbie did actually raise her shirt, but only just enough to show the bottom of her bra.

Later Jack told his friends that he and Debbie had been kissing after they left. Walt remembered, "He said, like, that him and Mrs. Beasley were like talking about like doing stuff.... 'Me and Mrs. Beasley are going to go out' or something.... I thought he was just kidding around. I was like, '*Shut up*.'"

Each year that Walt Grimes had been at Greco, his parents had thrown an end-of-school party on the last day of the school year. This time the invitation list had grown so large that Mrs. Grimes had moved the location from their own home to Riverhills Park, owned by the city of Temple Terrace

The party started around one. Debbie drove over a couple of hours later, bringing Jack, Walt, and I believe Walt's father. She introduced herself to all the adults and then said, "I'm going to play with the kids."

Mrs. Grimes recalled later, "A lot of teachers are that way and that didn't send any kind of signals to me, just that this is a teacher that has more of an affinity for the kids than she does for adults. And that's a trait I've seen in teachers before."

Still, Mrs. Grimes was captivated. "She had on long pants and heels. I remember thinking, *What a lovely, beautiful girl.*"

Later Mrs. Grimes noticed Debbie sitting at a picnic table in a gazebo with five or six boys. "I was curious that they were all boys, although she's a beautiful young teacher and it's understandable to me that 14-year-old boys are attracted to beautiful young women."

Something made her think she should check out the situation. "I went over and sat down to kind of chitchat for a minute. The kids were joking around and shooting the breeze. I asked, 'Who's in a class with her?' And it seemed like she didn't teach any of them. She was basically like a special ed teacher and these were not special ed students. These boys were all very handsome and very popular."

Mrs. Grimes sought out her son and asked, "Who invited her? How did she get here?" Walt answered, "Jack invited her." The questions reveal her suspicion; in granting a license for the party, the city had required that a number of chaperones be on hand, and several teachers had been asked to come. Almost none of them had showed up, so having Debbie there should have seemed like a blessing, yet Mrs. Grimes's protective instincts were aroused.

While continuing to play hostess, she kept tabs on the proceedings. She knew Jack by sight; as one of Walt's closest friends, he had been to their home frequently. Mrs. Grimes saw that Jack was playing basketball, and when that game finished, moved off to another game. "I noticed that when he moved from place to place, so did she. She shadowed him, in other words."

At six o'clock the DJ who had been providing music shut off his speakers and started packing up. The party was over, the kids began to drift away. Vicki Grimes and her husband Cliff stayed behind to clean up, along with a number of the kids. Only one other adult stayed to lend a hand: Debbie. "She stayed right until the bitter end, helping out," Mrs. Grimes remembered. Points scored in her favor.

Then there proved to be a transportation problem. The remaining youngsters were all headed back to the Grimes home, and they wouldn't all fit into the two Grimes cars. Debbie offered to drive the others, solving the problem.

At the Grimes home, most of the boys—about ten of them—would be staying for the night, but two girls who had been at the party were stranded without a ride home. Debbie to the rescue again, offering to provide transportation for the girls. Then she heard where they lived, in a neighborhood that is not one of the better areas. She said, "Oh, well, I don't feel safe driving there." But she offered a solution: Jack could come along to provide protection.

Mrs. Grimes thought, *You're the adult here, a 14-year-old doesn't need to be providing you with protection.* She told Debbie, "That's fine, I'll take them home." She loaded the girls into her car and drove off.

By the time she returned home, it had already grown dark. She discovered Debbie was still there.

Later on she found her suspicions confirmed by some of the youngsters. "It's no secret up at the rec center that there was something going on," she was told. A couple of youngsters whose father worked at the center added to the evidence. They said Jack had told everyone, "Oh, she's my girlfriend."

It sounded absurd. Yet everything she had witnessed for herself added up.

Young Walt Grimes provided the end of this story. When Debbie finally left the Grimes house that night, there were still some other kids who weren't staying for the night and needed rides home, Jack among them. Debbie took them all, dropping the others off first. Jack later told Walt of the conversation he had with Debbie when they were alone in the car together. He said that he and Debbie had talked about having sex "but she needed to prepare," and that she had bought some lingerie to wear for him.

She told Jack that she had never cheated on her husband, and no man had ever turned her head before him.

Man? Is that the way she was seeing the 14-year-old—as a *man*?

Chapter 10
NAKED LUST

We come now to what is for me the most painful, wounding part of the story. Thankfully at the time I had no personal knowledge of the events. In this chapter, my own comments and narratives are in italics to distinguish from the details based on the recollections of people close to the story and reports from official records.

Back in the real world, with school now over, students and teachers went their separate ways, each on his or her own personal schedule of summer activities. One thing that didn't change was the arrangement between Debbie and Jack, with Debbie continuing her regular routine of driving the youngster to his basketball games.

The Greco players would talk to Debbie before the games and briefly afterward, then Jack would go off with her. Jack's friend Bobby thought, "It just seemed kind of bizarre that she was coming to all the games." But it must have seemed not so odd once Bobby heard from Jack that he and the teacher had been "kissing and whatever" in the car en route to and from the rec center.

It was on one of these drives home that Debbie first opened up to the boy. "I have feelings for you that make me smile when I think of you," she said. "I can't get rid of the feelings." Those were words I will always wish were for my ears alone. Picturing that scene still makes me burn with anger and embarrassment. How could this seedy drama have been playing out in my life?

True to his age, Jack placed several calls to his cousin Cliff, keeping him updated on the newest developments in the unbelievable story about the super-hot teacher who liked him. Cliff says, "He didn't exaggerate over it." It was just, "I'm talking to this real good-looking teacher. I think she likes me. And she's really, really hot." Jack described her as having "long blond hair, very skinny, nice boobs"—that was the full description. Cliff thought it was "cool" but found it hard to believe. He had "a good-sized doubt" about whether it was true, and figured that even if a teacher really was coming on to Jack, "It wasn't going to be a good-looking teacher."

Later, Jack called Cliff to tell him about the kiss in the car. "The teacher," he said, "is trying to hook up with me."

Cliff said, "I don't believe you."

Jack answered, "I'll prove it."

On the first full week that school was out, the first week of June, Jack's mother drove her son to her sister's in Ocala, where he would spend a week with his cousin Cliff. It promised to be a week of lazy days with temperatures reaching the high 90s. For Jack it would be a momentous week, one that would change his life and the lives of many others.

By then Debbie's infatuation had heated to a boil. She and Jack were talking to each other over their cell phones several times every day, most of the calls made by Debbie. Jack allowed Cliff to listen in on one conversation; he heard Debbie gushing about how much she missed Jack.

On Wednesday, she called Jack on his cell phone to set plans. The next day she made the hour-and-a-half drive to Ocala, an inland town of about 45,000 people on the Florida peninsula, known for its horse farms, proud of its trees, popular for its Silver Springs nature theme park where tourists come to spend the afternoon spotting alligators from the safety of a glass-bottom boat.

Debbie wasn't coming for the alligators or the horses; she was drawn by an attraction of a different kind.

Arriving in Ocala about noon in her silver SUV, she picked up Jack and his cousin around noon, rather early considering that the excuse for her trip was to drive Jack back to Tampa to play in his regular basketball game, which wasn't until the evening.

She drove them to our townhouse. The boys sat in the living room while she ordered a Hawaiian pizza—not a favorite of hers, so she had apparently left the choice up to Jack. With her pizza, she drank a beer. Then she ordered a pay-per-view movie, *Stuck on You*, a comedy about two young men who are inseparable: they are Siamese twins. Why that particular movie, I wonder? Because she was feeling inseparable from the boy?

Cliff watched the movie sitting on the couch in our small living room. Debbie and Jack squeezed in together on a single chair.

When the movie was over, Debbie led Jack upstairs.

In the bedroom, he saw that the bedspread was pulled back. He sat down on the edge of the bed. Debbie sat down next to him and they started kissing.

This is not easy to write. The bedroom I shared with my wife. The bed that was our marriage bed. My bride of 11 months was sitting there with a 14-year-old boy thinking lustful thoughts. Desiring him.

I guess she would have had sex with him in our bed. I was saved that one small humiliation only because she was having her period.

After a while she stopped kissing and asked, "Are you sure you want to do this?"

"Yes," he answered.

He explained later that she had already told him she was having her period so he "knew she did not mean having sex."

She pulled down his shorts and began gratifying him orally.

Perhaps she was overcome by remorse, or guilt, or some previously missing and only temporary sense of decency. Before he climaxed, she suddenly stopped.

He had had a small taste of the forbidden but for the moment it was as much as he was to have. He put himself together. They went back downstairs in all innocence to rejoin Cliff.

They had not had intercourse but Debra Jean Beasley LaFave had crossed the line. She had violated a taboo, several taboos. Even if nothing further happened between them, she was a criminal in the eyes of the law and in the eyes of society. If she had stopped then and gone no further, she might still be teaching the children of Tampa.

This society makes it hard to learn the distinction between fantasy and reality. Today's teenagers think they can be as slim as a photo of an airbrushed model on the cover of Seventeen magazine. Disneyland confuses the young by having actors dressed up in the guise of Mickey Mouse and Goofy and the rest, creating in young minds the notion that the cartoon characters are real and have just stepped off the screen to shake hands, give a hug, and pose for a photo.

Teachers should be helping kids learn the distinction between fantasy and reality. Debbie, allowing a young boy's fantasy to become reality, was playing Mouseketeer with a mind-bending, brain-damaging result.

In late afternoon, Debbie drove the two boys to Jack's basketball game at the 22nd St courts in Temple Terrace. She and Cliff sat in the stands watching the game and talking. After a while she wanted a cigarette, and he walked outside with her. Cliff says that Debbie acknowledged she had had sex with Jack. As he remembered it months later, he asked her directly, "So you had sex with him?" And he says she replied, "Yeah, I did." She talked about how she liked Jack a lot and how weird she felt that she liked him so much.

Tom Grimes, whose son Walt played on the same team as Jack, knew that Jack was supposed to be in Ocala for the week and was surprised he had shown up to play. Debbie noticed Tom and said hello. During halftime, he saw that she got up and moved away from him, to the other end of the court. It was a simple enough act but something about it caught his attention, staying in his mind clearly enough that he made a point of mentioning it when questioned later by the police.

For the trip back to Ocala after the game, Debbie asked Cliff if he had a driver's license and Cliff said he did—even though, as a 15-year-old with a learner's permit, the law permitted him to drive only with an adult licensed driver on the seat next to him. Debbie didn't intend to be next to him. She got into the back seat with Jack. As Cliff drove, Debbie and Jack kissed for a time.

Cliff had seen the pair go upstairs together in the townhouse, but now was seeing the connection for himself. "I thought we were just really going to hang out," he said later. "And then I seen that they are acting more, you know, sexually than I thought. Because this was like the first time I had ever seen them together, you know." Cliff was taking it all in, somewhat dumbfounded. "I was amazed. They were talking about how she likes him and how he likes her. I'm, 'This is weird.' I didn't say much but I was in shock. Like, I didn't know what to say and so I really didn't say much."

After a while Debbie started giving Jack oral sex. This time she continued until he climaxed.

She told Cliff to pull over at a Taco Bell. Debbie and Jack got into the front. She drove the rest of the way, dropping the boys off near Cliff's home around 11 that night.

Young boys are inclined to brag about their sexual conquests. Often what they claim is a pack of lies. Jack had no need to lie. He called his friends Bobby and Walt to tell them of the momentous happening. Walt remembered later, "He told me like one day that she had given him oral sex or whatever. I was surprised, very surprised." Asked if he believed it, Walt answered, "I kind of did…like after I saw [her] at his basketball games and stuff." And he added, "He told me they were probably going to like have sex or something."

"Sex or something." There's nothing funny about this, yet at times you can't help but smile.

Debbie met with her friend Sandy for lunch at the Westshore Mall. Sandy noticed an extreme change in her friend's behavior. "Debbie and I were very close," she says. "We talked on the phone quite a lot. But for two or three weeks, I'd been leaving messages on her voicemail and she wouldn't call me back." That never happened before between them.

And there was the way she had put herself together. "I remember thinking, *Oh, my gosh, she's just like a 14-year-old.* She was wearing tiny gold shorts that had something written across the butt, and a kind of half-shirt. And she was in pig-tails. It was just really bizarre. It looked like something I would put on my four-year-old daughter—you know, cutesy." Also strange was the way she was sitting: "with her legs folded under her, cross-legged, like a kid."

Even stranger for Sandy was Debbie's conversation in the car after lunch, as they set out to go on an errand together. As they drove, Debbie talked about an educational conference in Denver the school had approved her to attend. Then, totally out of left field, she started saying, "I just am not ready for kids. I just feel like maybe I got married too soon. I just feel kind of trapped and smothered right now."

Sandy said, "Why? What's going on?"

"I don't know," Debbie said. "Sometimes I just want to be *free*, to do what I want to do."

"You're going on that conference," Sandy said. "That'll give you some time away."

Debbie said, "Maybe what I need to do is just find someone to have an affair with."

Figuring she was just kidding, Sandy laughed. "Oh, yeah," she said. "That's some solution."

Debbie joined her in laughing, as if confirming that it had indeed been just a joke.

Sandy was struggling with her friend having gone from a desperate feeling of wanting a child to this completely opposite attitude of "I don't want kids, I got married too soon." And "I feel smothered." The sudden transition was so jarring. Sandy now regrets she didn't pursue the subject. "Looking back, I feel if we had gotten more into that conversation.... I think she was really dying to tell me what was going on."

It doesn't pay to dwell on the past and wonder What if? *Even so, I can't help thinking: suppose Debbie had opened up to Sandy that afternoon. Would Sandy have told me? Or told her husband, who would have told me? And then what—would the joint efforts of Debbie's parents and me, perhaps with Sandy as well, have been enough to bring her to her senses?*

Or maybe I would have asked for emergency leave and taken her away on long a trip. Insisting that she leave her cell phone at home, of course.

Could we have saved her?

Two days later, our group of friends assembled for Saturday night dinner at Pam and Jeremy Jackson's. During the course of the evening, with the girls in the living room and the guys out back, Debbie said to Avery's wife, Beth, "Whatever happened to that intern at your school?" This led to a conversation I would later come to recognize as one of the most odd of the whole affair.

The intern Debbie was asking about was a young woman, Nancy Harris, who was in her senior year of college on the way to a degree in education. Just as Debbie had done, the lady needed to complete a teaching internship before she could graduate, and had come to the high school where Beth teaches. She turned out to be gifted in the classroom and became very popular with the other teachers.

One day a group of the boys who Beth had as students approached her with a story they thought was funny. They were giggling and laughing and nudging each other, dropping hints but not coming out and saying what was all about.

Finally one of boys in the group, Matt, let her in on the secret. He was having an affair with Mrs. Harris. Beth didn't believe it, of course. Torn between annoyance that they would make up a story like that and the sense that she needed to find out if something was really going on, she replied, "Oh, my goodness!"

And then, probing, she said, "That's not true—that never happened. You can't make up stories like that."

The boy answered, "She bought me the such-and-such DVD, she took me to…" and gave the name of a local area hotel. "It cost $63.50 for the room. She took me to Wendy's and bought us burgers," and so on, providing authentic-sounding details. Afterward Beth called the hotel and asked the rate for a standard room. She was told it was $63.50 a night.

She went to the teacher, mentioned the CD the boy said Nancy had bought him, and watched the reaction. The young woman's face turned into a mask of horror.

At that point Beth shared the details with the principal, who promptly called the police. But the boy was 18, no longer a minor. When the parents refused to press charges, the principal clamped a lid of secrecy on the whole thing. Nancy of course was booted out. Denied her teaching certificate and her university degree, divorced by her husband, she had moved out of state and taken up a different career.

One part of the business that Beth never understood, she told the ladies, was that she was treated to sharp, nasty comments from a couple of the other teachers, who insisted that she should have kept the whole thing quiet until Nancy had completed her internship and received her degree.

When Beth finished telling the final chapters of the story to the ladies sitting in her living room, she commented, "It's so insane. He was a teenager, and she was married."

Debbie agreed, adding one of those typical-Debbie comments. "It's really crazy," she said, and then continued, "If I weren't married to Owen, I would definitely go after Officer Chapman."

She was talking about a white-haired security guard at Greco Middle School, a man in his fifties. Debbie was always telling the other lady teachers at school how good-looking she thought Officer Chapman was, often saying things like, "Oh, there's something so sexy about him." The attraction was strong in both directions. Another of the teachers remembered something Debbie had shared with her: Chapman had told Debbie that he kept getting in trouble with his wife because he talked about Debbie at home so much. None of the young lady teachers at the school could figure out what she saw in him; to them, the guy was an old-timer, completely unsexy.

Beth says, "She really had the hots for him. And he was always coming on to Debbie."

Why would Debbie have brought up Officer Chapman to her lady friends at Pam's that night? In her confused state of mind, she must have thought she was throwing her girlfriends off the scent. By reminding them of her attraction to a much older man, Beth later realized, Debbie must have been thinking that it would somehow make people less likely to suspect she was having sex with a young boy.

To anyone of rational mind, the story Beth told that Saturday night would have been a cautionary tale of a life ruined when a young woman gave in to temptation. It should have been enough to make Debbie think, I must stop this, now, before my world collapses the way that other woman's did.

It was a chance for salvation. But the passions must have been too strong to overcome the voice of reason that had to be shouting inside her head. Here was another stop sign Debbie was speeding past.

The next day, Sunday, Debbie and I began packing for what I expected to be a relaxing week at the beach. We would be joining her parents on their annual pilgrimage to the same place they had gone for their honeymoon.

The week started off badly. Before we were even out the door, we had a fight. I had reached the boiling point, and told her, "Within a period of a single month you have completely changed personality. Who the hell are you?" I shouted, "You're not my wife."

So we set out with bad vibes for what should have been a carefree week.

We had hardly settled in the quarters we had rented for the week with Joyce and Larry before Debbie announced that she wanted to invite some of her students to come and spend a couple of nights. I thought it was an outlandish idea. Debbie and I were still newlyweds; even sharing this week of vacation with her parents was stretching it for me, yet Debbie was too close to her mother for me to object. But ask some students to join us? Debbie insisted she didn't see any problem with it—she had a personal relationship with these kids and she just wanted to share the beach experience with them.

What she really had in mind, I now understand, was that she didn't want to be without Jack's company for an entire week. I would find out later that she had already invited him, suggesting that he bring along a couple of friends who she must have imagined would provide a smoke-screen. If Jack had come, Debbie would have been in heat the entire time he was there, frantically scheming ways to be alone with him. Jack later told an investigator that he "thought it would be weird," after what he and Debbie had done together—which seems to show better judgment on his part than on hers.

The Beasley annual trips to Englewood beach are usually for a week. We had been there four days when Debbie announced that she had to drive back to Tampa for a job interview at King High School. I sat down with her parents and shared with them my concerns that Debbie's recent behavior changes had made me face an uncomfortable possibility: I thought she might be having an affair with the father of one of the students. Joyce, Larry, and I agreed that I should not let her go back to Tampa by herself; I would give up the rest of my week of vacation and go with her.

I knew Debbie had come to feel that teaching high school English would be much more rewarding for her than teaching remedial reading. So her applying for a job at King High didn't add to my suspicions. How was I to know that the focus of her passion, young Jack, had finished middle school and would be starting at King in the fall? How was I to know that she had only submitted her application to King High three days before the end of school?

Her father was alarmed by the suggestion I had made and took Debbie aside for a private conversation. He basically asked her whether anything was going on. She told me afterward that she was very offended and very angry with him. The conversation left her extremely upset and uncomfortable with her parents, and the three of them fell into a heated argument. She denied that she was involved with anyone. She sensed we were all suspicious about her reasons for wanting to return to Tampa alone, spending another three days and nights on her own.

Her denial was convincing to me. But at the same time, coming after all that business about going to every basketball game, and the sudden change in personality, it left me wondering.

The following day, after Debbie and I had returned early from the beach, she drove to King High School, a magnet school in Tampa, for her one o'clock interview with the principal, Dr. Steele. She didn't know he had no openings for another English teacher. But he welcomed the opportunity to interview any qualified applicant, keeping the information on file to refer to should an unexpected opening come up. Despite what I now know were her conflicted emotions at that juncture, Dr. Steele didn't notice anything unusual in her behavior. He later recalled her as mature and not rattled by the interview process, and as "having it together." One remark she made especially caught his attention and he jotted a note: she said she would do anything to help kids.

Later that afternoon, she dropped by the basketball court for Jack's game. She had a gift for him: a pewter keyring pendant with a butterfly on one side and the word "Hope" on the other. "I have one just like it," she told him. Like a teenager with a crush, she wanted them each to have something that spoke of an emotional attachment deeper even than the intimate bond of sex.

My suspicions about Debbie having an affair with the father of one of her students continued to gnaw at me. Leaving work that afternoon, I set out not on the usual homeward drive but headed for the basketball court, arriving about midway through the game. There was Debbie in the stands, dressed skimpy enough to show way too much flesh—but that was nothing new. Otherwise there wasn't anything to raise an eyebrow about. Some kids were sitting around her, natural enough for a popular teacher. She seemed pleased to see me, as far as I could tell, yet was unusually quiet for her and intent on the court action.

When the game was over, she said goodbye to some of the players, I walked her to her car, and we both drove to our townhouse. I would find out much later that Jack, stranded without his usual Debbie chauffeur service, had to impose on his coach, Steve Torkelson, to drive him home.

Sunday afternoon, out of my hearing, Debbie used her cell phone to call Jack, asking if he would spend part of Monday helping her clean out her classroom. He must have understood that she had something more in mind than she was willing to say over the phone. I can imagine his pulse beating faster as he agreed. They arranged that she would pick him up at the rec center, where his mother would drop him off.

Cliff decided he had to find a way to get down to Tampa and check out the progress for himself. Rounding up company for the trip wasn't any problem: he had been sharing news of his cousin's exploits with a few other guys, mostly friends from school and the neighborhood. Not specific details; Cliff and Jack weren't in the habit of sharing much in the way of details about what they did with girls. Cliff found three guys who said they'd be happy to join him for the trip, one of them, conveniently, old enough to drive and with access to a car.

The next Monday—June 14, 2004, "a day that will live in infamy"—Debbie drove over to the rec center around noon and found him standing outside waiting for her. He stepped into the car and she drove him back to the school. They worked together on the clean-up for a while, listening to rap music. I've never seen many classrooms with a sofa, but Debbie's portable classroom had a couple of them. After a while, Jack sat down on one, a couch with light blue cushions and wooden arms.

She bent down next to him and said, "I've been thinking about you a lot." They kissed. She asked, "Are you ready?" and he knew she meant ready for sex. Or maybe she asked more directly, "Do you want to have sex with me?" Afterward the climactic event overwhelmed the memory of the small details.

"Yes," he said simply. She knelt on the couch, straddling him. "Are you sure?" she asked.

He was extremely sure. He had fantasized about her hour after hour, talking to Cliff and the rest of his buddies about her, imagining this but never believing it would actually happen. Now it was happening. Probably at least a couple of seconds passed before he managed to croak a shaky, "Yes." His wildest fantasies were about to be handed to him—by the woman I was married to.

She stood up. Facing him so he could watch her, she stepped out of shorts—the black terrycloth ones I had seen her wear so often. Underneath she was wearing black thong panties with roses on them. He pulled down his shorts and underwear. She straddled him again and they kissed a while longer.

She pulled her panties to one side, reached down, and guided him into her.

He thinks they continued for about ten minutes until, for the first time in his life, he completed the act of sexual intercourse, that most secret, most sacred, most treasured of human communications.

Afterward she went to the bathroom in the portable to clean up. When she came back, she asked him, "Are you okay?" and he said, "Yes."

Jack was no longer a virgin. Debbie had robbed him of his innocence on an old, stained sofa in the metal coffin of a portable classroom with its windows blackened, the stain of guilt heavy in the room.

Not that virginity is a cherished concept for most 14-year-old boys in this society, but Debbie was an adult removing the possibility of Jack having that life-changing experience in any kind of wholesome context. She had prematurely plucked him from his adolescence.

Many men would refuse to condemn Debbie, considering what she did as satisfying a male fantasy; these are men who, like their ladies carrying status handbags, haven't learned to distinguish between fantasy and reality.

When Cliff and his friends from Ocala arrived and found their way to Debbie's portable, Jack announced that "We were just cleaning up her portable," but said it was such a smirk "that we knew what happened." Jack confirmed it to Cliff, who could tell that Jack "was pleased about it, proud of it." Cliff let the other boys know.

One of them sat down on one of the couches, the one they figured had been used for the sex. All the boys laughed, and the kid got right back up again. They were all treating it like it was a big joke.

The boys helped by carrying some boxes out. From the way the boys were smirking and clowning around, Cliff thought Debbie "knew what was going on"— she understood the boys knew that she and Jack had just had sex.

The plan was for them all to go together to the mall. Jack rode in Debbie's car, the boys from Ocala in the Jeep they had come down in. They stopped first for something to eat, Debbie paying for the food. The place they chose was a Subway—for me especially ironic, since it was at a Subway that Debbie and I had first encountered each other on the USF campus.

The Ocala boys wanted to go to the mall to "check out the girls" because "there's a lot of girls at the malls"—more girls than at the malls in little Ocala.

From the felonious to the ridiculous: Debbie had had a dental appointment scheduled for 1:40 that afternoon. She phoned the dentist's office and, showing a sense of responsibility in one area of her life that she clearly lacked in another, much more important one, said she couldn't make the appointment and wanted to pay the missed-appointment charge. She gave the dentist's assistant her credit card number to be charged the $20 fee.

If it weren't so sad, it would be funny: who wouldn't rather have sex than go to the dentist?

Jack called his local school buddies to tell them of the latest development with Mrs. LaFave. Bobby recalls Jack sharing that "he had had sex with her in the portable." Bobby wasn't sure what to think. "I really didn't believe him at first because I thought he was just messing around. But...I could kind of tell that that could be true."

Meanwhile Debbie had a problem. She couldn't keep taking Jack back to her classroom more than two weeks after school had finished. It would look too suspicious. Sneaking him into our home or her parents' home could set tongues wagging, just as had happened over her lesbian affair, when it seemed as if everyone in her parents' town of Ruskin heard the news.

She and the boy had already made out once in the back of her car with Cliff driving. Why couldn't they keep doing that? She called Jack, arranging to pick him up the following day, and telling him to call his cousin and say they would come by for him.

A few minutes before 9 on Tuesday, June 15, 2004, Debbie withdrew $100 from an ATM at the Publix Pharmacy on Winthrop Market Street in Riverview. Her hair was in a ponytail from the top of her head, and her height was boosted slightly by a pair of platform sandals.

She swung by Temple Terrace to pick up Jack, then headed north on Interstate 275 toward Ocala. They arrived on schedule at the designated rendezvous spot, Porter's Nursery in Ocala, not far from Cliff's home. (I won't even comment on the decision to set up for sex with her teen lover by picking up the boy's cousin at a "nursery.")

He got in and she drove to a BP gas station where Debbie asked Cliff to take over the driving while she got in the back seat with Jack. Cliff, maneuvering the car back onto the street, saw that Debbie was leaning against Jack. He drove past Wild Waters aquatic park and ended up at a McDonald's, where they stopped for lunch. He then drove to a Smoothie King where he treated himself to a smoothie.

From there Cliff headed west on Highway 200 while the two in the back kissed. Cliff heard Debbie tell Jack she knew what they were doing was wrong. Jack said he knew it, too.

That didn't deter them. After a while, Debbie and Jack stood up in the back seat, and she laid the seat out to form a large flat surface. She pushed his short trousers aside and gave him oral sex for a time. Then she lay down with her head toward the back of the car.

In the rear view mirror, Cliff could see Jack take off his basketball shorts, leaving his shirt on, then lay down on top of her. She placed her hand between his legs and guided him into her. Cliff could see that Debbie had her legs spread, his cousin moving up and down, pumping away in the act of sex. He could see her legs as well as her bare buttocks. The two did not talk.

Cliff kept driving on Highway 200. Shortly after he passed the I-75 overpass, Debbie moaned a couple of times. Then she laughed. Jack had climaxed.

Debbie sat up and asked Cliff for her sundress, which she had tossed into the front seat. He handed it to her. She brazenly faced forward to put it on. The 15-year-old, driving illegally, was now hazarding them all because his young eyes were glued to the rearview mirror. He would later accurately describe to the police the way her pubic area was shaved.

When she had her dress on, she asked Cliff to stop somewhere so she could clean up. He pulled into the parking lot of a pharmacy. Jack and Debbie went to use the restrooms. When Jack returned, he shared with Cliff his teenager's response to his second experience of intercourse with the woman who was then my wife and sexual partner: "It was awesome."

Cliff would later tell a police investigator that both boys thought Jack's having sex with the teacher was "cool."

It was now about 1 o'clock. Debbie drove to a liquor store, ABC Fine Wine & Spirits, where she bought two mini-bottles of Skyy vodka, one melon flavor and one berry. Though never a big drinker, Jack later reported that she added the vodka to a can of Sprite and drank the mixture.

Cliff called his friend Adam and invited him to join them as they headed to the local Best Buy electronics store. Adam met them in the parking lot and the four went into the store together. There would be no denying it later—the Best Buy security cameras captured a series of images that clearly showed all four.

In the store, Jack explained to Cliff and Adam that the gift she was shopping for was an iPod for her husband: my birthday was two weeks away. For all of us, our actions at times are filled with contradictions and absurdities. Having just had adulterous, felonious sex with her teenage lover, Debbie had come to Best Buy to purchase a present for me.

Adam says that Jack also told him that "Mrs. LaFave is transferring to my new high school because she wants to be with me."

The mini-iPod, brand new at the time, was in short supply. Debbie had apparently done some research to discover that this particular store had a few in stock. She picked one out and paid $299.58 on her Household credit card. The foursome then wandered around the nearby Paddock Mall, window shopping but not buying anything. By about 3 o'clock, Debbie, Jack, and Cliff were back in the car. She had Cliff call to make sure his mother wasn't at home; the coast was clear, so Debbie drove to the Corey home and dropped Cliff off.

She and Jack then headed back to Tampa, arriving at the 22nd Street basketball courts an hour early for his six o'clock game. For once she didn't stay to watch, instead heading off, stopping long enough at Starbucks to buy a grande iced coffee.

The next day, Wednesday, Debbie didn't call Jack until a little after noon. She told him it was pretty obvious he could not say anything to anyone. Jack assured her and said he was going to the rec center for the day. She called him again around six that evening to say she wanted to make another trip to Ocala with him the following day. Obviously this wasn't a couple of rolls in the hay with an ill-chosen partner while overcoming some peculiar 11-month itch; this was a sick passion she meant to continue pursuing.

She met Pam Glas and daughter Maddie at the mall, and bought some outfits for the youngster. Again she said she was in a hurry and had to be somewhere. "I have an appointment at one," she said. "I have to go somewhere. I don't have that much time, I've got to get going."

Debbie dropped into Tampa's Old Navy store and bought $90 worth of goods. And she headed to the Sports Authority store in nearby Brandon, where she spent another $43. Some of these purchases were gifts for Jack.

On Thursday they set out early, Debbie picking up Jack at a street corner near his house about 9 in the morning. That may have been rather early for him: he slept in the car on the way to Ocala. Debbie had used shopping for antiques as an excuse for the trip, and they stopped en route at one antique store so she could look around. She didn't find anything to buy.

Cliff had told his mother he was going out to shop for a Father's Day gift. Jack called when they were a few minutes away and Cliff again walked the couple of blocks to the nursery, where he was waiting when the silver Isuzu rolled up a little after 10:30. The boys remember differently how she was dressed. Cliff says orange Capri pants and blue tank top; Jack says both the Capri pants were pink and purple, the tank top in matching colors and tied at the neck. Perhaps this only demonstrates how unreliable witness reports can be.

Debbie got out to let Cliff into the driver's seat, showing no concerns about his driving her car. "Me and Jack thought it was cool," Cliff would later say. She told Cliff to find a spot where he could park. The two guys tried to think of somewhere they could go where they wouldn't be spotted.

Cliff settled on a dismally unromantic setting, a place called Brick City Park, pulling in and stopping the car just inside the fenced entrance, next to a dumpster. He got out to leave them alone, assuming they wanted to have sex again. He was right.

Debbie pulled off her pants and top. Jack saw she was wearing nothing underneath—no bra, no panties. She pulled his pants down and once again started by giving him oral sex. Then she guided him on top of her. Again she seems to have assumed he was still too inexperienced to know how to enter her himself. Jack says she again took hold of him and guided him inside her. A bitter example of Debbie still being the helpful teacher.

She again allowed him to finish inside her.

Cliff stood outside making cell calls. He strolled down to a quarry pit. He walked to a ball field where some kids were playing lacrosse. When he strolled back to the car, Jack was getting into the front seat, and motioned for Cliff to join. The three drove around for awhile. Debbie told Jack, "We have to hide our relationship. It would be terrible if your parents found out." Cliff thought she sounded "real scared" of their relationship being discovered. She told the boys she had "stopped kissing my husband much"—a sad attempt to justify her actions.

She talked about the age difference between them, but in Cliff's description "brushed [it] off like a joke," with some remark that makes it sound to me as if she was picturing the two of them growing old together: "When one is 40 and the other 50, it doesn't matter."

"She talked fast a lot," Cliff reported. "Always in a good mood. Happy."

Cliff had the impression that she was serious about the relationship, talking about her living together with Jack. As soon as Jack turned 18, she was going to tell people about them. She knew it wasn't right, he recalled her saying, but she couldn't help her feelings. Cliff thinks he remembers Debbie saying that when Jack turned 18, they might get married.

She promised that when he graduated, she would buy him a car as a present. A Lincoln Navigator or a Cadillac Escalade, as Cliff recalls — both large, expensive SUVs.

In recounting details (except the confusion about what clothes Debbie was wearing each day), the stories told by the two boys coincided in all respects. If the account of these statements was also accurate, it casts the episode in a different light entirely: She was imagining a future with herself and the boy—a Letourneau household.

After Debbie had cleaned herself, they picked up another of Cliff's friends, then headed once more to the Paddock Mall. At the Champs store there, Debbie bought Jack two pair of basketball shorts, one red, one black.

There are several different versions of the explosive event that happened during that afternoon, triggering all that would follow. Two of the versions are from the boys themselves, another from Cliff's mother, still another from the friend who was with them during part of the afternoon, and one more from a local newspaper reporter who said she heard her version from Jack's mother.

I'm going on the theory that what people told investigators initially is likely more reliable than what they think they remember after so many months had gone by. I believe what actually happened is that, in one of those unlikely coincidences of the kind Charles Dickens often used, the kind that can change the course of a life for good or ill, Cliff's mother chanced to see her son standing next to a silver SUV she didn't recognize, with her nephew and a blonde lady. Sensing something amiss, she called Cliff on his cell phone and watched as he answered the call. She asked what he was doing. He told her that he and Jack were with "Ashley," the sister of a friend of theirs from the University of Florida, and that they were going to Orlando to buy a Father's Day present. The explanation sounded reasonable on one level, yet her suspicions weren't entirely put to rest.

She called her sister and said, "Did you know Jack is in Ocala today?" No, Jack's mother said, she didn't know he was in Ocala; she had dropped him off at the rec center and he said he was going to be there all day. When they hung up, Mrs. Carpenter called Jack's cell phone and asked him for an explanation. He told her that a teacher from his school had come by the rec center and said she was on the way to Ocala to buy a present for her husband, and would he like to go along. Mrs. Carpenter was shocked that any teacher would take a student on an out-of-town trip without permission from a parent. She told Jack that she wanted to talk to the teacher, and he gave her Debbie's cell phone number.

Shortly after, Debbie's cell phone rang. She let the call go to voicemail, then checked. It was Mrs. Carpenter, leaving a message for Debbie to call her back.

When Cliff got home, his mother was already there, waiting to confront him. He remembers being "almost in shock... freaking out." He was panicked because his mother was "about to find out that I have been in Tampa...without her having any idea. My parents were going to go nuts."

He says, "Trust is a huge thing between me and my parents. You know, I have a hard time keeping their trust. And so I had their trust good, and then I, of course, ruined that."

His mother demanded, "Where have you been? Who have you been with?" and told him, "We know what's going on." She was, he says, "flipping out."

Cliff and Jack had made up a story in advance, a cover story in case they were spotted and needed to do some explaining. They would say that the teacher was looking for some type of present for her husband from an antique shop, an item they only had at a place in Ocala. Jack went along with her and she would be bringing him right back to Tampa. That was the story that Cliff first told his mother. She told him that she knew everything that happened and that they needed to sit down and talk about it.

Cliff blames himself for their getting caught, for telling too many people. "It was more my fault probably because... more people probably knew than should have."

Debbie and Jack were still on I-75 en route back to Tampa. As they talked, Jack caught Debbie by surprise, telling her he wanted to take a break from seeing her. He put it in such strong terms that Debbie apparently thought it sounded like "Goodbye." Providing an update to his friend Bobby afterward, Jack would mention the break and say it was because Debbie had been calling him on his cell phone too often.

In fact, the phone calls were not the reason but the symptom. Whether he consciously realized it or not, he was growing concerned about the depth of Debbie's emotional involvement. For Jack, the sex was an unexpected but much welcomed gift, yet he didn't want the rest of the package Debbie was so ardently pressing on him. Cousin Cliff undoubtedly diagnosed the situation correctly: Jack "didn't want the whole relationship thing."

Cliff quietly rang Jack and dropped the news: Cliff's mom had called Jack's mom about what the boys had been up to. The big secret wasn't a secret any more.

About five o'clock Debbie drove up to drop Jack off at the basketball courts where, just another teen athlete once again, he played until time for his mother to pick him up.

A youngster who seventy-two hours earlier was still a virgin, Jack had already experienced a day of extraordinary feelings and emotions.

His day was far from over.

Chapter 11
BUSTED!

DEBBIE ARRIVED HOME and asked me for advice, a request far less innocent than it sounded. She knew Jack's mother had been tipped off that her son had been spotted in Ocala with her. She needed to find a way of reassuring the boy's mother that the Ocala trip was completely innocent and nothing to be concerned about.

What she wanted was a lie to tell Mrs. Carpenter, and she began with a lie to me, a whole pack of lies. She said there had been some extra time before the day's basketball game and one of the players, Jack, had asked her if she could take him to the mall, so she did. I already knew that she had taken "some students" to Ocala a couple of days earlier, a trip she explained by saying that Jack had a cousin up there who kept emus, or llamas, or some other animal that's unusual in Florida.

I felt she was spending too much time on trips to Ocala, and her being alone with the children was even worse. I had expressed on multiple occasions that it was improper. "Something could come of it," I had told her. "One of the children could say that something happened." Even her parents had tried to make the same point to her.

I knew she would sometimes drive two or three kids home, which of course meant she would be alone with the last one. She had always been very argumentative, very defensive in her position. In these conversations, she'd answer me with things like, "I don't think it's a problem. I have a close relationship with my children and I'm just doing them a favor." And "It's innocent," she would say. "They're my kids, and they love me."

I was worried about it because I knew it wouldn't look right to other people and because it might land her in trouble. I never even dreamed there might be some more sinister explanation.

On this evening in June, she told me she had taken Jack on a trip without his mother's permission, and Jack's mother had left a message for her on her cell phone. She wanted me to tell her what to say to the mother. I advised, "Apologize immediately. You know she's going to be angry. Just defuse it and say that it was a lapse in judgment and it won't happen again without her permission." She did that, and Mrs. Carpenter seemed to accept it.

I had no reason to believe it was anything other than another example of Debbie using bad judgment in overextending herself to be a friend to her students. The blind, unable to see facial expressions, sometimes trust people when a person who can see would not. I was emotionally blind, unable to see that I was being played for a fool.

I had been taken in, but Mrs. Carpenter hadn't. Driving home after picking Jack up at the basketball court, she confronted him. "You need to tell me the truth. Because I know. You need to tell me about it right now."

Jack broke out in tears, perhaps tears of relief. He confessed he had had sex with the teacher.

When she reached home, Mrs. Carpenter called a deputy sheriff she knew and gave him a quick rundown. When you're upset, nothing is easy. She was told she needed to call her local police department. She hung up and redialed the Temple Terrace police.

Just after 8:30, Senior Police Officer David Thornton received a radio call directing him to the Carpenter home on Woodland Ridge Drive. He was there within a few minutes. Officer Thornton listened to Mrs. Carpenter's story and then asked Jack for a few details. He called the station and advised his supervisor, Corporal Hensel, that the case involved possible sexual battery of a minor under the age of 16. Corporal Hensel told the officer that a detective would be sent to of to join him and meanwhile he should continue working the case.

The officer prepared to interview Jack, first having him take an oath similar to the oath given to a witness in court before testifying. Mrs. Gardner, sitting close by, must have suffered on hearing her 14-year-old spell out his sexual encounters in exacting detail. Officer Thornton talked Jack through the entire story, drawing from him a description of each incident of oral sex, each incident of intercourse, writing down detailed notes. In law enforcement today, you don't have to be a police captain or a seasoned detective to know that unless you have assembled all the facts very thoroughly, no prosecutor will even bother considering the case.

At the end of his report, Thornton would write that Jack "is not prescribed any medications, and has not been diagnosed with any psychological disorders. He presents himself as an intelligent, mature 14-year-old."

Convinced by now about the likely truth of what he was hearing, he also placed a call to the sex offender division of the State Attorney's office and spoke with Carol Hooper, who recommended having the boy make phone calls to the suspect—"controlled" calls, meaning they would be recorded and usable in evidence.

The officer gave Jack a standard police form and guided him through putting down a brief summary in his own handwriting. Complete with a middle-schooler's errors and a misspelling of something he now knew how to do but not how to spell, Jack wrote:

> During the last week of school a teacher at Greco Middle School named Debra La Fave told me that she had feelings for me. —She told me that she was thinking about me a lot and had feelings for me that she didn't know what to do with them. —However we did not have sexual intercorse until the week of Monday June 14. On Monday she asked me to help her clean out her portable. That day we had sex for the first time. On Tuesday we drove down to pick up my cousin ______, on that day we also had sex. On Thursday June 17, we drove up to Ocala once more. My cousin drove us around again and again we had sex. That is all that has happened to this point.

The officer also interviewed Mrs. Carpenter, a classy, well-spoken woman of about 40, with reddish-brown hair. His write-up of this brief conversation ended with the notation about her phone call with Debbie. "She spoke with LaFave briefly on the phone and LaFave apologized for taking him out of town without her knowledge/consent. Mrs. Carpenter did not tell LaFave that she knew that they had been having sex." He noted that "She wants LaFave prosecuted." Mrs. Carpenter had not yet recognized what prosecuting the case would mean for her son.

From his interview with the boy, the officer knew Jack had not showered and was still wearing the same T-shirt and shorts he had worn during the sexual encounter earlier in the day. He hadn't paid much attention to that fact because Jack had originally said he had worn a condom. Later, as they continued talking, Jack admitted that wasn't true. Debbie had told him she was on the pill, hadn't asked him to use protection or offered any, and she was calling the signals.

MULTI-PURPOSE FORM - STATEMENT
PAGE (2)

I, ____________________ on the 17 day of JUNE 20 04 A.D. at (time) 9:25 P, at Temple Terrace, Hillsborough County Florida, freely and voluntarily make the following statement. I have been advised that I have the constitutional right to remain silent, than I need not make any statement that may tend to incriminate me, and if I do, that it may be used in a Court of Law against me. I have been advised that I have the right to the advice and council of a lawyer. ~~I have also been told that if I cannot afford a lawyer, then one would be appointed without cost to represent~~ me. No force has been used nor promises made in obtaining this statement.

Int. MM | I hereby swear and affirm that the following statement is the truth and nothing but the truth.

During the last week of school A teacher at Greco Middle School named ~~[scribbled out]~~ debra La Fave told me that she had feelings for me. — She told me that she was thinkin about me a lot and had feelings for me that she didn't know what to do with them. — However we did not have sexual intercorse until the week of Monday June 14. On Monday she asked me to help her clean out her portable. That day we had sex for the first time. On tuesday we drove down to pick up my cousin ____________, On that day we also had sex. On thursday, June 17, We drove up to ocala

Signed this 17 day of JUNE, 2004 at o'clock 9:35 am or (pm)

X ____________________

Signature

Witness

Witness

SPO David R [illegible] 623/80/E6aw

Officer

MULTI-PURPOSE FORM - STATEMENT
PAGE (2)

I, ____________________ on the 17 day of JUNE 20 04 A.D. at (time) 9:25 P., at Temple Terrace, Hillsborough County Florida, freely and voluntarily make the following statement. I have been advised that I have the constitutional right to remain silent, than I need not make any statement that may tend to incriminate me, and if I do, that it may be used in a Court of Law against me. I have been advised that I have the right to the advice and council of a lawyer. I have also been told that if I cannot afford a lawyer, then one would be appointed without cost to represent me. No force has been used nor promises made in obtaining this statement.

Int. MM | I hereby swear and affirm that the following statement is the truth and nothing but the truth.

once more. My cousin drove us around again and again we had sex. That is all that has happened up to this point.

The boy's handwritten statement; real names masked

He admitted having sex with the teacher, but had lied about using protection. On my part, maybe it's a self-defense mechanism that I keep finding instances of dark humor. The boy's claim that he had been using protection when he really hadn't suggests that sex education in the schools really is having an impact. His mother had just found out that her son, at age 14, had already had sexual intercourse, and with an adult woman, no less, but he was embarrassed for her to know he hadn't used protection!

Officer Thornton realized that Jack's clothing could have recoverable DNA evidence that could confirm the boy's story of having had sex with the teacher. He sent Jack to change clothing and bring him the basketball shorts, underwear, and T-shirt he had been wearing. He put the clothing into an evidence bag, gave the boy a receipt for it, and filled out a form for DNA analysis.

Detective Mike Pridemore was at home, off duty but on-call when the phone rang with the assignment that was to take so much of his time over the next weeks. He drove by the Temple Terrace Police Department to pick up a tape recorder and accessories for telephone monitoring, then headed for the Carpenter home. There, Officer Thornton briefed him on everything that had been done up to that point, and took a back seat as Pridemore assumed charge of the activities.

With Mrs. Carpenter as witness, Detective Pridemore had Jack sign a form giving consent for electronic and mechanical wiretapping for the next 30 days. He set up the equipment: a $300, three-head Marantz PMD-221 cassette tape recorder connected to the boy's cell phone, with a separate earpiece that would allow the detective to listen to both sides of the conversation. He briefed the boy, Detective Pridemore says, explaining that they needed to "substantiate the fact that he and Ms. LaFave had sex." Jack was told to "try and have a 'normal' conversation with her to obtain this information," which sounds as if it would be a challenge for most adults, most less an inexperienced teen.

Then he had the boy call Debbie's cell phone number. There was no answer. Jack tried again a short time later, with the same result.

Though it was now almost 1:30 in the morning, Detective Pridemore called Tampa's Crisis Center, a non-profit organization offering help to people with a range of needs, including treatment and support for victims of sexual abuse. No nurse was on duty at that hour, but the on-call nurse was paged. The detective spoke to her, arranging to bring Jack there for testing. She agreed, promising that she and a second nurse would meet them at the center. He loaded mother and son in his car for the 15-minute drive.

The experience was the first of the indignities Jack would undergo in the weeks and months ahead. In an examining room, the two nurses put on plastic gloves and told Jack to drop his shorts and underwear. They then combed his crotch area with a "pubic comb," which collects loose hairs, including any that may have been transferred from the pubic area of the other person. This must be embarrassing enough for a rape victim; for a 14-year-old boy who has spent the last few hours answering detailed questions about his sexual encounters over the last few days, being inspected and antiseptically combed by a pair of ladies in this way must have been terrifyingly humiliating.

For the DNA samples, as a standard for the victim's own DNA, the nurses swabbed the inside of the mouth on left and right sides. To collect possible specimens of the partner's DNA, they swabbed the sides of the face.

And, of course, the penis. No matter how reassuring the nurses, who had treated many rape and sexual assault victims of both sexes, I can't even imagine how a youngster in the boy's position deals with his embarrassment at a moment like this. In her write-up of the exam afterward, nurse Mollie-Rae Jerman would describe him as "alert, oriented," but showing his discomfort through "intermittent eye contact, speak[ing] softly, appearing uncomfortable with conversation." No wonder.

If Debbie was arrested, which already seemed more than likely, a DNA comparison would be made using material on the swabs from the boy, with DNA samples collected from Debbie.

When the nurses were finished their short but upsetting examination, Detective Pridemore took possession of the pubic comb and "sexual battery kit," then drove the pair home. It was now after 2 A.M., but the night's work wasn't finished. As the uniformed cop had done earlier, the detective had Jack swear an oath, then began conducting his own interview. Jack had to go through all the details of each encounter yet again.

Finally about 3 A.M., Detective Pridemore wrapped it up for the night and let Jack and his mother go off to bed.

Pridemore swung by the Police Department where he had the pubic comb and sexual battery kit logged in as evidence and placed into locked storage. His night was over at last.

But Detective Pridemore's night of rest wasn't a long one. He was back at the Carpenter home at 8:30 the next morning to start the phone-call attempts again. Jack placed the first call at a few minutes before nine. Debbie answered. With the tape recorder capturing every word, the call went like this; (some of the inanities and I-didn't-hear-you repetitions have been deleted here and throughout the phone transcripts):

Debra: Hello.

Jack: Hey.

Debra: Hey, what's up?

Jack: Nothing. What're you doing?

Debra: Nothing, just drinking coffee and watching TV.

Jack: Oh, really?

Debra: Yeah. What's up?

Jack: I got up early to talk to you.

Debra: Oh. Are you okay?

Jack: Yeah. I…me and my mom kind of had an argument last night but it's fine now.

Debra: Yeah?

Jack: Uh-huh.

Debra: I talked to her.

Jack: Oh, you did?

Debra: Yeah. I called her when I got home last night.

Jack: Oh. How did that go?

Debra: It was.... I mean I just told her, I was like, you know, I'm sorry, bad judgment and I should've double-checked with you, blah, blah, blah.

Jack: Uh-huh. Well, I guess I don't think we should be going to Ocala anymore.

Debra: No, no.

Jack: But everything went smooth in the portable.

Debra: Yeah.

Jack: So, whatever. If we decide to do anything again, then that should probably be our place for now.

Debra: That's true. Are you okay?

Jack: Yeah. I'm fine now.

Debra: Yeah?

Jack: Uh-huh.

Debra: I...Did you call me last night?

Jack: Yeah.

Debra: I can't remember if I can get or if...When are you leaving today?

Jack: I don't know yet. I have to talk to my dad.

Debra: I'm not sure if I'm going to go to Denver anymore.

Jack: Oh.

Debra: So maybe when...

Jack: Yeah.

Debra: Holy Lord, right?

Jack: Yeah, I know. It's kind of crazy, but I'm pretty sure everything's fine now.

Debra: Good. I totally got.... Well, I told Owen everything.

Jack: About what?

Debra: Like, oh no, no, no, no, no—chill. I just said that—I pretty much just told him the whole story.

Jack: Cool.

Debra: Except, you know why we went to Ocala.

Jack: Of course.

Debra: He actually gave me advice on what to say to your mom.

Jack: Yeah?

Debra: Yeah, yeah. So....

Jack: All right. Well, you enjoyed yourself yesterday, right?

Debra: I did. Did you?

Jack: Yeah.

Debbie then looked for reassurance, remembering that the last time they were together, the boy had talked about taking a break.

Debra: So it's not *over* over?

Jack: Nope, not yet.

And then she fell into a having-second-thoughts frame of mind.

Debra: God, Jack—why couldn't you just have said, "No, not yet?"

Jack: I'm sorry.

Debra: That kind of sucked. Oh, Lord, what am I going to do with you?

Jack: Sorry.

Debra: Did you end up playing last night?

Jack: Yeah.

Debra: Was it difficult to play?

Jack: A little. I did pretty good though.

Debra: Did you?

Jack: Uh-huh.

Debra: All right, my dear.

Jack: Okay. So you don't have any plans for today?

Debra: No…I'm just chillin' today. Hello? Are you there? Hello?

Jack: Hello?

Debra: Hey.

Jack: So after my dad's, after I get back from my dad's, do you want to get together again?

Debra: Yes, I do.

Jack: Okay.

Debra: Okay?

Jack: All right.

Debra: Did you miss me last night?

Jack: Yeah. What can we do this time, do you think?

Debra: We'll definitely figure out something very local.

Jack: Okay.

Debra: I'll be thinking. I'm going to think about it.

Jack: Are we going to do it at your place this time, or no?

Debra: We'll figure something out.

Jack: Okay.

Debra: I will have it all planned out.

Jack: Okay.

Debra: I hope you have a good weekend.

Jack: You, too.

Debra: Okay.

Jack: All right. Well, I guess I'll talk to you later.

Debra: Okay, honey.

Jack: All right.

Debra: Bye.

Jack: Bye.

From Detective Pridemore's perspective, "It was clear that there was some type of relationship but nothing to substantiate that there was any type of sexual activity." There would have to be at least one more call.

Meanwhile the detective started another conversation with the boy, this time learning about the "Hope" keychain pendant

Debbie had given him. Pridemore took possession of it, as well as the two pair of basketball shorts she had purchased for him.

He remembered Jack had told of an afternoon spent at our townhouse, and asked the youngster to describe it. Jack provided a detailed description, and then drew a sketch of the downstairs and the bedroom.

One other category of evidence any criminal prosecutor wants to have in a case of this kind is a description of "identifiable body features" that might help convince a jury the victim had indeed seen the other person naked.

Jack was full of details. He described Debbie's tattoos, saying that she had Chinese or Japanese writing on the small of her lower back, in the center, which she had told him were characters that sounded out as the name of her sister who had died. Jack thought he remembered the name as Jean, but otherwise the description was accurate.

So were the other details he provided: Two butterfly tattoos on one side of her lower back, though he was curiously uncertain about which side. A birth mark on each inner-ankle near the shin, both light brown like freckles, oval shaped with rough edges, about nickel-sized. He said she had prominent tan lines—she was still going to the tanning parlor—and described them as string bikini lines on each side, and a V in the crotch area, with most of the rear end covered.

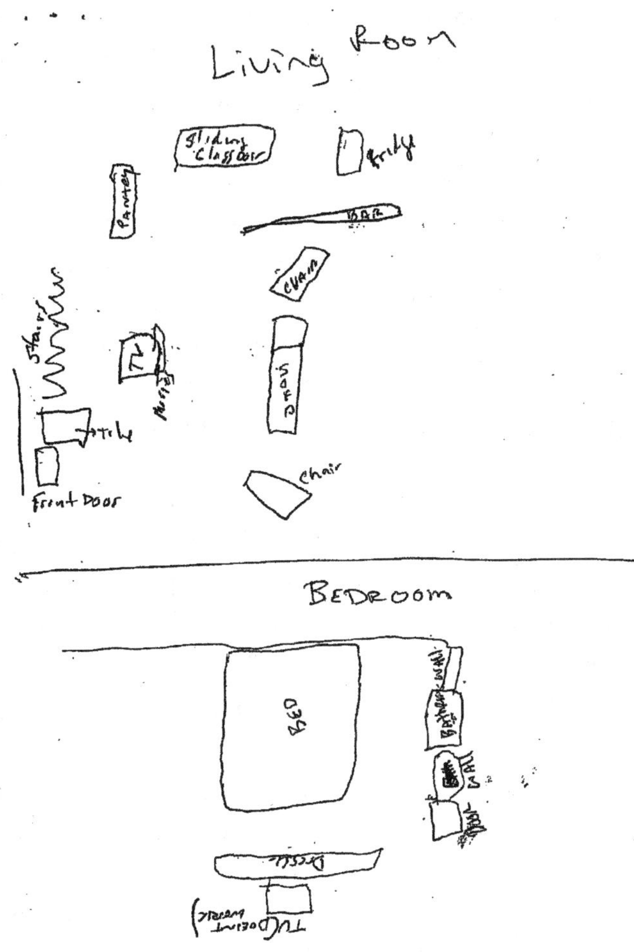

Jack's sketch of the LaFave townhouse

He described three belly-button rings—two in butterfly designs, and one pink, heart-shaped—but many of the students at Greco had seen her bare midriff.

His description of my wife's pubic area was detailed, specific, and painfully accurate: Light brown hair, shaved vertically into a thin rectangular shape, with the vagina itself clean-shaven.

Detective Pridemore knew his case was too sensitive for routine handling. The State Attorney's office would give him guidance and support every step of the way. And not just because of the nature of the crime, heinous enough to move it to near the top of the stack, ahead of more routine matters like liquor store holdups and identity-theft cases. As soon as the prosecutor heard that the suspect was especially good-looking, he recognized that the media troops were likely to descend en masse. He had seen it happen often enough. Sex between an adult female and a juvenile male is unhappily not a rare event, but when the woman is good-looking, the story makes headlines across the country and the evening network news.

With all the important events going on in the country and the world, how does a story like Debbie's become national news? A news producer on a major network says that in today's market, the national morning news programs "have to do what is important and interesting to the audience."

They're looking for stories that can turn into ratings gold, so a lot of the decisions are about audience draw. It's based on the honed instinct of "news nuns" like himself, people immersed all day, every day, in what's happening, people who have developed an instinct for what's going to grab audience attention. Any time there's a chance to take a bite at the apple, that's what you go for. Especially on a day when there are no major stories.

But network news can't be the *National Enquirer* wrapped in a nicer package, he insists. There's an art to covering sleaze in a highbrow way. When you're doing a story with a sex angle, you elevate it by talking about the issues, the psychology, the psychosis. Done with taste and sensitivity, pieces of this kind can become both interesting and worthwhile what might be called—"capital-J journalism, wrapped in a package that's watchable."

Which must be about as candid as a journalist with a major news operation ever gets. No wonder he insisted on speaking off the record.

Friday morning, following the first controlled phone contact between the victim and the suspect, Detective Pridemore again called the State Attorney's office, this time speaking with both Carol Hooper and with Hooper's boss, the head of Sex Crimes. Pridemore gave an update on the status, focusing especially on details of the phone call, which the detective pointed out had fallen short of anything clearly stating that a crime of sexual assault on a juvenile had taken place.

The prosecutor agreed with that assessment. He told the detective to try another phone call. It would turn out to take not one more but several.

Detective Pridemore sat down with Jack and had a conversation with him about what he might say in the next phone call, hoping to make it more valuable than the first one, yet without giving the boy specific wording that might not sound natural when he said it. He told Jack to "talk to Ms. LaFave about [your] fears about unprotected sex." Shortly before lunchtime he had Jack try reaching Debbie again. He connected.

Despite the hour, Debbie told him she had been asleep. They engaged in a little small talk, then Jack began by offering a bit of what was going on for him:

Jack: My dad cancelled for the weekend but my mom said I'm grounded, so I can't do anything.

Debra: Really?

Jack: Yeah.

Debra: Your dad cancelled?

Jack: Uh-huh.

Debra: That's kind of shitty.

Jack: Yeah, I know.

Debra: That sucks.

Jack: I know. I'm going to see him, though. Sometime.

Debra: Oh, that's good.

At that point Jack set a trap along the lines that Detective Pridemore had suggested.

Jack: I'm a little worried though.

Debra: Why?

Jack: Like I don't want you to like get pregnant or anything. I was just thinking about it and I was just thinking if next time, now that we've had sex about three times, if I should use like a condom or something.

Debra: Oh, you're being weird.

Jack: Why?

Debra: Why are you being weird?

She repeated the question, the second time asking why he was "being worried." He answered that it was "because all this happened," meaning the flap with their having been spotted in Ocala, which led to that painfully prophetic line from Debbie in response to his remark about having sex without protection:

Jack: It's just been, I've been thinking about it because I haven't used.... I'm just scared. I don't know.

Debra: Oh—that should be the least of your worries.

For the first time showing an interest in her life outside of her relationship with him, Jack asked the question that produced a revealing answer, though Detective Pridemore could not have suspected the significance:

Jack: Okay. All right. So are you probably going to Denver or no, you said?

Debra: No, I'm not going to go.

Jack: Oh, you're not?

Debra: Huh-uh.

In a conversation with Beth a short time before, Debbie had been so enthusiastic about the trip to this educational conference, suggesting that it would give her a chance to "feel free." Now, suddenly, after the unwholesome taste of almost daily sex with Jack, she had canceled a trip that she had been so looking forward to and that would have been good for her professionally—for the knowledge she would have gained, the contacts she would surely have made, and the addition of an impressive item on her professional résumé.

All of that she had decided to forgo rather than miss out on a few more abbreviated, foreplay-deprived humps with her inexperienced lover.

A few minutes later, Debbie rang on Jack's cell phone. He wasn't available but dialed her back a few minutes later for what turned out to be a short call that included this exchange:

Jack: Yeah. I was just thinking about it. It's just been like on my mind a lot lately.

Debra: Yeah? Are you freaking out?

Jack: No. I was just.... I was just thinking about it and I thought I'd ask you to see how you were feeling about it.

Debra: Yeah?

Jack: Uh-huh.

Grunting thoughts out loud that the other person makes no real emotional connection with, like a pair of tongue-tied teen-agers.

There wasn't anything further the detective could do for the moment at the Carpenter residence. The next phone call—and it was clear now that there would have to be others—would need to wait until a reasonable time had passed. No reason to alarm the lady over too many phone calls in quick succession.

Detective Pridemore returned to the police station. Among the items he hadn't found time for yet: Since two of the sexual contacts the boy had described allegedly took place in Ocala, in Marion County, he needed to let law enforcement authorities there know so they could open their own investigation. (A layman like me would have assumed that for offenses within the state, a single agency could handle the entire case, saving duplication of effort. It turns out that's not the way the system works.)

Saturday morning Detective Pridemore showed up at the front door of the Carpenter home about 10 A.M. Jack and his mother had finished breakfast and were waiting for him. This time Jack would try harder to set up a meeting with his sex partner.

He called at 10:15 and got no answer. The detective had him try again at 10:50, with the same result. At 11:18, Jack's cell phone rang. The caller ID showed a number the boy didn't recognize, and he didn't answer. But a voicemail message was left:
Debra: Hey, it's Debbie. I am at a kid's birthday party, if you can't tell. This is Owen's cell phone, so I'll try to call you later, okay? Bye.

Jack speed-dialed back to her cell phone, leaving a message, "Call me back as soon as you get this, all right?"

I had taken Debbie to a birthday party at the YMCA that Pam was having for her older daughter, Maddie. Debbie spent part of the time sitting on my lap, the loving wife. For most of that time, she was holding Pam's newborn, just like a loving mother.

Pam would later describe Debbie at that party as being "very laid-back and lovey-dovey" with me. "She was talking with our other friends and just being normal. She was very upbeat, her normal, happy-go-lucky self. And (she) doted over my children like crazy, the way she always did."

Debbie's cell phone rang. Carrying the baby, she walked out of the room to answer the call.

A pack of excited little girls can be noisy, and I didn't think anything of Debbie's leaving the room to take the call. Until later, when I read the transcripts of the recorded phone calls. I was shocked, but apparently not nearly so shocked as her closest girlfriend Pam, who thought she knew Debbie so well.

The conversation (parts repeated here from earlier in the book, for continuity) went like this:
RECORDING: Please hold while the Nextel subscriber you are trying to reach is located.

Debra: Hello?

Jack: Hey.

Debra: Can you hear me?

Jack: Yeah.

Debra: There's like 20 kids here, screaming.

Jack: Where are you at?

Debra: I'm at some YMCA...

Jack: Really?

Debra: ... in downtown Tampa.

Jack: Oh.

Debra: There's like 1,000 different kids.

Jack: Oh.

Debra: So what's up?

Jack: Nothing much. What are you doing?

Jack: Nothing. I'm actually holding.... Pam has a newborn baby, so I'm kind of holding her right now.

Jack: Oh, really?

Debra: Yeah, watching all the... My ovaries are hurting listening to all these frigging kids screaming.

Jack: (laughs)

Debra: You couldn't pay me enough money to have a kid right now.

Talk about Dr. Jekyll and Mr. Hyde: she was cuddling a newborn as if it were her own while complaining that you couldn't pay her to have a child. This from a lady who was having unprotected sex with the boy (and with me). Her attorney would later talk about an insanity defense. I wonder if he ever considered trying to claim multiple personality!

The phone conversation then swung into the part Detective Pridemore had been angling for:

Jack: So do you have any plans for Monday?

Debra: Nope, I don't think so.

Jack: Do you want to try to do something Monday?

Debra: Yeah, that's cool.

Jack: All right, because I'm grounded for the rest of the weekend. You could probably pick me up at the rec.

Apparently at this point Detective Pridemore began signaling frantically to Jack. The detective planned to make the arrest when Debbie showed up to keep a prearranged appointment with the boy, and he wouldn't want to do that at a public playground where the arrest would be noticed and draw a crowd. Worse, it would likely be a crowd that included any number of kids who knew Debbie and admired her. A pack of athletic kids who were enthusiastic members of the Debra LaFave fan club could be a big nuisance. Bad idea.

Pridemore seems to have gotten the point across; after a bit more chitchat, Jack suggested a revised plan:

Debra: Okay. So how... how... how did everything end up? Is everything okay right now?

Jack: Uh-huh.

Debra: Yeah?

Jack: All right. Probably, you could probably just pick me up here. Is that all right? That would probably be better.

Debra: Why?

Jack: I don't know. Because I don't know if I'll be able to get a ride to the Rec, because my mom is going to be working.

Debra: Okay.

With that problem apparently solved, Jack allowed the conversation to wander again before coming back to another point that was important to Pridemore.

Jack: All right.

Debra: So everything's cool?

Jack: Yeah.

Debra: Yeah?

Jack: Uh-huh.

Debra: Sure?

Jack: Yeah. All right, and everything's good with you?

Debra: Yeah, so far so good.

Jack: All right.

Debra: Yeah.

Jack: All right. Well....

Debra: I was a little worried yesterday, but….

Jack: All right. Well, about what time do you think you're going to want to pick me up on Monday?

Debra: I have no idea. I'll call you.

Jack: All right, because I don't know if I'm going to be able to talk to you because I'm going to be with my dad tomorrow.

Debra: Okay. All right.

Jack: All right.

Debra: Okay. Well, I'll just…. I'll talk to you later.

Jack: Okay, then.

Debra: Okay, bye.

Halfway there, but only halfway. Debbie had agreed to a rendezvous on Monday, but Jack hadn't been able to draw her into setting a time. It would have to do for now. The next call would wait until Sunday.

As Debbie and I drove home from Pam's party at the Y, another car pulled out directly in front of us. I couldn't swerve in time, and T-boned him. The airbags went off, a first for both of us. I hit my head against the steering wheel, which hurt like hell but didn't do me any real harm. Debbie received a burn from the seat belt. She was otherwise uninjured physically, but the shock of a serious traffic accident brought waves of painful memories about her sister's death, leaving her stunned. She took to her bed for the rest of the day.

The car wasn't totaled (though Debbie would later describe it that way), but was wrecked too badly to be driven. We waited for the tow truck to come and haul it to the body shop. Debbie's father picked us up and drove us home.

There was a party that night at Bernadita's. If I was superstitious, I might say this was an omen: I went to the party without Debbie. Very soon I would be without her forever.

On Sunday, Jack tried to reach Debbie twice, without success. Late in the afternoon, while I was watching a game on television, Debbie found a chance to call the youngster out of my hearing. She agreed to pick him up at his house at 10 o'clock Monday morning but said she'd have to call on Monday to let him know for sure because she was sore, and she told him about the car wreck.

Jack's friend Walt Grimes returned the next day, Sunday, with the rest of his family from a week-long cruise to ports on the east coast of Mexico. Their telephone held a string of voice-mail messages from Jack, eager to talk to Walt. Mrs. Grimes recalled later, "It was obvious to me that Jack was desperate, desperate to talk to his friend."

Walt remembers, "After I got back from my cruise, Jack called me and asked if I wanted to go to the mall with him and his dad." Jack needed to spill the whole story, as if his buddy Walt was hearing his confession. "We went up there [to the University Mall]. And he told me all about like everything that happened. He told me that he'd, like, had sex, like, in the back of Ms. Beasley's car while his cousin was driving them around, and he got caught."

For Catholics, confession brings absolution. For the rest of us, confession may ease the conscience but may not bring much peace of mind. Jack's thrill at being introduced to the experience of sex had lost its glow of pleasure and excitement.

Monday morning. Detective Pridemore, accompanied by Detectives Steven Sutter and Bernard Seeley, were already at the Carpenter's when Debbie called a little before 9 o'clock.

The entire conversation is worth repeating here—"pinky promise" and all:

Debra: Hello?

Jack: Hey.

Debra: Hey. What are you doing?

Jack: Nothing. What are you doing?

Debra: Driving.

Jack: Oh, you are?

Debra: I had to take Owen to work today.

Jack: Huh?

Debra: I had to take Owen to work today.

Jack: Oh, really? What's wrong with the car that you guys had an accident in.

Debra: Oh, we totaled it.

Jack: Oh, you did?

Debra: Yes. It's his car. It's totaled, yeah.

Jack: Oh, all right. So what time are you planning on heading over?

Debra: Are you sure? Like, I just feel.... I mean, I don't want you lying to your mom. I mean, it's like....

Jack: No, it's all right. She's gone in a sales meeting, like all day.

Debra: You're sure?

Jack: Yeah.

Debra: Positive? Because I'm like, scared. I don't want, you know....

Jack: Yeah, I'm positive.

Debra: I mean, I just.... I know you wouldn't, you know, do it unless you were sure.

Jack: I am.

Debra: I mean, we were just so close last time, you know?

Jack: Yeah.

Debra: Are you *sure*, sure?

Jack: Yes.

Debra: You wouldn't lie to me, would you?

Jack: No.

Debra: No what?

Jack: Why are you saying that?

Debra: I don't know. I'm just scared. It was a little freaky last time.

Jack: Oh.

Debra: And you were just like really dead-set on, you know, taking a break.

Jack: Well, I just want to… I just wanted to see you. I thought you wanted to see me, too.

Debra: No, no, no, no, no, no. Don't take it the wrong way. It's just, you know, I'm looking out.

Jack: Yeah, but I know we're fine today.

Debra: All right. Well, whenever, I guess.

Jack: All right. In fact, earlier the better, because….

Debra: Huh?

Jack: I said, try to come earlier the better because my mom is at a meeting.

Debra: What time is she supposed to be… Is she already gone?

Jack: Yeah.

Debra: You're positive?

Jack: Yes.

Debra: All right. Promise?

Jack: Yes.

Debra: Pinky promise?

Jack: Yes.

Debra: Say 'pinky promise.'

Jack: Pinky promise.

Debra: All right. Well, tell me a time.

Jack: 10 o'clock.

Debra: Okay, that sounds good.

Jack: Okay.

Debra: All right.

Jack: All right.

Debra: Do you want me to call you around that time?

Jack: Yeah, you can call me.

Debra: Are you sure? All right.

Jack: All right.

Debra: All right, bye.

Close to 10 o'clock, right on time, punctual to her own funeral, Debbie called again:

Jack: Hello?

Debra: Hey.

Jack: Hey.

Debra: What you doing?

Jack: Nothing. What are you doing?

Debra: Driving.

Jack: Oh. Where are you?

Debra: I'm almost there. Huh?

Jack: I was just asking where you were.

Debra: Oh, I'm almost.... I'm getting ready to turn on [Interstate] 75.

Jack: Okay.

Debra: You're sure everything's clear?

Jack: Yeah, everything's fine.

Debra: Promise?

Jack: Yeah.

Debra: All right.

Jack: All right.

Debra: Okay. Be outside, okay?

Jack: All right.

Debra: All right, bye.

Jack: Bye.

Pridemore's report describes this moment that would change Debbie's life forever, and mine as well:

"Detective Sutter and Detective Seeley were standing by in the area awaiting the arrival of Suspect LAFAVE. As Suspect LAFAVE pulled to a stop next to the victim's home, where she had picked him up previously, Detective Seeley pulled to the front of LAFAVE's vehicle and Detective Sutter pulled up to the rear.

"I made contact with Suspect LAFAVE and told her we needed to take her back to the police department to talk about the relationship she had been having with Jack Carpenter.

"She just looked at me blankly and shook her head up and down slowly."

Chapter 12
TSUNAMI

FOR THE THREE detectives standing at the curb along the side of the Carpenter home, the action taking place that sunny Saturday morning in June 2004 was routine. Between them they had made a great many arrests, and there wasn't anything about this one to mark it as particularly unusual. Sure, the lady was young, she was certainly beautiful, and even with little makeup she looked appealing in her Capri pants and tank top. But a woman teacher being charged with having sex with a teenage student is no everyday event in any police department.

Debbie didn't turn violent or lash out in anger or show any other sign of causing trouble. After the simple nod that seemed to acknowledge she understood what was happening and maybe had even lived this scene already in her mind, she stood passively, cooperating. Detective Pridemore spoke to Jack to receive his confirmation on the identity, then indicated to the others to proceed. Detective Sutter put handcuffs on Debbie, then helped her into Detective Seeley's car. Seeley climbed into the driver's seat and drove away with her.

For Detective Pridemore it had been a busy few days, and this one wouldn't be any easier. As investigating officer, he would be in charge of organizing an entire series of events that would now take place. He headed for the police station, while Detective Sutter stayed behind to take possession of Debbie's car and deliver it to the police impound lot to be examined for evidence.

When Detective Pridemore arrived at the Temple Terrace Police Department, on North 56th Street, he had Debbie taken into an interrogation room, where he sat down with her. He told her the charges she was being arrested on were two counts of lewd or lascivious behavior involving a minor between the ages of 12 and 16, a second-degree felony, and he read her the Miranda warning. Debbie and I had watched enough cop shows on television that she didn't have to be told it would be a mistake to say anything without having a lawyer present. Detective Pridemore noted in his report that "Suspect LAFAVE did not wish to answer questions without an attorney." Curiously, she also asked for a representative of the teachers' union to be sent for.

She was allowed the standard one phone call, and by now you won't be surprised to learn that the call was not to me but to her mother. Joyce made the perfectly natural assumption that the charges were completely untrue. She gave Debbie what reassurance she could and promised she would arrange for an attorney as quickly as possible.

Detective Pridemore filled out the standard arrest form used in Hillsborough County, called a CRA, or Criminal Report Affidavit, filling in the charge as "Lewd or Lascivious Battery," under Florida statute 800.04(4)(a). In the section for "probable cause that the crime was committed by the defendant," the detective wrote, "On 6-3-04 at appx 1400...Def. LaFave performed oral sex on a minor child (V[ictim]) John Carpenter, fourteen. Def. LaFave was positively identified by [the victim] as the person with whom he had sexual relations. Def. LaFave identified herself verbally to affiant."

At her booking, Debbie's statistics were recorded as 5'7", 135 pounds, build medium. The policewoman in charge of examining her noted, "Tattoo two small butterflies lower back. Tattoo Chinese symbol on lower back." Her clothing was described as "Pink/Purple Capri Pants, tank top type shirt."

As for underwear: No bra. No panties.

She had obviously left the house that morning geared for action.

Joyce Beasley had lost one daughter; now her only remaining child was in trouble, deep trouble. Joyce's first concern was getting her daughter out of jail. Within a few minutes, she had contacted attorney Fred Wollrath, and hired him.

Then she was free to call me. She reached me at work. I thought it was just a routine call and started joking with her. She said, "Owen, this is a serious matter. It's no time to joke. Debbie has been arrested. She's accused of having lewd and lascivious conduct with one of her students."

I was frozen in shock. I just sat there at my desk in silence, part of me thinking *No way,* part of me remembering how strangely Debbie had been acting, my suspicions of an affair with a parent, the late-night phone calls from the boy. I was emotionally shaken, very angry, deeply hurt. And profoundly humiliated: she was accused of cheating on me *with a child.*

Finally I collected myself enough to say, "Okay, Joyce, what do I need to do?"

Joyce's manner was very stern, yet I sensed she was trying to be strong for me. Amazingly, she seemed under control as always. Even when Angie died, she was a pillar of strength, consoling other people. To this day I don't know where she her strength comes from.

We worked out a plan. Debbie's father drove to the bank, picked me up, and gave me a lift to a car rental agency.

I started to replay the previous couple of months in my mind, reviewing all the suspicions I had had.

Meanwhile, under Mike Pridemore's direction, another detective, Paul Gilmore, was writing out two search warrants. One was unusual enough for the officers of a small police department that Gilmore, accompanied by Detective Seeley, drove over to the State Attorney's Office to ask for guidance. Based on this input, they finished the warrant, which a prosecutor then reviewed and approved.

Some of the most basic protections we enjoy as Americans were built into our system by the Founding Fathers as a rebuke to the British system that gave citizens few rights against agents of the king. Among the protections granted to Americans are limits on the powers of the police. When officers of the law want to inspect your home, search through your papers, or examine your banking records, they must appear before a judge, present a warrant offering compelling reasons in support of the request, swear to the statements in the warrant, and convince the judge that the reasons for the request are substantial. Judges don't take this responsibility lightly; it's not uncommon for a judge to send the investigator back to collect more evidence, interview a witness again, or obtain some other further justification.

After the prosecutor had approved the warrants, the two detectives took them to present to the Honorable Michelle Sisco. Asking for the warrants to be reviewed by a woman judge was particularly appropriate because of one particular sensitive type of information the detectives and the prosecutor were asking for. In the sort of case in which phony charges are too easy to make, corroborating evidence is essential. The police and prosecutor needed to know whether the boy had accurately described Debbie's body. And not in terms of satisfying themselves that the information was correct, but gathering physical evidence that could be presented to a jury.

In addition to the warrant that called for taking evidence from the townhouse where Debbie and I lived, the other one authorized taking photos of Debra's naked body.

Judge Sisco studied the warrants. She discussed them with Detective Gilmore and, after he had sworn to the truth of the statements in them, she signed. When the detectives had returned to Central booking at the Orient Street Jail, where Debbie had been transferred to be held, Gilmore had her brought to an interview room. With Detective Pridemore standing by to observe, Gilmore read the search warrants to Debbie and explained to her what was to be done.

The details of this I find painful to relate. I don't pretend to understand what demons led her into that sick behavior, but I loved her at the time and the indignity that her actions had brought her is for me an unhappy tale.

Detective Seeley and Detention Deputy Esther Moitt led Debbie to the jail clinic, where they were joined by a jail nurse. A drape screen was drawn, affording the female deputy, the nurse, and Debbie privacy from view. Debbie was told to strip. The detention deputy then took a series of digital photographs as called for in the warrant, starting with two showing her tan lines, and two showing her tattoos.

She was then told to lie down on the table and spread her legs. The nurse strapped her into gynecological stirrups. The deputy then took two pictures of her pubic area.

With the picture-taking done, Debbie was allowed to put her jail garb back on. In the presence of Sergeant Crawford, Detective Seeley reviewed the photographs for clarity and to confirm that they showed the items described in the search warrant. The disc was then removed from the camera, sealed in an evidence envelope, and signed to establish the chain of custody. The navel ring Debbie had been wearing when she was booked, described as having "a pink heart-shaped stone" which was also described in the search warrant, was placed in a separate evidence envelope.

(In another strange twist of an already twisted story, Detective Gilmore would later be arrested while Debbie's case was still unfolding. The charge was soliciting prostitution, and he was dropped from the force.)

In my rented car I drove to the Temple Terrace Police Department, only to be told that Debbie was had already been taken to the Orient Road Jail, the place in Hillsborough County where all people arrested are booked, photographed, and fingerprinted. I also learned that she would be held in jail until her trial or until she was released on bail at a hearing scheduled for the next day. Until that hearing, she would not be allowed any visitors other than her attorney.

It had not occurred to me before that whether Debbie did or did not commit the crime she stood accused of, she would have to spend the night locked up. On top of that unnerving news, I arrived home to be greeted with an unwelcome surprise. A team of six cops had picked the lock to my front door and was inside the house collecting items to be hauled away. One of them read me the search warrant, which I was too muddled to understand very clearly. He explained that they were gathering evidence. A Crime Scene Technician had videotaped the entire house before the search began.

They had pulled a pair of Debbie's black workout shorts from our bedroom laundry hamper, and taken out of our closet one of Debbie's sundresses—described as yellow, though I thought it was white, with a flower design (the dress, I would later learn, that she wore on the day of her Best Buy shopping trip), and even the sheets from our bed. They also took two belly-button rings they found on the counter in the kitchen—one brass color, one silver, both with a butterfly design.

Having strangers pawing through our possession and carting some of them away left me feeling violated. And the sight of curious neighbors standing in the street in little groups, drawn by the unfamiliar scene of half a dozen police cars parked in front on my house, only added to my sense of discomfort.

At Greco school, one teacher received a visit from principal Janet Spence. Knowledgeable about computers, he had attended special training given by the school district that enabled him to access files not available to other teachers or staff. Ms. Spence said, "I need you to get the picture of one of our teachers and send it to Public Affairs downtown."

"Whose?" he asked.

"Debbie's," Ms. Spence told him.

He figured Debbie had been selected to receive some kind of award or acknowledgement. "I thought she must have done something neat as a teacher," he said later. He asked Ms. Spence, "What's it for?"

Looking distressed, she shook her head. "It's not good," she said. "It's not good."

For a brief moment he thought of pretending to look and then telling her he couldn't find a picture. He didn't like the idea of helping do something that could hurt his friend Debbie but quickly realized that they would come up with a picture whether he helped or not, and they might come up with one not nearly as flattering as the one he knew was stored on the computers at the school. He pulled up the picture and sent it to the PR people.

Then he checked the Internet. Stories were already beginning to appear that a Tampa teacher was in custody for having sex with a student. He called his wife and told her he thought one of the teachers had been arrested, and told her the charges. She asked, "Who is it?"

He said, "Debbie."

The teacher's wife said later, "He did it for shock value because I was obviously just astounded. But my initial reaction was that someone is lying.... Obviously someone is making something up. And so I felt bad for her." She remembers feeling "in shock," and told her husband, "That's awful—you can be arrested just because of what somebody says about you." She thought, *This could happen to any of us.*

That evening, the teacher and his wife sat down together to watch the news. The report gave Debbie's name and showed pictures of the address where she had been arrested. At one time or another, the teacher had driven home a number of the students, following various after-school events that ended too late for their usual transportation arrangements. He recognized the neat, distinctive house with its white exterior and black trim. "That's Jack Carpenter's," he told his wife.

He remembered hearing that the boy had told another teacher how "hot" Debbie was, and that time a couple of months earlier when Jack had told the same teacher he was going to have sex with her. *Maybe Jack had done more talking and someone believed him*, he thought. *It couldn't be true.*

I called my mother and invited myself to dinner. To her credit, she never even hinted a single "I told you so." Instead she was consoling and supportive, with promises to be there for me in any way I needed her. I stayed a couple of hours, then drove to the Beasleys, pushing my way through a crowd of reporters to reach the front door.

Joyce and Larry, I learned, had already made arrangements with a bonding company for posting her bail once it had been set, and the new attorney had already visited Debbie in jail. Joyce had found him through a contact who had become a friend. Following Angie's death, Joyce had taken an interest in Mothers Against Drunk Driving; she had called a lady who volunteered at the local MADD group to ask for advice on a suitable lawyer and the lady had said, "My husband is an attorney." Joyce had been grateful to find someone so easily, and had signed him up.

I didn't want to face the crowd of reporters and camera people almost certainly hanging around outside my townhouse, and the Beasleys didn't want to be alone. I stayed at the Beasley home that night. The idea of sleeping in Debbie's bed would have revolted me, but, expecting that she had left home for good when she married me, Joyce had converted Debbie's room into a dressing room for herself. I asked for a blanket and tried sleeping on the living room couch, but found it cramped and uncomfortable so instead stretched the blanket out on the floor of the living room and wrapped it around me.

When you most need sleep as an escape from your thoughts, sleep won't come. I was racked with gut-wrenching distress. Thinking I was living a life something close to the life I wanted, the life I had pictured in my mind, I now knew I had instead been living a lie. Maybe it had never been true. In the darkness, I cried.

I think I fell asleep about half an hour before time to wake up.

The local newspapers the next day ran articles on the story, but without giving it any particular play. The *St. Petersburg Times* put the article on page 3 of the newspaper's second section. The piece, written by reporter Shannon Colavecchio-Van Sickler, carried the headline "Teacher Accused of Sex with Boy, 14," and began:

> A 23-year-old Greco Middle School teacher was arrested Monday morning on charges that she engaged in sexual activity with a 14-year-old boy on two occasions this month.
>
> Debra Beasley LaFave, a reading teacher at Greco Middle for the past two years, faces up to 30 years in prison if convicted of two felony counts of lewd and lascivious battery.

Talk about showing your dirty laundry in public: the story went on to specify dates and times Debbie was said to have had oral sex with the boy, and intercourse with him. It also gave my name—calling me by the first name Kristian that I almost never use—gave the name of the street we lived on, and revealed how much we had paid for our townhouse. As far as the press was concerned, Debbie's transgression made me fair game, too.

The story in the *Tampa Tribune* by Michele Sager cited its source as information provided in a press release issued by

Temple Terrace Police Chief Velong. Going for a more sensational approach, Ms. Sager chose to mention the oral sex in her lead paragraph.

The news that the student was 14 stunned me. For me, and I'm sure for Pam, the connection was unmissable: Debbie had been raped at 13. By a boy of 15. And now she had chosen a sexual partner in the same age bracket. A fleeting pang of sympathy washed over me as I wondered whether this could have been a subconscious effort to relive the past, a desperately misguided attempt in hope of wiping out a torturous memory.

But I was just making excuses for her… excuses I wouldn't have accepted if she had offered them to me herself.

At Greco Middle School the next day, Avery Hampton, trying to find a little inside information to confirm his sense that the charges had to be based on some kind of unfortunate mistake or inappropriate talk by the boy, sought out Cliff Carroll, the school's Resource Officer. Cliff wouldn't tell Avery anything except to shake his head and say, "It's not good," just as the principal had. Carroll accompanied his response with an expression that seemed to make it clear this was something more than a blip that would soon blow away and be forgotten.

Avery says, "The moment I realized they had a real case, it was like somebody had died. I sort of went into a mourning stage, depressed and upset, a major disruption in life."

There was, Avery says, "A shell-shocked sense among all of our friends."

Teacher Bernadita Natal remembers that, "I didn't think [Jack] made it up," but also says, "Half the people [at school] didn't believe Debbie could have done that. She had a lot of friends among the teachers."

The next day, Debbie was scheduled to appear before an administrative judge at a courthouse in downtown Tampa for what's called "first appearance," at which the judge decides on the amount of bond or may decide that the accused is too great a risk to society or may be tempted to flee, and denies bond altogether.

I drove home to shower and change into fresh clothes, then joined the Beasleys at the courthouse. Pam Glas, good friend that she was, came to the hearing and sat next to me on one side, Joyce on the other. Joyce kept saying, "I can't lose another daughter, I can't lose another daughter." Some 30 prisoners were brought in, all wearing the classic jail garb of loose-fitting orange pants and top. Debbie, who looked like what you would expect of someone after spending the night in jail, had not showered or washed her hair or put on any makeup. And that was just the physical part. Emotionally she seemed even worse. I had the sense that she was doing her best to protect herself by closing down her feelings.

When Debbie's name was called, she stood up in the front row of prisoners, a sea of orange outfits behind her. Judge Walter Heinrich (friends call him "Buzzy") listened to the charges and to the attorney's argument for reducing the $15,000 bail. The judge announced he was setting bail at $5,000, a gesture that showed he had little concern Debbie would try to flee. Then he gave her some fatherly advice about dealing with the media. "Don't talk," he told her. "The press is here. They have cameras. They have print media, and they're going to take down everything that you would say. That would not be in your best interest."

The hearing was over in a few minutes. She wasn't free yet and wouldn't be until later in the day, after being returned to the jail and processed for release.

Outside, a crowd of media pursued us down the street until we reached the safety of our cars. Debbie's attorney remained at the courthouse to make a statement to the reporters, repeating the arguments that had led to the small amount of bail. "She has no prior arrest record. She's an outstanding member of the community," he said. And "She's lived here all her life."

At Tampa's ABC television outlet, two different field reporters had covered the earliest stories about Debbie. With interest now escalating, the station's news director, Chris Jadick, decided to assign one of the station's most tenacious reporters who also serves as one of the two regular weekend anchors. The reporter, Sarina Fazan, dark-haired, intense and focused when doing an interview, was born in Kashmir and grew up speaking French and two Indian dialects, and fashioning make-believe microphones as toys. Her dedication combined with her earnest concern for the feelings of people involved in a story she's covering have often enabled her to get interviews not granted to anyone else.

Sarina was sent with her cameraman on Tuesday to cover the bond hearing, the first assignment in what would for her become a two-year journey.

Following the hearing, the Beasleys and I had a quick bite to eat, then drove to the jail to wait for the paperwork and processing to be completed. We sat there most of the day, anxious and miserable, with nobody able to tell us how long the wait would be. At last, toward the end of the afternoon, Debbie came out to join us, wearing the clothes she had been arrested in, which I now saw to be a spaghetti tank top that showed her cleavage, a pair of Capri pants, and flip-flops. She took the clean clothes that Joyce had brought—a pair of slacks and a long-sleeved button-down shirt—and went to change into them. The four of us headed back to the Beasley home.

At home, Debbie's first action was to take a shower, and her mother joined her there for maybe half an hour. When they came out, Debbie and I went in back to the pool area and sat down to talk.

I told her, "Look, I know you did it, I just want to know why."

She started crying. That was as much of a confession as I needed, or would ever have.

She said, "Owen, don't leave me. Don't leave me."

"It's well beyond that," I said. "You've shown no respect for our relationship. Why would you expect me to have any of that for you?"

She sobbed and didn't try to answer.

I gave up. "You threw our relationship away," I told her. "It's no longer something I intend to fight for."

Through her sobs, she said, "Please don't leave me. Don't divorce me."

I said, "I'll stay by your side till it's over. I won't leave you until after the criminal trial. But we're done." I knew there wasn't any good answer but I couldn't help asking again for an explanation. "I just want to know why."

"I don't know why," she sobbed. Then she screamed at me as loud as she could scream, "I just don't know."

The screams brought her parents. Her father said, "Come back inside. Someone might hear."

I shouldn't have been surprised. Larry is so reserved that he seemed as much concerned about the neighbors as about his daughter's emotional state and future life.

We all returned inside and sat down in the living room. Larry and Joyce both started working on me with comments like, "You're acting irrationally," and "Don't be emotional." As if it's possible not to be emotional in a situation like this.

Joyce tried to convince me that the charges against Debbie were nothing to be concerned about. With her husband sitting right there listening, she told me, "Larry cheated on me when we were young. I forgave him," she said. "We've had 30 years of marriage and two children together. Debbie's just having an affair. You can get past this issue if you'll only give it the chance." I thought it was bizarre. Her attitude was, *We'll get through this, it's not so bad.* It sounded like the same sort of thing she had said to her girls through the years, encouraging enough on the surface but with that dangerous underlying message of not having to take responsibility for your actions.

I said, "You're out of your mind. This wasn't just cheating, it was with a child."

"Don't leave Debbie," Joyce said. "Give her another chance."

I was in deep emotional pain and feeling very angry and humiliated. Yet at that moment I felt it was my duty to stand by Debbie and protect her through the trial.

Still, my dreams were crushed. I knew the relationship was over and no amount of pleading by Debbie or her parents was going to change that.

Larry begged, "This is my daughter, this is my baby. Her life is at stake here. We need you to stand by her."

"The relationship is over," I told him. I gave them both the same reassurance I had given Debbie a few minutes earlier. "I will stay by her side until all this is over. We'll act like the happy couple for the time being. "

I had no idea how difficult it would be to try to keep that promise.

On the Channel 28 ABC Action News that night, reporter Fazan's coverage showed she had been doing her homework and was willing to give a balanced account, despite the severity of the charges. She had gained access to the school district's personnel file for Debbie, and included in her report that the records "revealed high marks for the two-year teaching veteran. Before her time as a reading teacher at Greco Middle School, she received all 'excellent' ratings for her internship at a Pasco County middle school." Small praise, perhaps, but better than Debbie was receiving from the other local media.

Knowing I couldn't walk into my house without contending with another gauntlet of media people, I had brought a toilet kit and a couple of changes of clothes with me. I stayed again on the living room floor of the Beasleys. Debbie elected to stay with me. We both wrapped ourselves under the blanket. When she tried to cuddle up against me, I turned my back on her. She snuggled up against my back.

The next morning the four of us got up and had breakfast together as if we were a normal family, Larry and Joyce probably figuring that if they kept things on an even keel I might have a change of heart and not go through with the threatened divorce.

I couldn't face going back to work yet. The immediate agenda for the Beasleys was to search for a skilled criminal defense attorney to handle Debbie's defense. The original attorney had done well enough for the bail hearing, but it was clear she was going to need a big gun to handle the trial. I said I would help with the effort of gathering names and interviewing candidates, which became the project of the next several days.

We eventually settled on a highly experienced local criminal attorney who seemed brilliant and very genuine, with the kind of Southern accent that puts people at ease. But it wouldn't be inexpensive. Larry at that point was retired, and their little house on 12th Street was fully paid off. The easy golden years that the Beasleys had envisioned weren't going to happen. Larry started making arrangements for a new mortgage on the house and looking for a job that would provide income. Larry Beasley was giving up retirement and going back to work.

The voice on my cell phone sounded more enthusiastic than usual. Richie, my childhood friend, understanding from afar that I could do with some cheering up, was calling from his current home on Staten Island. "Dude, what's going on?" he said, laughing. "I knew she was crazy." By now I was laughing with him. Just talking to him put me in a little bit of a better mood. Richie said later, "I had never seen you like that before. You had always been focused, but that day, you were like a lost puppy."

His call had come not long after I had found Debbie sitting at her computer looking at the Internet sites dedicated to her case, like some Hollywood starlet excited to find herself garnering some publicity. Except that the starlet has a right to be pleased. Debbie's apparent fascination with these sites I found bizarre and sickening, and I turned sarcastic. "Are you proud of yourself?" I asked her. "You always wanted to be famous."

At work, I tried to keep up the image that the situation was under control, blindly hoping that if I didn't provide any details, people might go on believing the kid was lying. With Debbie, I didn't want to let her see how much pain and anger I was suffering. So I kept everything bottled up, a condition so painful that it threw me into a mild depression. I wanted to crawl into a cave.

One day Pam Glas had a surprising visitor. Debbie dropped in to see her.

While she was tacitly acknowledging to her parents and me that the charges were true, she somehow couldn't admit to her friends, not even her dearest friend Pam whom she had been so candid with in the past, what she had done. Instead she told Pam that she had "so much evidence" to prove that the charges weren't true. Pam says, "She gave me a rationale for every single thing that the accuser had said in his statements."

Pam had not had Jack as a student, and was having trouble placing him. Debbie reminded her, "He was on that field trip with us when we went to Universal Studios. That's how he got my cell phone number—because remember when we gave all the kids the cell phone numbers to keep in touch with us."

Pam asked, "How does he know what your house looks like?" Debbie answered that the boy and another student had "helped me pack up stuff from her portable and then drove over to the townhouse and helped lug stuff into the house and up to the bedroom."

Whatever Pam asked about, Debbie had an explanation. What about the report that the police had impounded her car and taken swatches of the fabric from the rear seat for testing? "They're not going to find anything," Pam remembers Debbie assuring her. "It's just lotion, I spilled lotion back there."

And then she said that the kid was having a rough time with the divorce of his parents, meaning, I guess, that she felt sorry for him. She was looking for an iPod for me, she told Pam, and had heard that they had some at the Best Buy in Ocala. She had taken the boy along with her and was going to drop him off at his dad's house because he desperately missed his dad.

Pam challenged Debbie just as she had on earlier occasions: "Do you see where this is bizarre, that you would take a student and drive them anywhere? That's totally inappropriate. Why would you even do that?"

"I don't know," Debbie answered. "It was stupid of me. But, you know, I didn't do this. The kid is lying." Then Debbie said something that Pam still remembers with wonder. "She told me she wanted me to picket. She said, 'We have to picket this.'" Debbie didn't say who "we" meant, or what she thought the picket signs were supposed to say, or where the picketing was to be done. Just "We have to picket." It made no sense.

But aside from that mysterious suggestion, "She was really convincing," Pam says. "She had a reason for everything that had happened." And besides, "She was one of my best friends.... Why wouldn't I believe what she was saying?"

Pam told the other teachers at school, "You know, maybe she is telling the truth." Looking back, Pam is embarrassed about being taken in. "I really believed her," she says. "I was a complete idiot." But she wasn't the only one taken in. Debbie was so admired as a teacher that colleagues found the accusations hard to believe. Jeremy Butts, for one, thought the charges were "ludicrous."

By Friday of hell week, five days after Debbie's arrest, the Sheriff's Office for Marion County had put together enough evidence to ask for an arrest warrant on charges for the sex acts in Ocala.

The Marion County Sheriffs had done their own interviews of both Jack and Cliff—the third police interview for Jack, and by no means the last for either of them—and had driven Cliff around, taking photographs of the routes and locations where he said his cousin and the teacher had had sex.

Sheriff's Deputy Patricia Quiggle prepared the arrest warrant and had it signed by Judge Victor Musleh, Chief Judge of Florida's 5th Judicial Circuit, in Ocala. When they notified Debbie's new attorney of the warrant, he advised them that his client would surrender voluntarily. His intention, of course, was to avoid the crowd of press cameras. Events didn't work out according to that plan.

I went up with Debbie the night before and we stayed together in a hotel, paying cash so the press wouldn't know we were there—that's how paranoid you become. We shared a bed but the passion level, at least on my part, hovered somewhere below the zero mark. I knew I would never have sex with this woman again.

Debbie put herself together the next morning with vivid red lipstick, her hair in a bun, and wearing a bright pink sweater. The instructions were for her to appear at the Sheriff's office instead of the jail. The reason became obvious when we arrived: the Sheriff wanted his department to have its share of the publicity, and had notified the press. When the deputies said they wanted to take a set of body photos, Debbie's attorney, who accompanied her for the arrest, pointed out that the Temple Terrace police had already taken a set. One deputy made a phone call and received confirmation, which saved Debbie the repeat embarrassment.

When the paperwork was finished, Deputy Patricia Quiggle put Debbie into handcuffs and walked her 200 yards across a parking lot to the jail, while the television cameras rolled and the reporters called out questions, the kinds of questions that almost always go unanswered, as they did this day.

The Probable Cause affidavit made out at the jail and signed by Sheriff's Deputy Quiggle says, "The Defendant was located and arrested at 692 NW 30th Avenue, Ocala, in Marion County, Florida," which is the address of the Sheriff's office. "The Defendant was transported to the Marion County Jail without incident," which is a curious way to describe having turned herself in and been walked across a parking lot.

The affidavit listed two counts of "lewd and lascivious battery" and one count of "lewd and lascivious exhibition," which I assume was based on Debbie having allowed teen-age Cliff to catch a glimpse of her naked in the rear-view mirror.

I'm reminded of the old saying about an ill wind that blows no one good. My father and I had been living far from each other for years; we had kept in touch but had not been what anyone would call close. I had called him when I first learned of Debbie's arrest, and he had called me almost daily since.

My mother was already a good listener and wonderful support. Now, my dad became that, as well, leading to a tremendously strong relationship that brought me feeling closer to him than I had ever been.

After Debbie had been bailed out on the new charges, I figured it was probably safe to return to our townhouse, which as I had hoped was by then free of doorstep decorations in the form of people armed with cameras. We moved back in and settled down to a kind of uneasy, arms-length truce.

I didn't see any reason why I should put up with the discomfort of sleeping on the couch—I was the one who had been wronged. But Debbie couldn't be induced into sleeping on the couch, either. We were at an impasse. I said, "Okay—you stay on your side of the bed, I'll stay on mine." And that's how we slept in our king-sized bed: a foot or two of distance between us that might as well have been a thousand miles.

The Debra LaFave saga remained a local item for a couple of weeks, then started coming to the attention of news outlets elsewhere. The episode was to remain an international story for the next two years. Avery Hampton noted that, "A couple of weeks before [the story] started popping up in the tabloids, we had friends from Germany who came for a visit and had already heard about it." Avery thought this "really, really weird."

Why so much attention to Debbie's story? Female teacher/male juvenile student incidents come to light with alarming regularity in this country, but very few become the focus of national attention beyond the initial reports. Debbie would be joining the ranks of Pam Smart, Mary Kay Letourneau and a handful of others. What accounts for the difference?

I think there are two answers: the age of the victim (Pam Smart's lover was 15, Mary Kay's, 13), and the attractiveness of the woman.

People flock to art museums to see beautiful works of art, we travel long distances to see the splendors of beauty in nature, we're drawn to movies and television shows, as well as rock concerts and music videos, that feature beautiful performers. It's human instinct. Newspaper and magazine editors aren't stupid people. They know they sell more copies with a beautiful face on the cover or front page. Ditto for television news directors: their show will draw bigger audiences if they run stories about beautiful people.

The Debra LaFave saga went international because she is so gorgeous. Damn it.

On July 12, the *National Enquirer* ran an article headlined "SEX-CHARGE TEACHER WAS NICK CARTER'S HIGH

SCHOOL SWEETHEART," accompanied in this case not by an appealing photo of Debbie but by a picture of Carter. He must have upset the *Enquirer* editors at some point in the past because the image they chose to accompany the article shows him with a grimace that is a cross between a sneer and a scowl, what must be one of the most uncomplimentary shots of him ever taken.

Describing Debbie as "the sexy blonde teacher whose scandalous relationship with a 14-year-old student has shocked America," the article went on to quote an unnamed "childhood friend" who told of Debbie's "steamy affair" with Carter.

But this supposed authority on Debbie's early life described the connection between the two as much later than it actually took place, claiming it was in Debbie's "sophomore year at East Bay Senior High," when in fact they had been close while she was in middle school; by her sophomore year in high school, the lesbian affair was already behind her and she was no longer at East Bay.

"He and Debbie were together all spring and through the summer…whenever he was in town," the informant claimed. "They were always holding hands, kissing and whispering to one another." Debbie "loved to show off jewelry Nick gave her" and was "especially proud of a pager he gave her" on which he "beeped Debbie several times a day to give her love messages like, 'I miss you' and 'I love you.'" The informant also told of a time when Debbie brought Nick to church services with the family at the Baptist church in Ruskin, and of a talent contest for which Nick sang a love song to Debbie, during which he "gazed at her lovingly through the whole song and even blew her a kiss. It was very romantic."

One sub-head in the article sounded a theme that would become painfully familiar to me in the months ahead; picking up on a statement Jack had made in his police interviews, something Debbie had said about me to give herself an excuse and justification, the sub-head read: "SEXUAL INADEQUACY."

In any case, Debbie LaFave had become a tabloid item.

Pam continued to hear from Debbie. One evening when Debbie was to have dinner with Pam and Jeff, Pam also called the Jacksons and the Hamptons and asked them to come as well. As each couple arrived, husband and wife each gave Debbie a big hug. They sat around talking about this and that, Avery says, "as if we were back having lunch at school." But Beth Hampton thought Debbie was different. "She was a lot more reserved and quiet than normally. And I think she was just sort of trying to assess how we were looking at her."

"Nobody," Avery says, "was mentioning the elephant standing in the corner of the room."

Debbie played with Pam's children and then, after a time, brought up the forbidden topic. But still, I guess, so embarrassed about what she had done that she continued with the same set of blatant falsehoods she had earlier tried to dazzle Pam with. Avery remembers Debbie saying, "They're telling these awful lies about me. I don't know why they're telling these lies."

Then Debbie started talking about "what they're saying about me on the Internet." She asked everybody, "Have you seen the things they're writing about me?" Debbie went to Pam's computer and called up the Web site debralafave.com to show everyone the stories about how she took part in orgies and other outrageous tales. Everyone there knew Debbie well enough to know those things weren't true. She was laughing at how ridiculous the stories were, and the others laughed with her. "These are all lies," she said, "And the boys are lying too."

The idea that Debbie was still spending time looking at the Debra LaFave web sites is appalling to me yet I understand that it was part of her line of defense with our friends, hoping to sound like a virtuous woman much maligned, hoping to keep the friendship of these people who cared about her, blinding herself to the certainty that the truth of the story would all too soon be plastered all over the newspapers and television. And what would she say to her friends when that happened? It was a question she obviously could not bring herself to face.

Someone in the small group asked, "How do you spell the boy's last name?" Debbie said, "I don't know—how would I know?" Beth Hampton, incredulous, said to her, "You know him personally, and his name is such a common word." Beth thought Debbie was being much too defensive.

When the Hamptons left at the end of the evening, Avery thought that "Debbie was clearly a captive of her own emotional needs, and out of control." Despite that, as Beth recalled it later, "My husband really believed that she was telling the truth. I sort of felt like she might be lying but I didn't know her side. And so I was saying, 'Okay, well I'm not sure what her defense is, so let's not make any assumptions.'"

Yet later, looking back, Beth remembered walking away that night saying to Avery, "Did you see the way she reacted? Of course she did it."

Three weeks after Debbie's arrest, the Channel 28 nightly news focused on those Internet sites that Debbie had become so fond of visiting. By then there were sites with names like DebraLafave.com, DebraBeasleyLafave.com, and DebraLafave.net. Another, DebraLafave.org, was home to what they called the "Save Debra Foundation"—though whether they intended to pass along any money that might have been collected by this "foundation" to Debbie's defense fund or to keep it in their own pockets wasn't immediately clear.

The site, the report said, "Takes a lighthearted look at the case but probably embodies the reaction that most men seem to have to the story," and quoted the site's owner who had explained in an e-mail, "...from what I've seen, opinions seem to differ based on gender. I have yet to find a male that does not wish that he had the experience of this 14-year-old (minus the getting caught, of course)."

I sat down for my monthly chore of paying the credit card bills. Among other routine charges I found the item for one $299.95 iPod from Best Buy that Debbie had bought me for my birthday when she went shopping in Ocala with Jack and Cliff. And charges from Champs, the sporting goods store, for two pair of basketball shorts that she had bought for Jack.

I wrote the checks with a heavy heart.

Chapter 13
THE STORY GOES GLOBAL

THE MEDIA INTEREST in the story was exploding. On June 30, CNN aired a segment carried worldwide about what they called "a sordid case that swept through" our Florida community. The Marion County Sheriff's office had made public the affidavit drawn up to obtain the arrest warrant on Debbie. Their media representative, Susan Livott, went in front of the cameras to provide details, which ended up as sound bites on CNN. "The teacher traveled to Ocala from her home and met with the student and also his cousin," Livott said. "And some of these activities took place in front of the cousin." In case the point wasn't clear, she also said, "All the contact has been sexual in nature."

In Tampa, Channel 28 news television reporter Sarina Fazan was telling her viewers, "These days, the Internet is the best place to judge who's popular and controversial in pop culture, and few people are better represented online right now than Hillsborough County teacher Debra LaFave." Incredibly, "Debra LaFave" had become one of the top search items on the Web.

St. Petersburg Times reporter Shannon Colavecchio-Van Sickler, the best of the print journalists who would find themselves covering the story on a regular basis, wrote that "The combination of her striking model-like appearance, the oddity of a woman being accused of predatory behavior with a boy, and the lurid details of the charges against LaFave have made the newlywed the fodder of talk shows nationwide."

Everyone directly connected with the story was being hounded by the national media. I was ignoring the calls, not returning voicemail messages, saying No to everybody who managed to catch me on the phone. Debbie's attorney told Sarina that he had "received calls from virtually every major media outlet in America," and complained that the press was "camping out at my office" (though I can't recall ever hearing of an attorney who shunned publicity). Debbie, apparently enjoying the celebrity status, was calling Pam and saying that she had received a certified letter from Larry King or a voicemail message from Matt Lauer, and the two of them would laugh about it together. As the case exploded onto the national scene, some of the publicity ranked as lurid—or revolting…pick your own term—like the remark on the air from radio host Howard Stern that Debbie "should be thanked, not jailed, for making every schoolboy's fantasy come true."

I had to stop watching the late-night talk shows, where the hosts were milking laughs out of Debbie's situation. To me it was painful. And I knew they wouldn't have bothered if Debbie had been plain or heavyset.

One day the prosecutor called the boy's mother to alert her that the tabloid *News of the World*, which lays claim to the title of being Britain's biggest-selling Sunday newspaper, had published a story of what they called the "school miss," including salacious details the American press had been too discreet to include. Worse, they had managed to find out Jack's identity and printed his full name along with a school yearbook photograph. And it was up on their web site, where anyone could see it. Mrs. Carpenter was panicked. She managed to find a solicitor in England who sent the newspaper a letter threatening action. *News of the World* backed off and removed the picture and name from their site. But it cost Mrs. Carpenter something close to $4,000.

By then, in addition to the multiple interviews with Jack and, separately, with Cliff, the police had interviewed a number of peripheral players (the Greco school principal, several teachers, some school janitors, and people at the playground, among others), examined Debbie's vehicle at the crime lab, and even collected the cushions from both couches in Debbie's portable.

The car, which was received at the lab by technician Angel Dawn Rainwater-Lumpkin, was searched for "hair, fibers, bodily fluids, trace evidence." As part of the routine, a complete inventory was prepared of every item found in the interior and trunk, which turned out to be a testimony that Debbie wasn't an entirely neat and tidy person. The hand-written inventory runs to 11 pages, with items ranging from empty gum and candy wrappers, an empty bottle of Dramamine, bottle caps, hairclips, Rolaids, and tampons, to a dozen beauty, skin, and make-up items, a crossword puzzle book, two wrist watches, five cigarette lighters and a pack of cigarettes, and more than 40 store receipts. Also two VHS tapes, five CDs, and an empty holder for a cassette tape of rock/pop religious music by an artist named Wiley Brooks-Martin, assembled into a collection with a title that is, under the circumstances, unfortunate: "On My Knees."

Police officers and Sheriff's deputies from the two counties were also tracking down the path that the three had traveled on the two days in Ocala, in part from information provided by the boys, in part from receipts found in the car. From store to store, from ATM machine to Starbucks, they were able to trace her steps accurately, providing one more confirmation of the boys' story.

Investigators visited the liquor store where she had bought the vodka, the Best Buy, Champs, and elsewhere, locating the clerks who had waited on her, and asking each if he or she could identify her photo. Everybody who watches crime shows on television knows the routine—the police put together a "six-pack," a set of head-shot photos of the suspect and five other people. In this case, the six-pack was actually funny: at least two of the others looked really scary, ladies you would not want to come face-to-face with on a lonely street at night. Even though these store clerks had seen Debbie only briefly, most had no problem picking out her photo.

A stack of material released by police to the media included a statement by the boy about remarks Debbie had supposedly made to him that her sex life wasn't satisfying. For the major national interview shows, that was an angle they could use to grab viewer attention. Having seen the earlier *National Enquirer* story, I could just imagine their promos: *Teacher Had Sex with Student Because Hubby is Inadequate in Bed.* The phone calls intensified, now trying to draw me in to confirm their suspicions: "Are you gay?" "Are you unable to perform?" And so on. In other words, was I somehow to blame for what Debbie had done—as if that would be an excuse even if it were true.

Just for the record, I'll say here what I've said on the air and to print reporters, repeatedly: I am not gay. I have no problems in the performance department. Other than times when Debbie herself refused sex because of her mood or depression, we had the sex life you would expect of any newlywed couple—as I've indicated earlier in these pages.

But my answers didn't stop the media from calling, and radio DJs in Tampa had been taunting me on the air, saying things like, "Hey, Owen, you've got to be impotent, you've got to be gay—call and let's talk about it." It was so painful that I quit reading the newspaper, watching the news, and listening to the radio.

Sharing the townhouse with Debbie, the two of us in about as much space as a moderate-sized RV, was not turning out to be anybody's vision of joy. We had our meals together, we slept together but only in the most literal meaning of the term, but the only thing we did well together was fight.

The school board had given her formal notification that she was on suspension until the charges against her had been resolved—no surprise there. She started spending a lot of time in Christian bookstores, coming home with stacks of religious material to read, and studying the scriptures. In her time of trouble, she was naturally enough following her mother's example by turning to God, and I hoped it would help see her through the difficult time ahead. Meanwhile she had become even more childlike and more dependent on Joyce, with her parents taking responsibility for the handling of legal matters and advising her what to do.

Despite her Baptist heritage that comes with a fervent disapproval of alcohol, Debbie never had an issue with drinking, though her own drinking was very modest; in our four years together I had seen her actually drunk on only two occasions. Even so, her use of any alcohol had been a source of friction with Joyce all along—only complete absence would satisfy her mother—and Debbie had always been frustrated whenever her mother started in questioning the two of us on the subject.

Now the tables were turned. Debbie started ragging at me about my drinking. She did have some grounds for complaint on that score. In my frustration over this depressing turn in my life, there was a period of a few months when I was occasionally drinking more than was good for me, willfully getting good and drunk, though never to the point of interfering with my work. It's not something I'm proud of, and I'm glad to be able to say I found my way through it without doing myself or anybody else any harm.

As I had promised Debbie and her parents, I was still keeping up the illusion in public that I was standing by her, even to the point of our going out to dinner together; she had no money and no income so, sap that I am, I paid for her meals. But I wouldn't be maintaining the togetherness pretense much longer.

I was sitting in the living room one evening listening to a new Dave Matthews CD I had bought. Debbie wanted to go out to dinner. I was enjoying the music and decided to have some wine with it. Since neither of us had been keeping up with household chores, I discovered that the only bottle of wine we still had in the house was an expensive one we had been saving for a special occasion. There would be no special occasions in our future. I opened the bottle and offered her a glass. She had one, I had the rest.

By then in a better mood for going out to dinner, I drove us to Tia's, a TexMex restaurant. Earlier she had tried to answer a question of mine about the significance of the beads in a religious bracelet she had started wearing, part of her new wave of religious fervor. At the restaurant, she announced that she remembered what the beads symbolized. She started ticking them off, explained the first two, and couldn't remember any more.

I had suspected that her suddenly embracing religion might be a sham. This seemed like a confirmation. I told her, "I think it's hypocritical when people wear something symbolic but don't know what it means."

When two people are on a warlike footing, it doesn't take much to trigger an explosion. Debbie answered me in a loud voice—in the middle of a crowded restaurant—"At least I'm not a f***ing alcoholic!"

I'm embarrassed to say she had sparked my anger and I answered, "At least I'm not a f***ing whore!" And realized I had never heard my own voice so intense.

Throwing down her napkin, she said, "That's it—I'm leaving." And she walked out. I paid for the meal and found her waiting for me outside. We got in the car and continued the battle all the way home, a very heated, immature, emotional, alcohol-fueled screaming match.

The alcohol unleashed all the frustration and emotion I had been holding in. This was not my finest moment, but I wasn't willing to listen to her sorry songs any more.

As soon as we walked into the house, I told her, "You're not welcome here any more. That's it. I can't take it. You've got to leave."

She shouted, "This is my house too. What gives you the right to stay here and I'm the one who has to leave?"

I shouted back, "Because I'm not the one who had sex with a 14-year-old."

We had each done enough damage to the other. She walked out to her car, and drove away.

At one time, when we had had a problem with the front and back door locks, I bought replacement locks that I had never installed. I fetched my toolset and put them in.

Early the next morning she was back, trying to unlock the door and discovering that her key didn't work. She rang the bell; I let her in and we sat down. Calmer now but no less resolved, I told her again, "I'm suffering emotionally. You can't live here any more." The conversation had started calmly but turned into another argument over who had to move out.

Then her parents showed up, adding fuel to the fire, insisting with Debbie that I should be the one to move out. I wasn't the sinner—there was no way I was giving up on this. It finally sank in that they weren't going to change my mind, and they went off to gather up her things and carry them out.

A week after Debbie left, I came home from work Friday night, sat down in the big chair in the living room, and more or less stayed there the entire weekend. I cried, I slept, I watched TV, I barely ate. When the sun went down I just sat in the dark until I fell asleep. I sat there all Friday night and all Saturday and all Sunday. I didn't have any desire to commit suicide but for the first time in my life I felt as if I understood people who did.

I woke up on Monday morning in time to go to work. I still don't know how.

Driving to work, I told myself, *I won't go in that direction. I have the rest of my life to live. I need to move on.*

My first step out of the darkest weekend of my life and back to sanity was to find a therapist and start regular sessions.

About three weeks after Debbie had moved out, she and I had arranged that she would come in over the weekend to pick up furniture and possessions. Much of our furniture had belonged to her sister, and it was fitting that those things go to Debbie. To make sure there wouldn't be any hassle or problems, I planned to have my attorney on hand, as well as an off-duty police officer.

Instead, the Thursday before, she called me and said, "I'm leaving."

"Leaving where?" I asked.

"The townhome. I took all the furniture."

All the furniture???

I said, "Why the hell would you do that!? Did you leave me the bed?"

"No," she said.

"The mattress?"

"No."

"What the hell am I supposed to sleep on?" I asked.

"You could go to Wal-Mart and buy an air mattress."

It was the final straw. I had spoken the marriage vows that I took very seriously. Then after her arrest I had told her the relationship was over but I would still stand by her and try to protect her. Even with our closest friends I had hidden the truth and maintained the façade that we were still living together. And this is how she saw fit to repay me.

Without even waiting for the next day's office hours, I called Laurie Ohall, an attorney who is an old friend of mine and my mother's, and told her to draw up divorce papers. Knowing my filing for divorce would create a media stir, I determined to tell the story my own way. Laurie knew a couple of the local media people, and we invited Samantha (Sam) Sodos from the CBS-TV affiliate, Channel 10, and Anthony McCarthy from the *Tampa Tribune* to view my empty townhouse. But I was unleashing a tiger; these would not be two media interviews but merely the first two of many to follow.

I can't say that my first television appearance went very well. Hurt, nervous, and unprepared is not the recommended frame of mind for going on television. Samantha's very first question was, "Owen, did she do it?"

I replied, "I'm not going to answer that," but in my uncomfortable, not-in-control state, my awkward smile told every viewer the answer was yes.

When the divorce papers were filed, Debbie and I had been married one year and sixteen days. I had enjoyed a fantastic relationship with her parents until then. At that point, they turned on me. Joyce took charge of the divorce negotiations for the Beasley side and made my life a nightmare.

Irony of ironies: we hadn't yet finished paying off the credit card expenses for our wedding and honeymoon. They were on Debbie's credit card, which I would not be making payments on any more. I was happy to let Larry and Joyce have the heartburn over paying off those costs.

Other than a couple of conversations with Debbie about the divorce details, I would never speak with her again.

The local media quickly picked up on my furniture-less plight and I found myself a subject of fun on a Tampa morning talk show called—I'm not kidding—the "Cowhead and Brent show" on FM 92.5, "the Outlaw Country station" that I regularly listened to on my drive to work. They were saying, "Oh, the poor guy doesn't have any furniture"—laughing and pretending to feel sorry for me.

Reporter Sam Sodos called the station and gave them my phone number. So they called me up on the air and said, "We can give you some furniture." One of the guys had a couple of couches in his garage he said he'd send over, and they knew a furniture rental place they thought would also send some items without charge. "There won't be any media people," the guys promised. "We just want to help."

I was so down at that point in my life that the idea of some strangers willing to do a favor was more than I could turn down. I agreed, and we made the arrangements.

Meanwhile, Channel 28's Sarina Fazan had been pestering my attorney Laurie for an interview with me. I was quite unhappy with Sarina because she had been the most persistent of the reporters—hounding not just me but my friends, guys I had gone to school with, guys who had been in my wedding party, even camping outside my mother's home. So every time my attorney asked, I said no. Finally Laurie said, "Sarina is sweet but she's driving me crazy." I gave in and said I'd meet with her in Laurie's office, not to do an interview but just to talk.

A couple of days later, we sat down together and I laced into her about bothering everybody around me. I really let her have it.

Sarina's eyes welled up. I hope it was an honest reaction; if it was just a show she was putting on for my benefit, I'll admit she was convincing. She said she was sorry. "I don't want to cause you pain. Please forgive me." There is something about her personality that kept me there talking to her for at least an hour, maybe an hour and a half.

The next day she was back on the phone with Laurie, again asking for an interview. As a compromise, I said she could come with her cameraman and film the arrival of the furniture, but that I wouldn't do an interview.

She came. I gave in and did the interview she had been pestering for.

At one point, speaking about Debbie having removed all the furniture including our marriage bed, I told her it was probably a good thing that I was rid of it. Too many memories.

I was particularly candid, admitting that it had been "like living a nightmare. I won't lie to you—there were times I just sobbed like a baby, especially at night, alone." About Debbie, I said, "She has a beautiful side to her. She's very compassionate. She's a very sweet person, intelligent and obviously beautiful. There's a lot of great qualities about Debbie. That's why I married her."

One statement I made was sincere at the time, but I would later change my view: "I hope that she doesn't go to jail."

When my mother saw the interview, she called Sarina to say it was the best piece that had been done since Debbie's arrest. Later I discovered just how personable and effective Sarina is: she also won over Debbie and her parents.

You would have thought that every major television interview show watched Tampa's local TV news broadcasts each night. I don't know how the word spreads in that business, but it was as if every national show had found out at the same time that Debra LaFave's husband was willing to do television. Even though I had come close to making a fool of myself in that first interview, my phone started to ring off the hook.

I called my attorney Laurie once again to ask for her help finding someone who could advise me on whether I should go on national television and what risks I would be taking personally. And, if I was going to do this, what shows should I go on.

I think the attorney did something I could have done myself, except that she knew the right term to use. She entered "publicist" into an Internet search engine, looked at the credentials of the name of the top of the list, and decided that looked like a good place to start. The name was Karen Ammond, who I would find out is president and founder of KBC Media Relations, based in New Jersey and Manhattan, with a satellite operation in Los Angeles. Karen turned out to be somebody who was a superstar in handling high-profile media stories, dealing with clients ranging from business leaders and newsmakers to film and television actors, musicians, and authors. We had a phone conversation that night, even though Karen was vacationing at her family lake house in Vermont and talking through a typical New England August thunderstorm that kept disrupting her cell phone connection. But she and I hit it off immediately and formed a bond that continues to this day.

Remembering that first call, Karen says, "I could tell you were anguished and suffering, and my heart went out to you." We talked for about an hour and a half, and, she says, "Two things particularly impressed me—how verbal you were, and your way of talking about the story that didn't involve trashing Debbie, but instead saying how much you had been in love with her and how this had broken your heart." Karen says she was touched, deciding "I had to help."

She told me, "You've done nothing wrong as a husband, but it's imperative you get out and tell your story, or the tabloids will continue to speculate."

By the end of the call I felt completely confident in putting myself into her hands. Karen phoned the next day to alert me that she had spoken to her contacts at two network magazine shows, finding the most sympathetic response from the producer at ABC's *Primetime Live*, who was newly married and especially sensitive to my position. So much so, Karen told me, that the producer promised they would stop any line of questioning I was uncomfortable with. According to Karen, "Most of the time, you have to be ready for whatever they throw at you."

Within a few days I was on an airplane to New York's Kennedy airport, in business class, met at the airport by a town car and driven into Manhattan, my very first time in America's premier city. The bustle and frenzy lived up to every expectation.

At *Primetime*, the interviewer was Cynthia McFadden herself, and the session was done on tape, not live, which made me a lot more comfortable. But she asked me questions for two hours, a grueling two hours, including the embarrassing, dreaded one about whether I'm gay. I told her, "I'm not gay—not that there's anything wrong with that."

At one point Cynthia stopped the interview, turned to Karen who was standing behind the cameras, and asked her, "Did you get him media trained?" Karen smiled and said, "No—we just met a few days ago." She told me afterward the question meant Cynthia was impressed with how well I was doing on camera.

The interview aired two weeks later, on the *Primetime* premiere show for the fall. Though the two-hour interview had been boiled down to a six-minute segment following a big Donald Trump story, I was very pleased with the result—even though my friends in Tampa gave me a lot of teasing about my comment in defense of gays.

I was flown back to New York to meet Karen the day before the *Primetime* piece ran, to promote it with an interview on *Good Morning America*, this time live before an audience of millions—which, as you can well imagine, is nerve-racking.

But apparently I hadn't done too badly, because when I returned home to Tampa, Karen called to say that other shows were phoning her and competing with each other to have me next.

I had meant to go on one or two shows, figuring that would be enough to make the interest in me go away. Instead my appearances were fueling the story. I began to wonder: Could I take this opportunity and use it to help prevent the sex-with-student situation from happening so often?

When Tampa public schools opened for the new school year, it was, Avery Hampton remembers, "odd coming back into that situation." Police had been stationed at the school, and nobody seemed to know why. Counselors were on hand in case any of the kids had a breakdown. The teachers had been required to attend an "ethics" session, which consisted mainly of watching a video produced by the school district, designed to convey little beyond the simplistic, too-obvious message "Don't sleep with students." (While the video was apparently too unsophisticated to help, I think the idea of requiring such training, but in a much more sophisticated and effective way, should be mandatory throughout the nation; more about that later.)

Principal Janet Spence over the summer had ordered all of the couches and easy chairs removed from throughout the school, which some of the teachers found both useless and laughable—as if the presence of the couches had led to the impure thoughts that landed Debbie in trouble, and without them the transgressions would never have happened. But Ms. Spence herself was apparently thought to be in some way responsible, perhaps for not having insisted more firmly that Debbie never come to work in short skirts, tight shirts, or showing her cleavage. If so, it's a view I agree with. Especially in middle schools, standing in front of students whose hormones are springing to life but whose values and emotions about sex are still immature, inappropriate dress by women teachers, as well as inappropriate remarks or behavior by teachers of either sex, is asking for trouble. That should be so obvious that it doesn't even need to be said.

When the head-count of students was tallied up at the end of the first week, it seemed clear that many parents were afraid to send their children back to Greco. The school had expected 1300 kids; only 1100 showed up. Despite the obvious fears of the administration, "Kids are pretty resilient," Avery Hampton says. "As after any tragedy, we quickly got back to life as usual."

That may have been true in most ways, but not in all. Avery found boys making salacious comments along the lines of "I wish it would'a happened to me," and "I guess I picked the wrong year to be your student assistant," a reference to Jack having been Avery's student assistant before becoming involved with Debbie.

Life as usual was not an apt description for Jack's situation, either. Some of his former Greco classmates now at King High School with him dropped by Greco to visit favorite teachers, bringing word that Jack was being subjected to two different reactions, neither of them welcome. Within a few days, every teacher and kid at the school knew he was the boy who had been involved with the beautiful teacher in a case that was still waiting to go to trial. Boys he didn't even know, passing him in the hall, would give him high fives—congratulations he did not want.

But even that wasn't as bad as the reaction from a few of the former Greco students, fans of Debbie's, the kind of kids who had written how "cool" she was in her copy of their graduating-class yearbook. "She was such a popular teacher," Avery says. "Kids worshipped the ground she walked on." These kids blamed Jack for Debbie's being caught. They thought it was his fault that she had been fired and would never teach again, and they let him know it.

The situation became so uncomfortable that Mrs. Carpenter pulled Jack out of King High and had him transferred, a striking parallel to Debbie herself having been pulled out of high school and sent elsewhere just ten years earlier.

Avery's take on the whole business is worth considering: "I think it was not the affair but what followed that has done the damage."

The situation for Debbie was growing worse and worse. She was already convicted in the eyes of most of the public. Unable to teach, she was working at an air-conditioning company as an office assistant for a scant $10 an hour. Her Citibank Visa credit card, with those charges from our honeymoon, still carried a balance of about $4,000. A paper filed with the court showed Debbie was financially under water by $31,575, but that must have been some sort of attempt at sympathy: the one large item on the debit side of her balance sheet was her half of the townhouse mortgage. But I was making the mortgage payments, so that wasn't a real debt of hers.

At least she didn't have to dig into her own pocket to pay her high-priced attorney. Her dad was handling that, out of the money from refinancing the family home.

A big break in the police case arrived in mid-October. The first set of swabs taken from the inside of Debbie's mouth had been found unusable for obtaining a sample of her DNA, so the police had needed to obtain a second warrant and had brought her back in for another attempt. Now, nearly four months after the arrest, a report came in from the Florida Department of Law Enforcement crime lab giving the new DNA analysis. "A DNA profile foreign to [the victim] was resolved from Exhibit 7B," the report stated in the formal language of the laboratory. 7B was identified as being material that had been obtained from the swabs used on Jack's penis.

Two additional statements made the case solid: "The foreign DNA profile matches the DNA profile from Debra B. LaFave." And, "Based on these results, the frequency of occurrence of the foreign DNA profile resolved from Exhibit 7B for unrelated individuals… is approximately 1 in 200 trillion…."

For the first time, the police had something more than testimony from the victim and the eyewitness, and the phone call recordings. They had solid evidence. Jack's penis had been in contact with a body fluid of Debbie's.

When an accused enters a plea of not guilty, it doesn't mean "I didn't do this," but only "I'm not acknowledging my guilt, so the government will have to present enough proof of my guilt to convince a judge or jury." And that's what it had meant for Debbie. The last day of November would be another sunny, warm day in Tampa but the temperature was still in the 60s at 8:30 in the morning when she and her attorney showed up at the courthouse. Her case was back on the court docket again. She would probably have preferred to stay at home and let her attorney appear in her behalf, but had been ordered to appear in person.

Though this was expected to be a routine pretrial hearing, her attorney sprang a surprise, telling the court, "There is some work being done by a doctor," and "We have accumulated medical records," he said. "To give the court a sense of the case, I anticipate that in the near future I will be filing a notice of insanity defense."

I learned of this from Sarina Fazan's report on television that night, which showed Debbie at the courthouse. It was the first I had seen of her in four months and I was distressed to find her looking terrible, with dark circles under her eyes and a genuinely frightened appearance. Her attorney had apparently suggested a more conservative look, and she had come to court without her familiar dark eye shadow and bright red lipstick but with a small gold crucifix prominently hanging outside her clothing on a chain. Despite an extra 15 pounds or so, she somehow appeared younger, yet stressed out. It pained me to read the signs of distress in her face.

The prosecutor would later file a paper with the court giving the wording that the State wanted to be used in the instructions to the jury about the insanity plea. In part, it read, "All persons are presumed to be sane. To prove the defense of insanity, the defendant must prove the following two elements: 1. Debra Beasley LaFave had a mental infirmity, disease or defect. 2. Because of this condition, [she] did not know what she was doing or its consequences, or although she knew what she was doing and its consequences, [she] did not know it was wrong."

The trial had been scheduled to begin the following week. Because of the change in defense strategy, the judge granted a request for a delay to allow time to prepare the insanity defense.

Outside the courthouse, her attorney told the cameras, "Debbie has some profound emotional issues." True enough. But was that supposed to mean she didn't know what she was doing? That she didn't know adultery wasn't okay? That she couldn't understand sex with a 14-year-old student was unacceptable? Defending her on the charges was going to be difficult, and I suppose her attorney saw an insanity plea as the only course open to him.

Two days after that court appearance, the Debra LaFave case exploded into the national news once again. The Tampa State Attorney's Office released transcripts of the "controlled calls"—the recorded conversations between Jack and Debra, transcripts that contained what amounted to Debbie's admission of sex with the boy. They showed Jack saying, "I was just thinking if next time, now that we've had sex about three times, if I should use like a condom or something," followed by Debbie's reply that doesn't challenge or deny the "sex three times" but simply says, "Oh, you're being weird.... Why are you being weird?"

That, along with the "pinky promise" that the media would latch on to as if the phrase captured something significant about Debbie's entire personality.

The package of materials released also included photos the police had obtained from security cameras at Best Buy. Despite the somewhat fuzzy quality of the stills lifted from the store's security videotapes, Debbie can be clearly seen looking cute in her short white sundress, her hair in a ponytail, the boys seen investigating other parts of the store while she buys that iPod for me.

The timing of the release of this material made it sound as if it was part of the elaborate chess game between the defense attorney and the state. The defense had just unleashed plans for claiming insanity, and the prosecutor, in making the material available to the media, said, "If insanity is raised in any particular case, controlled calls could...be valuable so you could see the defendant's state of mind at or near the time of the crime."

I hope this doesn't begin to sound as if I am promoting one favored reporter over all the others who were covering the story in Tampa, but I was particularly impressed by a perceptive remark from Sarina's report on the release of this material. "From the evidence," she said on air, "It would appear that the relationship was not just a physical one for LaFave. Between May 27 and June 21, records show she called the boy 108 times, an average of four times a day."

That left me wondering—which did I find more disturbing: that my wife had sex with a 14-year-old, or that she had become emotionally attached to him?

When Pam Glas read the phone call transcripts, she was struck about remarks Debbie had made the day she was at the birthday party for Pam's daughter, complaining that "my ovaries are hurting listening with all these frigging kids screaming." Pam wondered about her former friend, *Is she the wicked witch of the West?*

The documents and photos that the prosecutor had handed over to the press launched a new round of media mania. By that time I had appeared on *Inside Edition* twice. The following week I did the show a third time, as well as appearing on *Good Morning America* again, plus *Deborah Norville Tonight*—three shows, all in the same week.

Of the millions of searches done every day on Google, the search term "Debra LaFave" was now one of the top ten.

In December, as Christmas approached, Debbie went to dinner at the Red Lobster restaurant with the guy she was then seeing, and the man's son. In another of those small-world coincidences, they were seated in a section assigned to server Lisa York, who was engaged to and living with Andrew Beck—the guy who had been Debbie's boyfriend when I first ran into her on the college campus. Lisa of course recognized Debbie; you could hardly watch television news during that period and not have seen Debbie's face, all the more so for residents of the Tampa area.

Andrew, Lisa says, had been contacted about possibly being called to testify at Debbie's trial concerning things she had told him of traumas in her past—principally, I suppose, the teen rape. Lisa recognized an opportunity.

As the group was leaving, Lisa spoke Debbie's name, and she stopped. Lisa said, "Debbie, you don't know me, but I'm Andrew's fiancé. I know you and Andrew have been friends for years. He has a family now, and he has a business, a moving company. Do you think you could please spare him any hardship, any bad publicity."

Lisa describes the scene in a way that you can tell she still feels the pain. "She looked at me as if I was out of my mind. She laughed and said, 'You know, Andrew and I talk.'" Lisa replied, "I know. I was there once when you talked to him."

If Lisa's story is accurate, Debbie must have been hurting badly, her jealousy instincts at a peak. According to Lisa, Debbie answered, "No, Andrew and I talk *all the time*, and you'll never stop me from talking to him." And she added, "You know what? I'm Andrew's first love and he would do anything for me. He'll do whatever I want him to do." With that, Lisa says, Debbie walked away.

Lisa's relationship with Andrew had begun four years earlier, when she started going with a friend from work to watch his team play sandlot baseball. She soon met Andrew, another of the guys on the team. He moved the relationship forward very quickly, from friends hanging out together, to becoming a couple, to moving into her house in St. Petersburg with Lisa and her six-year-old daughter Taylor.

Lisa says Andrew wanted all the same things she did— kids, house, white picket fence. He was "a loving, caring person," she says. "He kept a Bible on his side of the bed, reading in bed before going to sleep.

Then the relationship began to change. Lisa becomes teary as she continues, describing how Andrew "started begging me to have a child." Lisa, already divorced once, wanted to make sure first that they had a solid relationship. But under pressure "I finally gave in." Soon after she found she was pregnant, Andrew asked her to marry him. Lisa happily agreed. They made plans to marry after she gave birth. Their daughter Abby was born in June 2003.

Andrew was "a wonderful, wonderful father to both the children," Lisa says. "He always promised Taylor that he wouldn't ever give up on her. 'No matter what happens with your mother and me, I'll never leave you,' he told her."

Taylor asked Andrew to go with her to a father/daughter dance, where a reporter for the *St. Petersburg Times* was so impressed by the relationship that she wrote an article on the affection between the two.

The thorn in the Lisa York rose bush turned out to be Debbie LaFave. After Debbie was arrested, Andrew's attitude changed. He became withdrawn from Lisa, perhaps feeling pulled apart by his divided loyalties, in love with Lisa and her two daughters, while an old, never-dead love for Debbie was being rekindled.

The situation became uncomfortable enough that Lisa gave Andrew back his ring, packed up, loaded the kids in the car, and drove off to stay with a girlfriend in Georgia.

When she returned from Georgia, the repentant Andrew went to her in hopes of working things out and was convincing enough that they rented an apartment in Riverview and moved in together—the two of them and the two little girls. Eventually it slipped out that Andrew had gone to visit Debbie. "I wanted to hear it from her," he said.

Whenever there was something on television about her, Lisa says, Andrew would always defend her with a comment like "There are two sides to every story."

Some time after the release of the transcripts and the announcement about the insanity defense, Debbie's mother called Pam. "I hadn't heard from her in a long time," Pam says. "I'm not a huge fan of Joyce." Calling their relationship "bizarre," she described Joyce as "always having to be involved in every aspect of Debbie's life, including her marriage with Owen, I think in a very intrusive way."

Joyce said Debbie had moved in with her parents for a while, then moved into an apartment of her own. She didn't offer much other news beyond that, explaining that she had called Pam about her memories of Debbie having highs and lows and having to be sedated by medication. "I told her I did remember that," Pam says. Joyce asked Pam if she would be willing to talk to the investigator who was working for Debbie's defense attorney. Pam, though she did at one point talk on the phone with the investigator, now told Joyce, "I'd rather not be involved in the case at all, to be quite honest with you."

That turned out to be the last contact Pam would have with Joyce or with Debbie, bringing to an end what had been a very close, meaningful friendship for Debbie as much as for Pam. Joyce had Debbie's cell phone shut off, Pam believes, and bought her a new one. "I was never given the new number, and she hasn't called me. So I don't have any way of getting in touch with her except through Joyce. And I did call a couple of times to try to talk to Debbie. Joyce didn't say I couldn't, but it was pretty clear. She said, 'I'll have her call you back,' but no call ever came."

"I've had to go through a great deal of mourning over this whole situation," Pam says, "because I've lost my friend."

In late January I did a television interview that was the experience of a lifetime. Publicist Karen Ammond had arranged for me to appear on *Larry King Live*, as the sole guest for the entire hour.

My first contact beforehand and when I arrived at the studio in Los Angeles was with the show's producer, Hunter Waters, a smooth, polished professional whose way of preparing me for the interview I especially appreciated.

When I met Larry King himself, two things surprised me. His athletic build: he is a trim, lean man. And his clothing: in addition to the familiar dress shirt, tie, and trademark suspenders visible to television viewers, he wears jeans. I liked that—it immediately put me at ease.

This man who lives in a world of superstars and decision-makers treated me with respect and showed keen sensitivity to my situation. He is the gold standard of interviewers, the ultimate pro.

I sat in the chair that presidents have sat in, and royalty, the biggest movie stars, the most powerful corporate leaders. Larry started off breaking the ice with an easy question on the personal level. "First," he said, "what happened to your arm?" He had put me into such a relaxed, comfortable mood before going on the air that I answered the same way I might have answered a question like that from one of my fraternity brothers. "Don't you remember—you beat me up in the hallway." I guess it was pretty gutsy of me to give a flip response like that on national television, but I got away with it. Larry laughed, and I gave the real answer, which was that I had injured my arm in the gym lifting weights, and it had required surgery.

You would think that a man like Larry King, with the thousands of interviews he's done, would have covered just about every topic under the sun. Yet he showed a certain discomfort when he said, "This is...this is kind of strange to even talk about. It's not the sort of thing you can prepare for."

Being interviewed by the estimable Larry King is a humbling experience, but I couldn't afford to be awed because he kept throwing questions at me—including, of course, the one I was growing used to but would rather not be asked all the time, about whether I was able to satisfy my wife. He asked about my relationship with my father—better than ever—and about whether I thought Debbie should go to jail, which by then I was changing my mind about and still uncertain. He asked about the anger directed at me from Debbie's parents. I said, "I think it's a means for them to shift focus off of what really happened, and allow them to vent some of their anger towards me."

I found Larry very easy to talk to. But then, if you've ever watched his show, you already know all that. The way he comes across on the air is the same way he is in person. He kept the conversation going with me even during the commercial breaks. I think that says a lot: he doesn't just come in to earn his paycheck and then he's outta there—he truly enjoys talking to people, finding out about you. The American humorist Will Rogers once said, "I never met a man I didn't like." I came to believe that the same is true of Larry King.

The interview must have gone well. They received something like a thousand e-mails, and, I suppose because of that response, reran the show another three times.

Months later when there was another big news break in the Debra LaFave story, I was asked to appear again on all the top-tier shows, including Larry King. I flew to New York, where Karen met me. It turned out the schedule for the Larry King show had been shuffled—something that often happens in television, I learned—and I was no longer to be a guest that night. But I had an experience I would not have wanted to miss. Invited to watch the show in the studio, I was introduced to one of the guests, Jerry Seinfeld, and stayed to hear his interview with Larry, which was hilarious. And not just when the camera's red light was on; he was also a laugh riot during the commercial breaks. A front row seat, and I didn't even have to buy a ticket.

Larry chatted with Karen and me during one break and asked, "What are you doing about a book?" Karen, a heads-up publicist who is always on top of every situation, told him,

"We're working on it." She smiled, and so did I. That spark of encouragement from Larry King started me on the path that led to what you're now reading.

I look forward to sitting across from him again so I can thank him for that nudge, and for the kindness he showed me on my first appearance when I was still hurting emotionally. I'll never forget it.

Karen Ammond had become more than my publicist. Although she had originally signed on only to get me onto one or two shows, she had come to believe in what I was doing and to dedicate an enormous amount of time to working with me. She had become something like a personal manager, the kind that show business people have. And she had become a close friend and adviser. Karen observed changes in me that I wasn't even aware of.

"I saw him gaining strength," she said much later. "At first he was just telling his side of the story. Then he began researching, studying, talking to prosecutors. He became an advocate for the children and knowledgeable about the subject, so the shows were all the more eager to have him."

Thanks to Karen, I was discovering a talent I didn't even know I had. More important, I had the sense that I was doing some good. I never imagined I would be in position to play a role in bringing about changes in the society.

Just in case anybody is wondering, television shows don't pay people like me to do an interview. There was no money in it for me, even though I had to take time off work.

Some things you do because you know they're the right thing to do.

Chapter 14
LEGAL SKIRMISHING

WITH A TRIAL DATE of July 18 fast approaching, the Tampa prosecutor's office started to focus on the case, launching a phase that you might have thought would have been done very much earlier: they began in-depth interviews—"depositions"—of people able to shed light on the facts of the case and Debbie's state of mind. I was "asked" to come in to the State Attorney's Office on the first Monday in March.

The session began at 1:30 in the afternoon and lasted until a little after 4:30, three almost-nonstop hours. Though I never read the transcript, I understand it ran to 180 pages and that the cover, in bold capital letters, gave my name with the first name spelled wrong—"Christian" instead of "Kristian." The questioning was a good deal more uncomfortable than any of the television interviews. I was asked about Debbie's orgasms and whether we performed oral sex on each other. (I wasn't sure why they were asking, and wanted to know whether the act was legal in the state of Florida. They assured me that between consenting adults, it is legal.) And about Debbie's sometimes skimpy clothing, her changes in behavior in the months preceding the incidents, her depression and social anxieties, her medication and therapy, her childhood rape, her high school lesbian affair, even her mother's breast cancer. You would have thought they were planning to write Debbie's biography.

By the end of the month they had also taken depositions from two fellow teachers who had known her well, the couple who threw the end-of-school party and that couple's son, who was a friend of Jack's, and at least one couple who were part of our social circle. Later they would also take the deposition of the lady who had been Debbie's high school lesbian lover.

I don't pretend to understand police matters, but it seems strange that the prosecutor would spend time interviewing people like the party-givers but not sit down with the victim himself, or even the victim's cousin, who was the only other actual eyewitness to the events. Mysterious.

In the March 23 edition of the *St. Petersburg Times*, Shannon Van Sickler's story began "Camera crews manned every entrance to the courthouse Tuesday morning to capture the arrival of Debra LaFave.... It was only [another] pretrial hearing. But it was a glimpse of what is likely to come during the trial, given the international attention already focused on LaFave's good looks and the case's salacious details." Debbie showed up modestly dressed in a white collarless T-shirt under a light blue cotton pants-suit that didn't fit well, as if she had gained more weight, with the jacket buttoned so that her bosom was on less obvious display.

A pretrial hearing is usually an opportunity for the attorneys to present motions and for the judge to issue any special orders or instructions about the case. This one didn't take the usual course. The prosecutor and the defense attorney jointly told the judge that they wanted another delay (the trial had been originally scheduled to begin in April) so that both sides could review the psychological evaluations of Debbie and then see if they could come to an agreement on a plea bargain.

Debbie, asked if she had anything she wanted to say, replied that she had "no comment at this time," and then grimaced in a way that I thought revealed her emotional anguish and was painful to see.

It's an eye-opener to discover that many aspects of our right to privacy cease to exist when the government starts to investigate us in connection with a serious crime. In some ways, that's obvious; in others, it's surprising.

Because your doctor, lawyer, and therapist are granted the right of remaining silent about things they know of you, it stands to reason that your list of prescriptions would never legally fall into the hands of the police or prosecutors—right?

Wrong. Your doctor and therapist can refuse to provide information about your medications, but your druggist without batting an eyelash will hand over the information in response to a subpoena. On March 28, our pharmacy printed out the list of prescriptions they had filled for Debbie, from April 28, 2003, through early July 2004, some two weeks after her arrest, and handed it over for use by the prosecutor. It showed all of her depression and anxiety meds, and her birth control pills, together with the doctor's name for each prescription and the date it had been refilled. So much for illusions about the privacy of our medical records.

Though Jack and Cliff still hadn't been deposed, they were being called back from time to time to answer yet more questions for the prosecutor. Given the DNA evidence, it hardly seemed necessary, unless it was an intentional step in trying to toughen the boys up for the difficult questioning they would face on the witness stand. If that was indeed the reason, it would explain some particularly demeaning questions Jack was challenged with in a session on April 1.

He told the investigator that Debbie didn't ask him about having oral sex, she just did it. But before intercourse the first time, she asked him if he was ready, and he said yes.

The investigator—a lady, no less—asked the now-15-year-old if he had been the aggressive one in initiating the sex. He said no. Then she actually asked whether he had held Debbie's head down while she performed oral sex on him. He told her he had not.

By the end of March 2005, the blitz of TV appearances had tapered off. I had by then been on 16 shows, on the air with personalities like Sean Hannity and Alan Colmes, Geraldo Rivera, and Greta Van Susteren. Meanwhile a resolution of the court case seemed to be growing no closer. The principal players were back before Circuit Court Judge Wayne Timmerman again on May 18, with the prosecutor telling the judge that the government had just heard from the psychiatrist they had hired, so they would "convey a plea offer in the near future," and expected to be able to tell the judge by the scheduled status date on June 16 "whether this case is resolved." The judge granted a continuance until June. The hearing was over in less time than it takes to read this paragraph.

Outside the courthouse afterward, Debbie's attorney once again tried arguing his case to an audience of reporters. "There are probably not going to be any doctors in this case who are going to disagree with each other that Debbie is ill," apparently trying to strengthen his position with the public—and maybe with the prosecutor as well—that an insanity defense was valid and would be strong enough to convince a jury. But Sarina Fazan was on the air that night with a report that included a quote from the prosecutor, who said, "Our expert finds that she was sane during the time of the event." If the case went to trial, it was clearly going to be a battle of psychiatrists, which can be an extraordinarily difficult challenge for a jury to sort out.

Ms. Fazan also reported that Jack's mother was "pushing for a plea deal in hopes of avoiding a trial." Both Jack and his cousin had been through a tough time ever since that first phone call to the police. Seeing her son go on the witness stand to describe in detail all the sexual activities in front of a packed room of strangers and the press would be something any mother would dread. And the cross-examination would be vicious, trying to tear apart the stories of each of the boys, trying to make them contradict themselves and each other, trying to confuse them, trying to make it look as if *Jack* was the wrongdoer. Little wonder Mrs. Carpenter was hoping for a plea deal.

When the June 16 court date arrived, the prosecutor said he had not yet had time to study the report of his medical experts. He ask for another delay, but tried to make it sound as if he was only doing it out of respect for his courtroom opponent. "In fairness to the defense, they need time to contemplate" the report, the prosecutor told the judge.

Given the pattern of delays, Judge Timmerman, instead of setting yet another trial date, set July 18 for a hearing, leaving the trial date completely up in the air.

After months of wrangling over the terms of our divorce settlement—mostly a waste of time, since we didn't have enough assets to make the battle very worthwhile—I called Debbie and asked, "Why are you making things so miserable?"

She said, "It's not me, it's my mother." And I knew it was true—Joyce had been calling all the shots. Debbie said, "I've tried to talk to my parents. They say my vision is skewed. They don't want to listen." As the negotiator for the Beasley side, Joyce was insisting I pay off Debbie's credit card bills, wanted some money back that she had let me have to buy my way out of a car lease, and get this: she wanted me to give back the iPod Debbie had given me for my birthday, the one she had been filmed purchasing at Best Buy just after having sex with the boy. I guess I should have given it back; it was an unhappy reminder. Maybe I was just being stubborn. But even if it was a guilt gift, it *was* a gift, and I was hanging onto it.

Nonetheless, the phone call broke the dam. We reached a settlement, and in April the divorce at last became final.

Early in July, a Florida teacher's aide was sentenced for having sex with two teenagers. Though neither was a student at her school, she was given three years in prison and 12 years of probation. The judge said he was giving less than the maximum sentence because the boys had been "in some regard willing participants." Debbie and her parents must have been shaken on hearing the news.

In June the prosecutor finally put together a plea deal. Debbie and her parents considered it at length and finally turned it down, which could not have been an easy decision. This is a poker game for very high stakes. Mrs. Carpenter was still pushing hard for a prison sentence, and the prosecutor was steadfast in refusing to consider any deal that did not involve Debbie serving time. But the Beasleys were just as steadfast: no plea agreement would be acceptable that called for time behind bars. Nobody wants to go to prison, especially not someone as sweet, gentle, and vulnerable as Debbie.

Yet turning down the plea deal meant putting Debbie's fate in the hands of a jury and, if convicted, putting her sentence in the hands of a judge. And then facing a second jury and a second judge on the charges in Marion County. In the previous two years, five women had faced the same charges as Debbie in Florida's 5th Judicial Circuit. One of the five had been given a sentence of a year or less, to be served in jail. Two others had been sentenced to prison. Three out of five were serving time.

Judge Timmerman told both sides to be ready to start trial on December 5.

In his "courthouse steps" statement after the hearing, Debbie's attorney made a remark that triggered something of a furor: "To place an attractive young woman into that kind of hellhole is like putting a piece of raw meat in with the lions. I'm not sure that Debbie would be able to survive." Many people who heard the statement understood him to be saying that a gorgeous woman should never be sent to prison. *If you're beautiful enough, the laws and the rules of society don't apply to you,* he seemed to be arguing.

In fact, I believe the attorney's remark was calculated and extremely clever, in being addressed to one single person.

The victim.

Without compelling testimony from Jack, a jury would be much less likely to convict. Debbie's attorney would have found out how enormously popular Debbie had been as a teacher and how much this one boy had been attracted to her. It stood to reason that the boy was suffering at the idea that his testimony could send Debbie to prison.

"I'm not sure that Debbie would be able to survive." No matter what pressure the boy was under to testify, a statement like that would go a long way to make him change his mind, or even to take the stand and intentionally botch his testimony.

If this really was an intentional maneuver on the part of the attorney, it was brilliant.

In August, Debbie and Joyce had dinner together in the Red Lobster restaurant. Lisa York wasn't pleased to discover the pair, by now suspecting that Debbie was a full-fledged rival for Andrew's affections. "I knew he had gone to see her," Lisa says. He had been noting calls to and from her in his business log, and had even written down a visit to her. Lisa had noticed the entries. Andrew had tried to deny it. When Lisa showed him the items in his book, he had said, "No, no, we're just friends."

So for Lisa to see Debbie in the restaurant wasn't comfortable, and the situation became worse than she could have anticipated. Debbie had apparently come with malicious intent. She waited until Joyce went to the restroom and then confronted Lisa. "Ha, ha," Lisa reports Debbie as saying. "I had him, and he was good."

The attorney made another carefully timed strategic attack weeks later, clearly intended to embarrass the prosecution and taint their case in the public mind as he filed a nine-page motion concerning the photographs that had been taken of Debbie's body when she was arrested. Calling them "pornographic," he said, "They could not be any more explicit."

The local ABC news story that night began with "Just when it appeared the Debra LaFave case could not become any more salacious, a legal battle has erupted over the nude photos taken by police during the initial course of their investigation."

But it wasn't a battle. The State Attorney's office tried to defend the photos by explaining that when the victim of a sex crime gives explicit details of the perpetrator's anatomy, it's common for detectives to determine if the description is accurate. At the same time, they agreed the photos should be suppressed.

That was an appropriate decision. Under Florida's very liberal public-information laws, if the photos had been admitted into evidence in court, they would have become public information and been all over the Internet within the hour.

By seeming to cast the police and prosecution in a bad light and putting the prosecutor on the defensive, Debbie's attorney had scored again.

With the plea bargaining ended and the trial placed on calendar for a definite start date of Monday, December 5, interest in the case was once again drawing the attention of the national news shows and the cable television networks. *Inside Edition* and Court TV both notified the judge that they wanted permission to set up cameras in the courtroom, while other TV units from Germany and Japan also announced plans to cover the trial. Court TV indicated an interest in possible start-to-finish coverage for the anticipated two-week duration of the proceedings.

Jack's mother, already bothered by the idea of her son having to testify in court, was appalled by the possibility of his identity being revealed to a national television audience. Court TV, for its part, gave assurances that the identities would be hidden. Small relief, but if she had to, she could live with that.

Friday, November 22, 2005. If the Debra LaFave case had brought some surprises, none was as unexpected as this: with the trial less than two weeks away, the opposing attorneys and Debbie appeared in court to advise Judge Timmerman that a plea agreement had been reached.

After the months of negotiating, and after the earlier announcement that no agreement was possible, at the last minute a deal had been struck. Debbie stood in front of the judge, said that she understood the terms of the plea agreement and accepted them, and entered her plea of guilty to the charges.

The standoff over a plea agreement had finally shaken out in Debbie's favor. While she and her parents had adamantly refused to accept terms that included any prison time, Mrs. Carpenter had been just as insistent that any sentence without prison time would not be adequate punishment. But the difference had been resolved.

By then I had concluded for my own part that a sentence with no prison time would be outrageous, sending a bad message. Yet on a personal level I couldn't help but feeling pleased for her.

The terms didn't exactly give Debbie a free ride. It's not as if she was being let off with no punishment. The agreement listed 28 separate conditions she has to live by, the chief of which were three years of "community control" (house arrest), followed by an additional seven years of probation, and to become a registered sexual offender, required to notify the police of her address every time she moves, within Florida or anywhere she goes, for the rest of her life. Her neighbors will always have access to information that a sexual offender is living nearby.

House arrest requires her to be at home from 10 o'clock every night until six o'clock the next morning. Any time during the ten years of house arrest and probation that she is found in violation of any of the terms of her sentence, even the smallest infraction, she can be picked up and sent to prison to serve the remaining years.

She has to maintain a driving log and cannot drive alone except by permission of her community control or probation officer. She has to take an annual lie detector test and submit to warrantless searches of her person, residence, and vehicle at any time. She is not allowed to live within 1000 feet of any school, park, playground, or other places where children congregate. She has to complete a sex offender treatment program, continue in psychiatric treatment, and pay for therapy of the victim. And she cannot receive any financial compensation "from any celebrity, fame, infamy or notoriety achieved as a result of committing the crimes in this case."

A strict interpretation of one provision would mean that, until she completes the sex offender treatment program, probably two years at a minimum, she would be required to obtain court permission before having in her home any child she might give birth to unless supervised by an adult approved by the court. She could not even be in the presence of the daughter of her ex-boyfriend Andrew Beck without court approval. And if Debbie's taunt to Lisa was true, Andrew had already become something more than an ex-boyfriend.

What happened so suddenly to break the months-long stalemate over the sentencing terms? And to convince the prosecutor to agree to terms that involve no prison time, which he had been so insistent upon?

Not long before, the Tampa State Attorney's Office had written to Mrs. Corey, the mother of Jack's cousin, setting a date for her to bring her son in to be deposed. It seems curious they would want to interrogate the witness when they had not yet deposed the victim. But I think the prosecutor knew he was treading on thin ice.

The mother of the victim was already distressed over thoughts of her son having to sit in the witness chair for hours, maybe days, in a room packed with strangers, curiosity seekers, and reporters scribbling notes, as he was required to recount every sensational detail. It was the stuff of nightmares. It didn't seem possible, but the picture was about to get worse.

A phone call came with upsetting news from the Hillsborough prosecutor, on the road en route to Ocala for her nephew's deposition. In a conversation with the attorney for Court TV, he had learned that the plans called for hiding the identities of the boys, but that the Court TV cameras would *not* be masking the identities of the mothers.

Everyone who knew either of the families—every friend, every neighbor, every teacher at the boys' schools, every merchant the mothers dealt with, everyone they knew from their various organizations and activities—would see the mothers and immediately know who the boys were. Tabloid reporters would be scrapping with one another to see which among them would be the first to find some talkative local who would reveal the names of the families. The boys' identities would quickly become a national news item.

To Mrs. Carpenter, it seemed certain that the infamy of these events would pursue her son—to college, no matter where he went, and then dog him for the rest of his life, following him everywhere, marking him as different, making this unhappy time a subject of conversations and questions, accusations and off-color wink-wink jokes—forever.

There was additional, even more troubling news from the prosecutor. Court TV would not agree to a time delay that would enable bleeping out or cutting off the audio in case anyone inadvertently mentioned her son's name during trial. With 40 to 50 witnesses expected to testify, the chance of a slip seemed almost inevitable.

What the prosecutor had told Mrs. Carpenter in that phone call was the tipping point. Court TV had tipped the balance. While still on the phone with him, she asked the prosecutor what other options were available.

The question meant she was putting a mother's protectiveness of her son above her burning desire to see Debbie in prison.

The prosecutor would shortly amend the plea agreement to delete the term calling for prison, and also draw up an affidavit for Mrs. Carpenter to sign, stating her objections to allowing her son to testify and asking that the judge agree to the plea terms. The affidavit didn't state the most compelling reason: the powerful hand of Court TV.

The deposition of Cliff Corey took place on schedule, beginning at noon in the State Attorney's office on Pine Avenue, Ocala. His mother sat there for hours, listening to her son being gently questioned by Debbie's attorney. Though the boy had read through some of the police records the night before trying to refresh his memory, eighteen months had passed. The details had grown so cloudy that he had entire days mixed up, thinking he had driven them to Brick City Park for sex on the first Ocala trip, when it was actually on the second one. Debbie's attorney, who had been in trial on another big case, did not catch the mixup, though the Tampa prosecutor did.

The day after Cliff's deposition, the victim himself, Jack, was scheduled to be deposed in Tampa. With his mother's decision to accept a sentence for Debbie calling for no jail time, that deposition would not be needed. So the change in plans brought Mrs. Carpenter an additional benefit: saving her son the ordeal of bearing up under what his cousin had just gone through.

So almost everyone was ending up with what they wanted. Jack wouldn't have to testify, nor would his cousin. Mrs. Carpenter and her sister could go back to a semblance of more normal lives.

Debbie was getting off with no prison time—though with the constant threat of going to prison after all if she was caught violating any of her strict plea-agreement terms any time in the next ten years.

This wasn't the last act of the drama. Debbie was not off the hook yet.

She still had the charges in Marion County to face. And it was by no means certain that the prosecutor and the judge there would also agree to a sentence with no time behind bars.

Chapter 15
BACK FROM THE BRINK

"THE PRESS WENT wild."

That was publicist Karen Ammond's phrase to describe the few days immediately following the announcement of the plea bargain and Debbie's guilty plea. The network and cable interview shows clamored for some way to explain to their viewers how a teacher could have sex with a student and get off with no prison time. And they were looking to me for answers.

I had agreed at the beginning to do just a couple of interviews as a way of putting to rest all the foolish questions about whether Debbie did what she did because I was gay or had some performance problems. What was meant to be a short, one-topic effort had morphed into my becoming an "expert" whom the programs called on whenever there was another sex-with-student breaking story.

And on this one, of course, I was *the* expert.

In the two days after Debbie's sentencing, I appeared on an incredible eight shows, practically a non-stop 48 hours—with Greta Van Susteren, Nancy Grace, Rita Cosby, and *Inside Edition*, *Fox News*, *The Early Show*, and more. On top of that, *Today* and *Good Morning America* ran stories using archive footage from my earlier interviews with them.

Greta asked me, "If I met [Debbie] in a social situation, what do you think my impression of her would be? What's she like?"

I answered, "She's very reserved for the most part, quiet, very friendly. She's been portrayed as somewhat of a monster in the media," I said, "but she does have some great qualities and I think for the most part when people meet her they do generally like her."

In answer to a question about whether there were any signs I might've seen, I said, "I think there were signs, some flags that I ignored at the time. She was being treated and I thought the treatments would allow her to live a normal life. But I think generally it came as a surprise to everybody. She seemed fairly well grounded for the most part and seemed like a normal, everyday person."

It's a weird experience for a young banker from an off-the-beaten-track Florida city to find himself sought after by network television shows. But I wasn't in much danger of growing a swelled head. This story would soon be yesterday's news, and I fully expected to be yesterday's expert. As much as I enjoyed flying around the country at the networks' expense, being driven around in chauffeured town cars, being catered to, fussed over, tended to by a make-up lady, and sitting in front of the lights and cameras to talk to famous television personalities, I had no illusions it would last.

Nor would all the letters and e-mails. I know I'm considered a reasonably good-looking guy, but I was amused, bewildered, and somewhat dazzled by the entirely unexpected deluge of communications from ladies who wanted to introduce me to their daughter, a niece, or a coworker. Or themselves. Can you begin to imagine how weird this is?

I did not take up any of the invitations.

After Karen Ammond placed me in my first national television interviews, letters and e-mails began to arrive from many people who had connections to a similar story of a female teacher involved in a sexual relationship with a young boy, many of them pleading for advice. Karen and I began to sense a need, and that recognition led us on a path to launching a documentary film project. *After School,* now in production, explores the minds and personalities of the teachers who have committed these crimes, and examines the impact on students, families, and school officials.

On a higher level, the film is looking for solutions. The film will awaken and, I hope, even shock the viewer. We want people to be aware of what's going on in their children's schools and in all aspects of their children's lives that involve supervision by adults.

One of our producers with Karen is actor Efren Ramirez, who played Pedro in the film *Napoleon Dynamite.* He's a young man who when not filming a movie actively speaks to middle school and high school kids, offering them encouragement and motivation to reach their dreams. Efren saw the potential in our documentary and was enthusiastic about becoming part of it.

The website for the show, AfterSchoolDocumentary.com, had over 400,000 visitors in its first two months and became one of the most visited of any documentary sites on the Internet—testimony to the intense interest in the subject.

Debbie had told me stories about her relationship with Andrew Beck that made him sound like someone well below the standard of what she deserved and what she could have had. But now she was apparently glad to have him back in her life—although the way Lisa York tells the story, Debbie wasn't being very gracious about her triumph. The relationships were complicated, and becoming nasty. Lisa and Andrew were no longer living together, following a second break-up. Andrew, to his credit, still felt emotional ties both to Abby, his daughter by Lisa, and to Lisa's older child, Taylor.

It's understandable that Lisa, the jilted fiancé, wouldn't be very happy about having Debbie in her children's lives. She thought that Debbie had talked on the phone at least once to her younger daughter Abby. When she complained to Andrew, he claimed it wasn't true, that Lisa was just trying to stir up trouble.

Only Debbie and Lisa know the facts of the situation for certain, but Lisa's version is that Debbie began phoning her "excessively—calling me a bitch, laughing at me. I had to change my cell phone number three times."

Finally, Lisa decided it was time for action. She tracked down Debbie's Probation Officer, Mike Cotignola, and called him up. He listened to the story, she says, and told her, "You can come down and sign an affidavit, we'll present it to the judge and see if the judge believes there's enough evidence to revoke her probation. Or I can sit down with her and remind her of her freedom."

Lisa agreed to let the Probation Officer try to handle the issue by speaking to Debbie. He did, and Debbie denied she had ever spoken with Abby. The Probation Officer explained to Debbie what would happen if she ever had contact with a child without permission of the court, a warning that could not have failed to leave Debbie shaken.

Still, Lisa was distraught. The girls were having a hard time adjusting—Taylor because she had more or less "adopted" Andrew as a loving father to replace the real father who was no longer in touch, Abby because Andrew was her birth daddy, the only father she had ever known. Lisa was happy to see Andrew spending time with the girls, but the thought of their being in Debbie's company was scary. Debbie's behavior on the phone calls seemed so erratic. Andrew was defending her, telling Lisa that Debbie was good for the children. That wasn't what Lisa wanted to hear.

She went to court, filing a paper that spelled out Debbie's taunting conversations at the Red Lobster and the phone calls, and asking in effect: "Give me a protective order to keep Debra

LaFave away from my children." But it didn't work. The judge told Lisa no protective order would be issued unless there were grounds for believing that Debbie offered some threat of violence toward the children.

I thought Debbie must be in a very sad state indeed to have made those restaurant visits that sounded as if they could have served no purpose at all other than to flaunt her power over Andrew.

Lisa's older daughter Taylor, looking back months later, admired Andrew for "having done a great job of letting me know that it's not my fault my real father is not around, that it's my father's loss." Yet Taylor clearly felt betrayed by the way that Andrew, who had shown such love as surrogate father to her and as father to his biological daughter Abby, had left them and their mother for another woman. "As long as he's with Debra, he will never be the fit father that he wants to be, not even 4 Abby," she wrote.

The child's love had been shattered, just as mine had—and both by the same woman.

The whole cast of characters in the Debra LaFave drama reassembled once again on Thursday, December 8, this time in a new setting: the courtroom of Circuit Court Judge Hale R. Stancil in Ocala. Debbie arrived smiling and joking, confident in the outcome of the day's proceedings. The first ill omen came when she walked through the courthouse metal detector and set off the alarm; the problem turned out to be the electronic ankle bracelet she was already required to wear, to verify she's at home when she's supposed to be.

When the court session started, her smile faded quickly. The judge announced that "The court is not going to, at this time, accept the plea that has been presented."

Jack's mother was stunned. In one of those odd shifts that sometimes happen in life, the two women were on the same side about this. Both wanted it over, the uncertainties put behind them. For different reasons, both wanted Debbie's plea bargain accepted—Debbie because it would mean no prison, Jack's mother because it would mean her son would not have to testify.

After the hearing, Debbie's attorney told the crowd of reporters in a grand understatement, "There were some unexpected developments today in court."

It was three months before the case was ready for another hearing before Judge Stancil. Once again the action didn't play out as expected.

The prosecutor, Stacy Youmans, explained to the judge that the settlement terms with no prison time were based on the psychological damage that would be done to the boy if he were forced to testify. She introduced Dr. Martin Lazoritz, of Gainesville, a psychiatrist and professor of psychiatry at the University of Florida. Based on 90 minutes spent meeting with the boy and his mother, the doctor described the youngster to the Court as "not a very verbal, talk-about-your-feelings kind of kid" who "needs to be able to play basketball in anonymity."

Though 90 minutes sounds like a very short time for forming a professional opinion in such a complex matter, the psychiatrist told the judge that the teen "would be revictimized by the system" and "would always be plagued" if forced to testify.

Judge Stancil wasn't buying. "While the victim may have been 14 when the incident occurred, that was in June of 2004. A year and a half has passed since that time." In fact, Jack had turned 16, he was 6 feet tall, on the honor roll in high school, and some who knew him thought he could easily have been taken for a college student. Would this young man really suffer an emotional trauma from testifying?

It's not uncommon in a case like this—it happened in the OJ mess—that the victim's family files suit for damages against the perpetrator. In this case, a lawsuit would require that the boy testify in court. Reasoning that if the youngster could testify in a civil suit, then he was fit to testify in the criminal case, the judge asked the mother whether there would be a civil action.

In the view of some observers, the mother saw this as an attack on her integrity. I wasn't there, but people who were say that she told the judge it was none of his business. Strong words. But it wasn't the only slap in the face Judge Stancil would be stung with before this was over.

Despite the mother's outburst, the judge went on to make it clear that he didn't feel under any obligation to accept a plea bargain just because the prosecution and the defense had agreed to it. "I think I need to give it a little more thought," he announced. "Then I'll be in a position to let you know." His decision might take as long as 10 days, he said.

Many in Tampa and elsewhere applauded the judge's reluctance to let Debbie off with no prison time. Sure, it would be uncomfortable for the kid to testify, but the need for justice demanded that he bite the bullet and take the stand. At least, that's the way lots of folks saw it.

Ric Ridgway didn't see it like that. As the boss of the State Attorney's Office for the 5th Judicial Circuit of Florida, overseeing the work of 75 Assistant State Attorneys in a five-county area, Ridgway was now the man calling the shots for the State in Debbie's case.

As for whether women are treated differently than men in these cases, he says, "Gender is not [a question] that enters into our treatment of a case; it simply doesn't matter. I read a letter to the editor in our local newspaper that said the boy couldn't testify because he hadn't gotten the grin wiped off yet. I understand those attitudes exist out there. To a prosecutor, [the sex of the perpetrator] is just not a factor."

On the issue of taking the case to trial, he believes there was no way the case could have gone to trial and still protect the interests of the youngster.

"First of all," he argues, "they had raised an insanity defense. They were prepared to put on certain testimony of her version of what happened. [The boy] would have been the only person who could have rebutted that. And he would've had to testify, at least in rebuttal, to say, 'No, that's not really what happened.'"

And even if the state had put on its case without calling the boy, Ridgway maintains, there's no way his identity could have been kept secret. "He would be identified at some point in the proceedings by somebody. His name and identity would have been out there—somebody would have mentioned it. And that was the problem—what that would have done to him."

This wasn't just his own opinion, Ridgway says. "The psychiatrist that we retained to examine this boy is probably one of the most qualified in this state, board certified in child, adolescent, and forensic psychiatry. His opinion was that it would cause severe trauma to the boy that would take four to six years to recover."

But what kind of message would it send if Judge Stancil followed the example of the judge in Tampa and agreed to a sentence without prison time? Wouldn't that be the same as saying, *Oh, this really isn't such a serious crime after all*?

Ridgway answers that challenge by offering a different scenario: "What kind of message does it send to a young person who comes home and tells their parents what their teacher has done, and the parents have seen what [the boy in this case] got dragged through on national television. These parents think, 'You know what? We're not dragging our kid through that. We're not calling the cops.'"

It wasn't that Judge Stancil didn't appreciate the potential damage to the boy. He told an interviewer, "Any time you have a case where you have a child victim who has got to testify, you run the risk of traumatizing the child further. That's always an issue." But he went on to say, "Each case is different. Each individual is different. You have to consider their education, their background."

Yet the written statement from Jack's mother had to be

weighing heavily on the judge. Her paper said in part, "Because of the media coverage...I fear that proceeding to trial will negatively affect my son's emotional and psychological well-being, and will have an immediate and long-term negative impact on him." The document went on to say that her son had "made it clear to me that he does not want to testify and wants to resume his life in as normal a manner as possible."

Although Judge Stancil had promised to make his decision within ten days, it was nearly twice that long before he held another hearing in the case. Tuesday, March 21, turned out to be the most explosive day yet.

When court was called to order, Judge Stancil handed down a decision that was highly critical of the prosecution. The document was in fact a lengthy series of complaints aimed at both prosecutors—Mike Sinacore in Hillsborough County, Ric Ridgway as the head prosecutor for the area that includes Marion County—and it ran to six pages.

The judge wrote of his understanding that "Certainly, no 16-year-old male wants to be examined and cross-examined in a public forum regarding every minute detail of a sexual encounter, which very well may be viewed by some as entertainment." Yet he noted that from reports of interviews with the boy, "It does not appear that the victim had any difficulty describing the incidents in question" to the investigators—leaving the obvious question for the listener or reader to fill in: So why should it be such a problem to repeat the same statements in the courtroom?

"The victim," he wrote, "does not have a constitutionally recognized right of privacy in the context of a judicial proceeding, which is a public event that by its very nature denies certain aspects of privacy."

Judge Stancil complained about the failure of the prosecution to present more experts to bolster their case of the damage the boy would suffer by testifying, and that he had not even been presented testimony from the investigators who had interviewed the victim and "could have been called to testify regarding their impressions of his ability to give testimony." He complained about the failure to use the services of a victim advocate, even though "There are victim/witness advocates available in the State Attorney's Office, the Ocala Police Department, and the Marion County Sheriff's Office." (The prosecutor had failed to let the judge know that advocates had, in fact, been on hand for sessions with both boys.)

The Court had not been presented any evidence that the victim had been deposed, which "could have...demonstrate[d] his difficulty in testifying."

About the psychiatrist, Dr. Lazoritz, the judge complained that his testimony was "somewhat less than convincing" and that "meeting with the victim for 90 minutes or less seems to this Court inadequate if the victim has in fact suffered mental damage as a result of the incidents in question."

He also appeared annoyed that the State Attorneys had not pursued other ways of proceeding to trial that would have avoided the possibility of revealing the boy's name. "Finally," Judge Stancil wrote, "the parties could have requested the Court meet with the victim in camera"—that is, with the courtroom closed to all but the participants in the trial.

In summary, he found that "the parties have failed to present sufficient justification to accept the...plea agreement" that calls for a lighter sentence than the minimum spelled out in the Florida sentencing guidelines.

All of this led up to his concluding statement, a very strong condemnation of the State's position:

"It is the opinion of this Court that accepting the proposed plea agreement would undermine the credibility of this Court, and the criminal justice system as a whole, and would erode public confidence in our schools. Accepting the proposed plea agreement would likewise send the message that if enough publicity is generated, and the media's interest continues long enough, and because of that interest the victim does not wish to testify, a defendant can avoid an appropriate sentence.

"Quite frankly," Judge Stancil had written, "if the allegations against the Defendant are true, the agreed-upon sentence shocks the conscience of this Court."

The final statement, in the formal language of the law, said, "It is, therefore, ORDERED: The proposed below-guidelines plea agreement is hereby rejected."

Judge Stancil confirmed to those in the courtroom that the trial would begin on April 10.

It's likely that Debbie was not upset by what seemed to be a huge setback for her. I believe the prosecutor had already told Debbie's attorney a startling secret: Judge Stancil thought the decision about going to trial was his, but the prosecutor intended to have the last word.

The judge who had been critical of the prosecution was being repaid with a slap in the face. The Florida State Attorney for the 5th Judicial District, Ric Ridgway, issued an order called a writ of *nolle prosequi*—which can be translated as "unwilling to proceed" or "unwilling to attack." In legal-speak, it means "we are not going to take this case to trial." All charges in Marion County were being dropped, leaving Debbie to serve only the sentence already imposed in Hillsborough County.

Ridgway was too tactful to point out that months earlier, in a case involving a 37-year-old woman and a boy of only 13, Judge Stancil had accepted a plea agreement that involved probation alone, with no prison time. Why then and not now? The answer should have been obvious: the other lady wasn't a teacher.

Nonetheless, the judge was being overruled by the prosecutor. Not the first time in history, but extremely rare.

Before the afternoon was over, Debbie was holding a press conference. This was not a spur-of-the-moment reaction to unexpected happy news from the prosecutor. In fact, early that morning, Debbie's attorney had notified the local media. Key reporters received both a phone call from the attorney's office, and a 911 ("urgent") on their pagers. So it's clear that the prosecutor's rebuke to the judge was pre-arranged.

Soon after the news had come from Ocala, Debbie was sitting in front of a crowd of cameras and print reporters. Reading from handwritten notes on a piece of yellow paper, she began by thanking her lawyer for "believing in me and my illness," a curious statement that seemed to say "for believing that an illness really caused me to do what I did." But then she referred to "illnesses that can cause good people to do bad things," which sounded very much like a person still not ready to take responsibility for the harm she had done.

"I pray with all my heart that the young man and his family will be able to move on with their lives. Again, I offer my deepest apology." That sounded sincere; *Great*, I thought. But then she immediately shifted gears, once again focusing not on any misdeed of her own but on the "illness": "I have been undergoing extensive therapy and believe it has helped me tremendously."

And she concluded with a little finger-pointing at the press. "I would hope that all media outlets would let us peacefully move on."

Missing from the statement was anything about taking responsibility or holding any feelings of remorse, and the first question, from Sarina Fazan, was about whether she did feel remorse. Debbie answered, "Absolutely. Absolutely, Sarina," an answer that avoided saying directly that she was remorseful or that she took any blame. *It wasn't me but my mental condition that was to blame*, she seemed to be saying yet again.

Answering another question, Debbie acknowledged the young man standing behind her alongside her parents was her fiancé. This was Andrew Beck, the same on-again/off-again boyfriend who Debbie had enticed away from the girl he was engaged to and had fathered a child with. Debbie and Andrew were engaged but had no fixed plans for marriage, Debbie suggested. "I've known him for 20 years now," she said. But "We're just going to take it day by day."

Asked about the victim's mother, she said simply, "I pray for her."

A mention that "my family and friends are all that matter," must have sounded curious to people like Jeremy Jackson, Avery Hampton, and Pam Glas, who Debbie (or her mother) had cut off. Then Debbie attacked the press, sounding almost hostile. "If anything I am tired of the media. I don't think that one time has the media brought up the subject of my bipolar. And I challenge you to read a book or article on bipolar illness."

Asked about her future, she replied, "Right now, I'm going through a class that's online for journalism. I think that God has given me a great outlet to write and I would hope that I could reach people through writing."

One reporter saw the humor in this, exclaiming with a smile, "After all this, you want to become one of us?!" At last Debbie softened and showed that she, too, had a sense of humor and a touch of humanity. "Yes!" she said, adding, "Because, you know what? Some of you have a great heart and I am able to see that, through your writing and your expressions on TV."

Another reporter asked a question about her "greatest regret in this whole ordeal."

"My greatest regret," Debbie answered, "would be that I put this young man through this." She was skirting close to a sincere expression but again couldn't stick with it. Without pausing for breath, she once more shifted the blame: "The media has totally taken it out of proportion. He's suffered even more so by the media's actions. He is a young man and his privacy has been violated by the media."

Should I praise Debbie for her new-found religion? Or accuse her of using it as a crutch? "I'm a strong Christian woman," she told the reporters, "and I believe that God has a path for me and this was just a bump in the road." I was incredulous that she could dismiss her actions with a trite phrase that made them seem so small and insignificant.

She said, "I know that I'm a good woman despite everything that's been said about me."

Asked if, through therapy, she'd come to any understanding of why this happened—the same question I had asked over and over—she shrugged and said, "Why it happened? I don't know. That's a lifelong... I'm going to be in therapy for a *long* time."

They finished then, and the family group walked out, Debbie's left hand tucked ever so slightly under Andrew's arm, Andrew walking ahead of her just as I had seen him do on campus all those years earlier in what seems now like another lifetime. Some things never change.

At least no one can claim this outcome was made in Debbie's favor because she or her parents are powerful, connected, influential, or monied. Sometimes, apparently, "gorgeous" trumps all.

Chapter 16
LOOKING BACK, LOOKING AHEAD

WHY?

THE QUESTION that plagued me—and I think the question Debbie must have been referring to in her final press conference when she talked about expecting to be in therapy for a long time—has several possible answers, none of them an excuse, none of them really satisfying, none of them winning any kind of universal agreement among the experts.

Even if there aren't any definitive answers, the question deserves to be considered.

Could her deviant behavior be an outgrowth of her childhood sexual abuse? A two-year study sponsored by the Centers for Disease Control and Prevention, Atlanta, involving 17,000 adults, found that an extraordinary *25 percent* of women reported some form of childhood sexual abuse. Those in the group who had experienced abuse were more likely to attempt suicide and to suffer from depression.

Looking at this question in another light, though, Professor David Finkelhor says that an early rape experience can leave a female "more sexualized and responding more in a sexual dimension." Dr. Finkelhor, who was educated at Harvard and the University of Paris, with a Ph.D. from the University of New Hampshire, has been called the number-one authority in the U.S. on childhood sexual abuse, and he's authored or co-authored a dozen books on the subject. While there is "some disagreement" on the question of long-term impacts, he says, the research shows that it's "more frequent to abuse among those who were abused." He explains that "abuse survivors often have a sense of being 'defective' that might lead them into wanting validation from others."

Dr. Finkelhor also says, "There is a considerable body of research that suggests that one reason why many sex abusers choose child partners is because they feel more in control and less vulnerable to judgment and manipulation. They may have fears, anxieties, and traumas about relationships with peers, and they can overcome these in relations with children."

Los Angeles psychiatrist Mark Goulston, a former professor of psychiatry at UCLA, says that childhood rape can lead to choosing a series of bad partners, exactly as Debbie had told me happened in her relationships before me. Choosing bad partners, Dr. Goulston says, is based on a fantasy of choosing people who treat her as badly as the rapist while telling herself, "But I'll get him to love me."

Another suggestion comes from psychiatrist and University of Connecticut psychiatry professor Catherine Lewis. Women teachers who sexually assault a boy "tend to be socially naïve and have a desperate need to be liked by their students," Dr. Lewis said in an interview with *Time* magazine's Melba Newsome. Lacking emotional maturity, they feel more comfortable with a young boy because the relationship "feels less threatening."

As if describing Debbie, Dr. Lewis said, "They typically have had…poor relationships with their fathers as well as a pattern of abusive relationships." And they tend to connect with the boy in "a very idealized, romanticized and intense relationship, almost like a fantasy."

Could a devout, caring, supportive, loving mother be a contributing factor? If she's also domineering—domineering to the point of leaving the child feeling powerless—the answer appears to be yes.

Mark Goulston: "If you have an over-controlling mother, you can become desperate to become free of that." In addition, "In a household with an over-controlling mother, there is frequently a passive father who is not really effective in keeping the mother under wraps." This can lead to resentment, Dr. Goulston says, a feeling of disrespect towards men "because you see your father is not doing enough to protect you."

Out of this can come a feeling that "either someone's going to control you or you're going to control them. So having sex with a younger boy could be an expression of 'I'm going to be in control now.'"

In addition, this psychiatrist says, "In a sick way she might have been deriving a double benefit: getting even with people who scarred her when she was young, and also getting to model what she saw from her mother, which was, 'If you don't control others, they're going to control you.'"

There's another possible explanation to this ultimately unanswerable question of why: Debbie's depression and anxiety, and the medications she was on for these conditions.

If Debbie had gone to trial, her attorney had decided to stake everything on being able to convince a jury that her actions with the boy were caused by a mental condition so severe that she was entitled to a verdict of "not guilty by reason of insanity." He was prepared to introduce psychiatrists who would testify that the acts were beyond her control because of her bipolar disorder.

A person with bipolar disorder passes through moods that cycle from depression to a highly energized manic state, a condition that can be disabling. In Debbie's case, it would explain a lot about the changes I watched her go through in things like coming home and falling asleep naked in the middle of the afternoon, canceling social plans at the last minute, and unwillingness to do housework, which could all be signs of a depressive state. It would also explain those flights of unchecked enthusiasm when she would start talking and go on and on and on without letting anyone else say a word, and the moment in grad school when Pam wanted to tell her to shut up.

Insanity may have been the best defense tactic, given all the evidence that the police and prosecutors had gathered, but it was risky on two grounds. If she had been found not guilty by reason of insanity, she could then have expected to be placed in a mental institution and held there for some unspecified length of time, until the doctors decided that she could safely return to society. Since Debbie was unlikely to re-offend, that might have meant a short stay. But in fact, doctors tend to err on the side of caution, and many in her shoes have ended up remaining confined longer than they would have if they had gone to prison.

And then there's the other problem: trying to convince the jury that her illness kept her from knowing the nature and quality of the act she was doing, or knowing the act was wrong. This might have been especially difficult given the testimony that the boys would have presented about Debbie saying she knew what she was doing was wrong.

Experts who work with this subject every day thought that the defense tactic strained credulity. The director of the National Child Protection Training Center, Victor Vieth, said in a public forum, "The argument that some mental illness so lowered her inhibitions that she couldn't control her sexual activity is ridiculous. If that were the case, she'd be having sex on the street randomly with passersby." He went on to insist that, "If you can control when, where and how you're going to have sex, you can control whether or not you'll have it in the first place."

In addition to which, "It is," says Del Mar, California psychologist Richard Levak, "extremely difficult to get a verdict of not guilty by reason of insanity." Bipolar disorder might be used as an argument in favor of mitigating the sentence, according to Levak, but "I've testified as an expert witness in at least half a dozen cases" where that defense was attempted, and "it wasn't successful in any of them."

All of this means that Debbie was incredibly fortunate that she didn't have to go to trial. Did the criminal justice system act appropriately in Debbie's case?

The prosecutors could have required that the boy testify. Yes, certainly it would have been difficult for him—I'm sympathetic to all the reasons why he and his mother were so eager that the boy not testify. But as Judge Stancil in Ocala pointed out, he was 16 years old by then, no longer a kid. For his protection, arrangements could even have been made for him to testify in a closed courtroom. Beyond that, there's legal precedent that would have allowed him to testify over live closed-circuit video from another room, with his face obscured.

Even without his testimony, the prosecutors had ample evidence: The testimony of the boy's cousin, an eyewitness to Debbie having sex with the boy. DNA evidence irrefutably proving that the boy had had sexual contact with Debbie. The Best Buy photographs showing Debbie and the two boys together. The boy's highly detailed and accurate description of Debbie's naked body, even of the way her pubic hair is shaved.

And those phone calls, those inescapable, joyously depressing calls in which Debbie herself admits by inference that she has had sex with the boy on three occasions.

No one wanted to see the victim or his mother suffer more than they already had. Still, allowing Debbie to evade a trial and to get off with no prison time was unwise, inappropriate, and a travesty of justice. I agree with the statements made by Judge Stancil in rejecting the plea agreement and calling for the case to go to trial: "[A]ccepting the proposed plea agreement would undermine the credibility of this Court."

And I applaud his courage in writing that the proposed plea agreement "shocks the conscience of this Court."

Although it's natural enough that we ask *Why?* when confronted with a mystifying behavior like Debbie's, there isn't any answer, no matter how compelling or convincing, that excuses the behavior.

Childhood rape? Vast numbers who have suffered that trauma have gone on to live productive lives without assaulting others.

Bipolar? Other victims of the syndrome, law-abiding and respectable, are distressed by its being used as an excuse for behavior like Debbie's.

A side effect of her medications? That's the "Twinkie defense." Again, millions use those drugs without crossing a line anything like the line that Debbie crossed.

There is, very simply, no explanation that could serve as an excuse.

As for Debbie's statements at the press conference after the charges were dropped, I think they were, to put it politely, unfortunate. In her prepared statement, she had not a single word to say about having acted in a repugnant, indefensible way and causing a young man irreparable damage. Instead she focused on statements about her "illness," going only far enough to offer her "deepest apology" to the boy and his family. She had no apology for her own parents, who now have a mortgage on their once-paid-off house, and she had none for me.

Only in answer to a reporter's question did she finally acknowledge that her "greatest regret" was that she had "put this young man through this," a statement for which she earns no praise because it was immediately followed by her attempt to shift blame to the media for having "totally taken it out of proportion."

Worst of all for me was her inadvertent admission that she has not accepted responsibility, in her unfortunate statement that "I believe…this was just a bump in the road."

A bump in the road!

And what about the victim? How do male students who engage in sex with female teachers fare later in life?

Another of the most respected experts in this field is Robert J. Shoop, a professor of educational law at Kansas State University who has served as an expert witness in nearly fifty cases of sexual harassment and sexual abuse in schools. Dr. Shoop points out that for many boys in this situation, the initial reaction may come when the relationship ends: "A boy sexualizes the relationship, has an experience beyond his years, and then may experience trauma when the relationship breaks off." But the opposite may also be true. While "some seem not to be very affected in the immediate aftermath," Dr. David Finkelhor points out, others "have serious developmental reactions."

This view is confirmed in a U.S. Department of Education study of literature on the subject conducted by Professor Charol Shakeshaft of Hofstra University, an internationally recognized researcher in the area of gender patterns in classroom interactions. Her much-quoted 2003-2004 effort, titled *Educator Sexual Misconduct*, found that "For most children, being the victim of sexual misconduct does damage that lasts well into adulthood, and for most it is never fully repaired.... Child sexual abuse targets lose trust in adults and authority figures, suffer physical ailments and lowered immune systems, and do less well in school." Many become school dropouts or cut classes, and they are more likely to be substance abusers.

Dr. Finkelhor has found that abused youngsters are more likely to have difficulty forming intimate relationships and more likely to experience a sense of betrayal and shame similar to a victim of incest.

Psychiatrist Mark Goulston says that at the time, "a boy could feel macho and the envy of his friends. But as you get older, often in the mid- to late-twenties, you often look back at something you did when you were younger and feel a sense of foolishness—'I can't believe I did that' or 'I can't believe I thought that was so cool.' Along with this may be a realization that 'I was just perpetuating a sickness in her.' The more bizarre the act, the more likely it will kick back."

But he, too, stresses that every individual responds differently, and the reaction of this particular boy might not be negative. "He might well go through life looking back happily on what happened," Dr. Goulston says.

In fact, three of the men interviewed for this book acknowledged experiences with an adult woman they had themselves had in their teens. All three independently volunteered the information, remembering the experience as happy and beneficial, with no later negative consequences.

Dr. Levak offers what he acknowledges to be a "very politically incorrect" observation: "I know a number of young men for whom it has been a positive experience. It can be validation for a young boy's sexual prowess. In my 25 years of practice, I've heard both very positive and very negative."

But psychological damage is more likely, Dr. Shoop says, when they boy realizes this is something most people feel was wrong. Apparently the boy's reaction afterward and in later life depends to a great extent on how the relationship ends, whether it becomes known, and if so, how the parents react. Dr. Richard Levak says that in his psychology practice, if parents come in because they have learned that their teenage son has had sex with an older woman, sometimes they "make it into a huge catastrophe. In some cases the way parents respond can frighten the child more than the actual event."

It's the isolated case with some particularly attention-getting feature—a victim of 11 or 12 or 13, or a spectacularly good-looking teacher—that draws national attention, but as I began to research the subject for my increasingly frequent appearances on television interview shows, I was appalled to find out how common this offense is. Robert Shoop said the estimate that one in 10 children is subjected to abuse is not an exaggeration. The actual number may be larger, he said, because of underreporting of the problem.

In her study for the Department of Education, Professor Shakeshaft concluded that "More than 4.5 million students endure sexual misconduct by employees at their schools, from inappropriate jokes all the way to forced sex. About 7% report physical sexual misconduct."

Based on the studies she cites in her paper, Dr. Shakeshaft also notes that "About one-third of those cases are female teachers to male students"—which seems an extraordinarily high proportion, much higher than I would have imagined.

Hostile Hallways, a 2001 study sponsored by the American Association of University Women on sexual harassment in schools, found a significant increase in the percentage of schools that now have harassment policies in place—policies that the students themselves are aware of.

If schools can take action against sexual harassment, they could certainly be doing the same about teacher sexual abuse. But as the AAUW study points out, machines can detect guns in book bags; identifying inappropriate behavior demands that we all work together.

Devising a prevention program for this type of crime becomes complicated, of course, when the victim doesn't feel victimized but instead welcomes or even seeks the relationship. For boys in particular, who are taught by society and their peers that seeking sexual conquests is normal and desirable, a connection with any older woman, teacher or otherwise, may be seen to confer special bragging rights. Dr. Leo Cotter, a Tampa therapist who specializes in dealing with sexual offenders, speaks about males who describe the goal as "score as much as possible, double the number, and brag to your friends."

Another complicating factor, oddly enough, is that the women who are guilty of these crimes are often the ones least likely to be suspected. Dr. Shoop: "Some of these women who have sex with children go to Sunday school every Sunday, dressed very demurely, never use profanity, and are very discreet in their personal lifestyles," (a description that largely applies to Debbie, with the exception of the skimpy clothing she sometimes wore to work). "Once you cross the line into a school," Dr. Shoop says, "most adults have an ability to set up a screen that understands which times and which places certain behavior is inappropriate." From what he knows about Debra LaFave, Dr. Shoop sees her as fitting the pattern of other prominent cases.

Two of the specialists whose views are presented in this chapter, David Finkelhor and Charol Shakeshaft, have offered ideas about warning signs of behavior: things teachers and school administrators can watch for that may suggest a staff member is tending toward sexually inappropriate acts. From their ideas, I've compiled a list of possible warning signs:

- Adapting behavior like the students and treating students as if they were peers—trying to be "cool"
- Allowing one student to spend time in the classroom during their study hall or after school when there is no academic reason for them being there
- Buying gifts for a student
- Engaging in flirting or teasing remarks and behavior
- Telling sexual jokes or making sexual innuendos
- Frequent touching, patting, or hugging
- Repeatedly contacting the student at home
- Locking classroom doors

To these lists, I would add an item of my own:

- Dressing inappropriately, especially in a way that seems provocative—short skirts, low-cut blouses, tight, form-fitting shirts or sweaters.

Dr. Shoop is quick to point out that "Any of these signs taken individually may be perfectly innocent." Each, though, should be seen as an alert message. He describes a process called "grooming," in which the adult, sometimes consciously, sometimes unconsciously, progressively erodes the child's self-defenses, leading the child to bond with the adult.

"This is normally an incremental process," he explains, "where the child might initially be told simply, 'You're very mature and grown up, and talking to you is just like talking to an adult.'" This might be followed by an off-color joke or sexual innuendos and might proceed from there to buying gifts.

(The above list of warning signs, I note unhappily, could have been assembled just by watching Debbie in the school setting, early in 2004 and especially in the couple of months leading up to her offenses.)

Hofstra's Professor Shakeshaft insists that schools could do a much better job of spotting predatory teachers in time, and Professor Finkelhor suggests a place to begin: by making certain everyone in the field recognizes that "it's inevitable and normal for people working with adolescents to experience sexual feelings, and it's inevitable and normal for the kids, as well." Accepting the feelings is a first step to dealing appropriately with them. "Teachers need to learn to identify the signs in themselves, and in the students."

And that's not difficult. What's needed for all adults who work with children—and for the children as well—isn't so much training as raising awareness. With teachers in particular, who are pressed by so many conflicting demands, calling for yet another training program would probably be mostly ignored anyway. What I'm proposing could likely be handled in a single session early in the school year, with appropriate reminders every month or two in the form of a memo from the principal or an item or article in the teachers' newsletter from the school district. For clergymen, Scout leaders, Little League coaches, ballet teachers and all others who take part in activities that make them authority figures to children, the messages are just as important, even though the practicalities of delivering them would differ.

Note that part of every awareness session needs to be aimed at increasing the empathy of the adults by leading them to an understanding of how sexual contact with an authority figure damages the youngster. Adults generally have little understanding of the long-term damage that could result. Gaining an appreciation of this makes them far less likely to overlook danger signs they might observe in their peers.

From Professor Finkelhor and others who contributed input for this chapter, I've assembled just a few ideas of the kinds of elements that might be included in an awareness session on the subject:

- Appreciating the ways in which an inappropriate relationship is damaging to a young person and is contrary to the values of the profession and the norms of the society
- Presenting ways for teachers to recognize warning signs in themselves, in other teachers, and in students
- Empowering students to report suspicious or inappropriate behavior
- Offering concrete procedures for teachers who recognize they are being tempted (such as speaking to a peer or a counselor about their feelings)
- Reminding that those whose jobs include time with students individually, such as music teachers or coaches, are more likely to succumb to the temptation to sexually abuse than other teachers—and thus need to be even more on guard
- Offering guidelines for recognizing when a teacher needs to take himself/herself out of contact with a particular student
- Providing pointers that teachers can use for talking to young people about these issues, in a way that is compassionate but makes the boundaries clear.

On that last point, Professor Shakeshaft comments that we don't yet have any programs for students to tell them that in school, at church, or in a youth organization, an adult they trust might turn out to be an abuser or someone who crosses boundaries. "We need to help kids understand that and be prepared for that...help them understand what the boundaries are."

One other issue is more challenging to organize and carries the potential of being more controversial: In line with comments above, how the parents handle a situation may be the most important factor in the long-term impact on the student. Providing parents with guidance on the danger signs would be valuable; providing parents with guidance on appropriately calm and reassuring ways of dealing with the child could make a huge difference in whether the child will be plagued for years, or will take the incident in stride and make appropriate adjustments.

The preceding paragraphs sound like an exploration of what "they" can do to stem the flood of child sexual abuse cases involving adults in trusted positions. But to borrow inspiration from President Kennedy's famous phrase, my job isn't done unless I can stir you to ask, "What can *I* do to protect my own children?"

Or better still, to ask, as well, "What can I do that will help protect *all* the children in my area's schools?"

I want to end this book with a story that offers one crucial answer, the story of a lady named Terri Miller. Some 20 years ago, not long after she settled in a remote town in the Nevada desert with the unlikely name of Pahrump (from Shoshone for "water rock"), Terri was taken into the confidence of a local woman who said she was going to file for divorce and move away because she had found her husband, a teacher at the local high school, in bed with a student. Terri, thinking of her own small children who would eventually be going to that school, called the principal to start an investigation toward having the man fired.

But she hit a stone wall. The principal wouldn't investigate, saying his hands were tied unless the victim herself came forward. Eventually Terri would find that this simply wasn't true, that a complaint from the victim is never a requirement for looking into serious charges. She also found that this unwillingness to move against a teacher—even when the allegations involve sex with a student—is extremely widespread.

By the time a new principal took over at the local high school, Terri had heard reports of the same teacher having sex with other students. She called the new principal, whose response was even more extreme: "Hearsay," he declared. Then he hung up on her.

Many people would have become discouraged at that point and dropped the effort. Terri instead launched her own personal research, which led to the discovery that the Federal legislation referred to as "Title IX" provided a weapon. If she filed a complaint, the school district would have to investigate or risk losing government funding. She drew up a complaint on behalf of her daughter, by then a student at the school. The school district hired a private investigator, who interviewed some 40 students and filed a report recommending the teacher be fired.

But he wasn't fired. He was merely given a five-day suspension.

Are you indignant yet?

It gets worse: the teacher filed suit against the school district. Absurd, you would think. Apparently the school board didn't see it that way. Instead of counter-suing, they capitulated. As hard as this is to believe, they settled with him.

You might think at that point he would have fled the town and the state, and looked for some school far, far away. No, he stayed in Pahrump. Incredibly, he then filed to run for election to the School Board.

An incensed Terri began her own investigation, tracking down former students willing to come forward and tell their stories of abuse at the hands of this one man. And she found them—*sixty* of them. She turned the information over to the District

Attorney's office. While they began an official investigation, the ballots were counted in the School Board election. Somehow, the disgraced former teacher had won a seat on the Board.

But Terri's efforts prevailed. In 1995, charges were brought on a single count, the man was arrested, and pleaded guilty—presumably believing this would bring him a lighter sentence. It didn't. He was sentenced to life imprisonment.

That was ten years ago. The saddest part of the story, the most alarming part, is that this failure of school administrators to act on reports of teacher sexual misconduct is unacceptably common. Protecting predatory teachers, or allowing them to resign with no blot on their record, has been common for a long time and is still common today. In the words of physician and scientist John Rootenberg, "We can't afford to be complacent. We need to come together and say, 'No, that's not all right and we're not going to stand for it.' We need to make it a tipping point."

If a Debra LaFave case receives massive publicity because the assailant is a beauty, at least the publicity brings one benefit to the society by calling attention to the problem. State legislators have begun to respond. A number of states now have laws on the books to insure that school administrators do not ignore charges of teacher sexual misconduct. Arizona has gone further, with legislation calling for pressing criminal charges and revoking the license of any school administrator who fails to report misconduct allegations within 72 hours.

These laws, together with awareness programs for teachers, parents, and students, will make a difference in protecting future generations of children from predatory teachers and other adult authority figures.

The message is that each of us can make a difference.

We all share the dilemma of too much to do and not enough time to do it all. Despite that, my primary purpose in writing this book has been in hope of stirring public action to help make our schools and communities safer for our young people. One by one we can make a difference if we know the danger signs and remain vigilant. We must summon the strength to see through the golden haze that a teacher's intelligence, command, and aura of authority bestow. We must have the self-confidence and the courage to speak up.

Our schools will be better, safer places when rumors and suspicions are reported. And when we insist that our legislators recognize the extent of this problem and work to enact appropriate laws.

By the time you read this book, my own first child will have been born. In the few years until that child starts kindergarten, the efforts of concerned parents can create an environment where all young people will be in less danger of sexual predators than they are today.

I'll be trying to do my part. In the coming years, I will be dedicating my efforts (as well as a share of my royalties from this book and the *After School* documentary) to advancing knowledge about educator sexual abuse of children and to promoting actions that can make the occurrence less frequent.

If progress is made in that effort, then the sorrowful story I have made public in these pages will have been worth the pain of sharing these most private and embarrassing details.

Afterthoughts

THE BOY WE have been calling Jack Carpenter still lives with his mother in the same well-cared-for black-trimmed white house where Debbie was arrested. His mother grounded him that summer, taking away his cell phone and denying him use of his computer so it would be clear that his actions have consequences.

Her goal was to see their lives restored to normal, and they seem to be making good progress. Jack is doing very well now, starting his senior year of high school and thinking about the University of Florida, to follow in the footsteps of his college-student older sister. He still plays basketball and is on his high school football team. He understandably doesn't like to talk about anything to do with the LaFave part of his life.

Mrs. Carpenter received two reminders that Debbie was required by the plea agreement to pay for her son's therapy; she has not asked for payment. Perhaps the change of schools and his basketball and football are serving as the only therapy he needs.

His mother has a message for all parents, the biggest lesson she learned: "Be attuned to your kids. They've got to be able to tell you anything."

For whatever it's worth, in the 2004-2005 school year, with Debbie no longer teaching at Greco Middle School, the reading scores on the statewide exam in the seventh and eighth grades—the grades she had taught—fell by several percentage points. One student who had Debbie in seventh grade posted a note on a school site on the Internet, "Thanks to her my fcat scores went from the level of a 5th grader to the level of a 10th grader" in the single year, which suggests that Florida has lost a fine teacher, one who was capable of making a powerful difference in the lives of her students.

What authority did the prosecutors use in allowing the wishes of the mother to be the deciding factor in Debbie's sentence?

The language from the pertinent Florida statute (960.001) provides the right of a victim, including the victim's parent or guardian if the victim is a minor, to be present, and to be heard when relevant, at all crucial stages of a criminal proceeding. And in the case of a felony involving physical or emotional injury or trauma, the family of the victim "shall be consulted by the state attorney in order to obtain the views of the victim or family about…Plea agreements…and Sentencing of the accused."

The key word is "consulted." What the statute specifically does *not* say is that the victim or the victim's parent is granted the right to make the final decision.

In one sense, credit needs to be given to the prosecutor in Hillsborough County and the Chief Assistant State Attorney in Marion County for following their consciences in allowing the wishes of the boy's mother to be the deciding factor—especially in Marion, where this meant going against the explicit order of the judge.

Whether these two gentlemen each made the appropriate decision is, I suspect, a question that will be debated among attorneys and argued among law students for years to come.

As these words are put to paper in the spring of 2006, my own life is looking a great deal brighter than it did two years ago. At Gasparilla this past January, I had a chance meeting with a lady named Amy. We started getting to know each other over the phone and by e-mail, and when I asked her to go to an outdoor art exhibit with me, she said yes. I was pleased because, after what

I had been through the last time around, Amy seemed stable, normal, well-adjusted, and fun.

Then she realized who I was—the ex of that lady she had seen so much about on television. She had second thoughts; she shared her hesitation with her mother but, lucky for me, her mother had seen me on Larry King and been impressed, so enthusiastically encouraged her daughter to keep the date.

On March 4, I married Amy.

The wedding took place at the house where we now live, an 80-year-old bungalow in the heart of Tampa, with an old-fashioned front porch big enough for a couple of rockers.

As I told one local reporter, "This just feels like the way a relationship is supposed to be."

In addition to a new wife and a new house, I also have a new job. Parlaying the experience I gained in commercial lending at Mercantile Bank, I've joined with two old friends to form our own commercial lending business, Nationwide Capital. The hours are long but I am essentially self-employed, which is what I had been aiming for. And I'm beginning to dabble in my own real estate development projects, as well.

For me the experience, despite all its unhappy consequences, turned out to be a positive influence. It brought me to examine who I am and what I want in life. And it has given me an acute awareness of how fragile life can be, how quickly everything can change.

I've undergone an extraordinary transformation, becoming more confident, more sure of myself. The day Debbie was arrested altered my life in a curious way: that terrible time changed me for the better, though of course it took months to gain the distance that made this change possible.

My mother has often told me, "You were not born to me, you were born to the earth to do something great. You will have to find your own way." I suffered through my mistake with Debbie, but I am now finding my own way.

Through a curious, most unexpected path, I've found a new role in life, a mission—if it doesn't sound too self-important to call it that. Having been cast in the role of an "expert" on issues about teachers who sexually abuse students has given me a platform to offer views about guidelines, awareness training, and legislation, to a national audience. The feature documentary *After School*, in which I appear as the host and narrator, provides another opportunity. And by the time you read this, Karen Ammond and I will have launched a lobbying effort, carrying the message about this subject to legislators on Capitol Hill in Washington.

Debbie walked away from court that last afternoon a free woman, but free only in a very limited sense. She is now living under the three years of house arrest, a world better than prison yet by no means easy. Even Martha Stewart, living in a mansion, found house arrest hard to bear, and Debbie, once more living in her parents' small house on 12th Street in Ruskin, has to contend with slightly smaller quarters than Ms. Stewart. Her supposed fiancé, Andrew Beck, visits her there. Of course he never brings the children, which would violate Debbie's probation terms; he sees daughter and her sister only rarely, once or twice a month, if that.

Debbie is now working as a waitress, slinging salads and sandwiches at a restaurant that bears the name of an old Irish song, in Sun City, Ruskin, not far from her parents' home.

Once the house arrest is over, Debbie will still face the seven additional years under the thumb of the legal system, subject to a battery of restrictions including, at any moment, a warrantless search of her person and her possessions, until March 2016, when she will be 35 years old.

That entire time the threat will be hanging over her head

that any infraction of the rules could see her clapped into handcuffs and sent to a high-security women's prison to serve out the rest of her sentence.

In the end, I don't have it in my heart to despise Debra Beasley. I pity her and hope she manages to make the best she can of whatever lies ahead.

Acknowledgements

THIS BOOK OWES its existence to the many people who squeezed into their packed schedules the time to be interviewed, in some cases interviewed repeatedly. We're especially grateful to the people who are not recognized by their real name in these pages because they preferred, or required, anonymity.

After four months of collaborative conversations and research and writing, my co-author Bill Simon and I acknowledge the admiration and respect we still have for each other. Bill, having been through the process many times before, was able to make the effort smooth and mostly painless for me. For what he has taught me, I am indebted to him.

We both have truckloads of appreciation for the remarkable, extraordinary, unflappable Karen Ammond, of KBC Media (www.kbcmedia.com), America's number one publicist, who brought us together and helped us all the way. To watch her work is to appreciate what it means to be a true professional; Karen delivers in ways that continue to surprise and please. We also both owe a special debt of gratitude to foremost entertainment attorney Steven Beer, whose wide contacts resulted in bringing us together.

Bill Gladstone, founder and CEO of Waterside Productions, in Southern California, was the prime mover in making this project come to life; he is a gift of an agent.

A tip of the hat to Phoenix Books' publisher Michael Viner, and to Sonia Fiore for the design. To Julie McCarron, who went beyond the call of duty in overseeing the book through production, you have earned our gratitude and esteem.

It's always rewarding when you discover someone in a highly competitive field who still manages to be authentic and graciously helpful. Sarina Fazan of Channel 28, Tampa, is a television star in our book, and we expect to see her go far in her career as a TV journalist.

Thanks as well to a pair of *St. Petersburg Times* reporters—Sue Carlton for obscure facts she gathered that were nowhere else available, and Shannon Colavecchio-Van Sickler for her singular assistance. Mel Carber, of MC Enterprises, Tampa, duplicated official documents that provided us with a valuable source of facts and quotes; and also we appreciate the work of Richard Weerts, of 411XML, for his support in locating people involved in this story. Mike and Chris Steep, and Nick Muccini, raised relevant points on the societal issues.

And our hats off to the studied authorities in the field whose contributions add wisdom and the benefit of experience to the final chapter. We're grateful to Drs. Leo Cotter, David Finkelhor, Mark Goulston, Richard Levak, John Rootenberg, and Robert Shoop.

ACKNOWLEDGEMENTS FROM OWEN LAFAVE

The past two years would have been nearly impossible to get through, coming out comparatively unscathed, without the unflagging support of my devoted father, Larry LaFave, and my adoring mother, Sallie Turko. Most especially, thank you to my new partner, my wife for life, Amy, who has been amazingly supportive and understanding through the entire process. I couldn't have done it without your selfless love and support.

I would be remiss if I didn't mention my friend and counselor, Dr. Larry Vickman (Vickmangroup.com) who graciously offered his professional advice and encouragement.

For me, the journey of reliving this story in order to get it into book form has been painful but vastly rewarding, yet it was only possible thanks to the emotional strength given without question by each of these very dearest of people.

ACKNOWLEDGEMENTS FROM BILL SIMON

This book would not have been finished on deadline without the love, patience, and intellectual encouragement and support of my darling wife, Arynne, who contributes her wisdom diplomatically in the form of insightful questions that hold the power to transform my approach, themes, and conclusions. Arynne did this along every inch of this precarious project, saving me from going astray and being tempted to take some tangential course that would have been detrimental to the telling of the fascinating story.

Daughter Dr. Victoria Simon added to my knowledge base (she is a forensic psychologist) and allowed me to bore her incessantly with details of my creative dilemmas.

For perceptive comments and insight on the manuscript as it took shape, a nod of appreciation to Patrice Montpetit and Peggy Dixon, and a special thanks to writer Sheldon Bermont, whose suggestions and phrasings were a valuable addition in this book as they have been in other books. Sheldon (sbermontwriter.com) is a word-generator beyond the ordinary.

A nod as well to Steve Sharp, my favorite commercial artist, whom I overlooked thanking for his much-appreciated contribution to a previous book, *The G.O.D. Experiments*, and to Kaha Jgarkava, the best masseur in all of Los Angeles, who came to the house regularly to soothe shoulders sore from long hours at the keyboard.

Owen LaFave
Bill Simon
Tampa and Los Angeles
June 2006